MILTON AND THE CLIMATES OF READING:
ESSAYS BY BALACHANDRA RAJAN

EDITED BY ELIZABETH SAUER

Milton and the Climates of Reading: Essays by Balachandra Rajan

with an afterword by Joseph A. Wittreich

UNIVERSITY OF TORONTO PRESS
Toronto Buffalo London

© University of Toronto Press Incorporated 2006
Toronto Buffalo London
Printed in Canada

Reprinted 2007

ISBN-13: 978-0-8020-9105-5
ISBN-10: 0-8020-9105-9

Printed on acid-free paper

Library and Archives Canada Cataloguing in Publication

Rajan, Balachandra
    Milton and the climates of reading : essays / by Balachandra Rajan ;
edited by Elizabeth Sauer ; with an afterword by Joseph Wittreich.

    Includes bibliographical references and index.
    ISBN-13: 978-0-8020-9105-5
    ISBN-10: 0-8020-9105-9

    1. Milton, John, 1608–1674 – Criticism and interpretation.   I. Sauer,
Elizabeth M., 1964–   II. Title.

    PR3588.R375 2006   821'.4   C2006-900116-2

University of Toronto Press acknowledges the financial assistance to
its publishing program of the Canada Council for the Arts and the
Ontario Arts Council.

University of Toronto Press acknowledges the financial support for
its publishing activities of the Government of Canada through the
Book Publishing Industry Development Program (BPIDP).

Contents

Preface

Balachandra Rajan's first published essay on Milton appeared in 1945, just over sixty years ago. It was followed two years later by his landmark study '*Paradise Lost' and the Seventeenth Century Reader*. His second book on Milton, *The Lofty Rhyme*, was published in 1970. Two subsequent books he produced, *The Form of the Unfinished* and *Under Western Eyes*, were strongly concerned with the presence of Milton in poststructuralist and postcolonial environments of reading. But no book wholly on Milton had appeared since *The Lofty Rhyme*.

The climate of criticism has changed more than once since 1970. In the many essays on Milton that he has published since then, Rajan's consistent endeavour has been to show how Milton's work engages and critiques these changing climates. This book is a selection from these essays and also includes four essays not so far published. It indicates the different ways in which Milton can be read. Reading in both directions is needed if we are to maintain a dialogue with the past and not an appropriation of it dignified as relevance.

Note on Editions

Unless otherwise stated, references to Milton's poems are taken from *John Milton, Complete Poems and Major Prose,* edited by Merritt Y. Hughes (New York: Macmillan, 1957).

Except where noted, references to Milton's prose are from *Complete Prose Works of John Milton,* edited by Don Wolfe et al., 8 vols (New Haven: Yale University Press, 1953–82), and are cited parenthetically in the book as *CPW.*

Acknowledgments

This book was conceived during a special session I organized at the 1997 Modern Language Convention in Toronto, Ontario. 'Milton Studies and Critical Practice 1947–1997' was devoted to changes in critical perspectives on Milton's work since the publication of Professor Rajan's landmark *'Paradise Lost' and the Seventeenth Century Reader* in 1947. For encouragement received from both Claude Summers and Arthur Kinney in the production of *Milton and the Climates of Reading*, I am especially grateful. Claude Summers also kindly supplied me with a copy of C.A. Patrides's 'The Nature of Inconclusiveness: The Achievement of Balachandra Rajan.' For her professional advice, I extend many thanks to Jill McConkey, editor of the University of Toronto Press. I benefited greatly from the thoughtful, incisive critiques of the anonymous readers of this book. Barbara MacDonald Buetter deserves much credit for assisting with the editing of the project, and I wish to recognize her valuable work, as well as that of Miriam Skey, who meticulously copyedited the manuscript. Special thanks are due to Joseph A. Wittreich, without whose support and scholarly contributions to Milton studies and to *Milton and the Climates of Reading* this volume would have remained unrealized. Additionally, I gratefully acknowledge the generosity of Brock University and of the Social Sciences and Humanities Research Canada Council for considerable funding awarded during the period in which *Milton and the Climates of Reading* evolved.

I acknowledge with thanks permission from the publishers to reprint, with modifications, several essays by Rajan in this volume:

'Osiris and Urania,' *Milton Studies* 13 (1979), by the University of Pittsburgh Press.

'Banyan Trees and Fig Leaves: Some Thoughts on Milton's India,' in *Of Poetry and Politics: New Essays on Milton and His World*, edited by P.G.

Stanwood (Binghamton, NY: Medieval & Renaissance Texts & Studies, 1995). I am grateful to the Board of Regents for Arizona State University for permission to reprint this essay.

'Milton Encompassed,' originally published in the *Milton Quarterly* 32.3 (1998): 86–9.

'The Imperial Temptation,' in *Milton and the Imperial Vision*, edited by Balachandra Rajan and Elizabeth Sauer (Pittsburgh: Duquesne University Press, 1999).

'Milton and Camões: Reinventing the Old Man,' 'Post-Imperial Camões,' Special Issue of *Portuguese Literary and Cultural Studies* 9 (fall 2002).

MILTON AND THE CLIMATES OF READING:
ESSAYS BY BALACHANDRA RAJAN

Introduction: The Art of Criticism

ELIZABETH SAUER

> Mee of these
> Nor skill'd nor studious, higher Argument
> Remains, sufficient of itself to raise
> That name, unless an age too late, or cold
> Climate, or Years damp my intended wing
> Deprest; and much they may, if all be mine,
> Not Hers who brings it nightly to my Ear.
>
> (Milton, *Paradise Lost* 9.41–7)

> Wait for the silence to come and for the right way, like a finger of light in the silence. Then do what you know to be right and do it without fear.
>
> (Rajan, *The Dark Dancer*, 1958)

This book undertakes the daunting literary, cultural, and political work of developing a narrative of Milton criticism over the past sixty years. Its organizing principle is the scholarship of the acclaimed literary critic and Miltonist, Balachandra Rajan. Rajan's contribution to Milton studies during the course of his writing and publishing career offers a major corrective to the methodological prudence that often distinguishes Milton studies from many other forms of literary criticism.[1] From his publications on Milton, Eliot, and Yeats; English poetics from Spenser to Pound; representations of India in English literature; and imperialisms, Rajan's scholarship – the expression of his distinctive voice in the profession – provides evidence of his mastery of the English literary tradition for which he was honoured by the Milton Society of America and by the Royal Society of Canada. His contributions to Milton studies in particular remain among the most influential in the field.

While presenting a range of New Critical, contextual, poststructuralist, and postcolonial approaches within the continuity of voice of the same scholar, *Milton and the Climates of Reading* also charts future directions in the field of Milton studies. Accomplishing this goal involves locating the individual talent of Balachandra Rajan in terms of the evolution of Milton scholarship since the 1940s. This book offers ultimately a timely statement about the ways in which Milton's writings not only addressed their own era but also speak profoundly and powerfully to ours, especially through the application of diverse methodologies.[2] In fact, the whole of Rajan's oeuvre exhibits his efforts at connecting Milton to our contemporary preoccupations.

The Tradition and the Individual Talent

Joseph Wittreich's most recent book, *Shifting Contexts: Reinterpreting 'Samson Agonistes'* (2002), begins with an insight into the self-conscious, revisionary nature of the critical endeavour: 'Criticism is cumulative and, as it accumulates, assumes a corrective function, emending both a critic's own errors, as well as the mistakes of others, in the process setting the record straight. That is a first imperative when criticism, in this instance of Milton, risks coming to a standstill, largely through its resistance to theory.'[3] The self-contained truths of New Criticism that shaped Milton scholarship and literary criticism generally have long given way to numerous other critical and theoretical approaches: reader-response criticism, narratology, structuralism, feminism, New Historicism, postcolonialism, textual studies, and cultural criticism, to name but a few. Each has transformed our responses to literature, offering new interpretive experiences. Changes in the methodology of reading have significant consequences for the study of canonical texts in particular, marking them as sites of irresolvable conflict rather than consensus. Interdisciplinarity, postmodernism, new historicism, and cultural studies all question boundaries between literary and nonliterary discourses and remind us that the writing of the past and construction of literary history are never disinterested practices.

And yet, as Wittreich has recognized for some time, Milton criticism in particular and 'especially of late, has been paralyzed, indeed impoverished, by the suppression of such conflicts or just plain avoidance of them.'[4] In a recent and influential study of Milton, *How Milton Works*, Stanley Fish assertively justifies critical approaches that defend Milton's will-to-order, arguing that 'conflict, ambivalence, and open-endedness – the watchwords of a criticism that would make Milton into the Romantic liberal some of his readers want him to be are not constitutive features of the poetry but products of a systematic misreading of it.' 'Milton criticism,' he observes, 'sometimes offers us the choice between an absolutist poet with a focused vision and a single overriding message and a more tentative, provisional poet alert to the ambiguities and dilemmas of the moral life. The truth is that Milton is both, and is so without either contradiction or tension. He never wavers in his conviction that obedience to God is the prime and trumping value in every situation.'[5] The practice of reading into Milton coherence also characterizes the approaches of most Miltonists and 'Romantic liberals,' who, Wittreich maintains, argue for an alternative construction of Milton.

In a paper presented at the 2002 Modern Language Association Convention, Fish reminded us that Milton must matter first and foremost – and exclusively – as a poet. The best scholarship on Milton is designed to ensure that Milton will not in fact matter for most, since the majority of critics now foreground social, cultural, historical, or political issues at the expense of poetic and aesthetic concerns. But if Milton is made to 'matter' for his contributions to history and politics, then his poetry is doomed to failure, Fish contends.[6] One might ask, however, whether there are ways of making Milton matter for both constituencies. Milton himself seems to have anticipated such a question in wrestling with the conundrum of the aesthetics-politics relationship. The political content of so much of Milton's verse, from 'In Quintum Novembris' and *Lycidas* on, tears the worlds of art and politics together – a dynamic with which the early modern world was more familiar than our own.[7]

Those Miltonists who can best navigate these worlds are themselves poets and critics in a 'well-ballanc't' equalibrium.[8] Constituting the 'fit though few,' such scholars also recognize that the contributions of Milton's right and left hands – that of the verse and that of the prose – produce a creative tension, originating in the same mind. Those who can negotiate the many different, if not also competing, mandates of poetry, prose, politics, and aesthetics help ensure that Milton will continue to matter for the diverse worlds that Miltonists inhabit. This book is in part a testimony to Rajan as one who locates himself between various cultures and climates of reading without wholly occupying any one in particular. A celebrated scholar who likewise entered Western academia from its peripheries, Professor Nabil Matar recalls: 'As undergraduates studying English Literature, my friends and I were of course taught and instructed by American or British academics and scholars. We always wondered how we, Arab students, would ever make it in a world that really belonged (and was dominated) by Europeans and Americans. And that is why I remember Dr. Rajan's book, *"Paradise Lost" and the Seventeenth Century Reader*: Here was a man with a name that was not European, obviously Indian. In many ways, he became a reference. Here was a non-European who had made a place for himself in the bastion of English literature – Milton!'[9]

Both the life and the work of Rajan have in various ways become an extension, if not a part, of the legacy of Milton, the poet-revolutionary who inspired and challenged him the most. Rajan produced two books on Milton: *"Paradise Lost" and the Seventeenth Century Reader* in 1947 and *The Lofty Rhyme* in 1970, though Milton works his way into all of Rajan's scholarship. The earlier book dealt with a single poem in the seventeenth-century reading climate while also anticipating reader-response criticism: 'A poem cannot be defined genetically through its evolution in the mind of the poet. It can only be approached, as it was meant to be approached, through its effect on the audience for whom it was intended. Seen thus, the work of recent scholarship ... is useful and even indispensable. But the evidence needs to be rearranged and revalued, to be studied, not as the raw material from which the poem was built up, but as part of the equipment which the typical reader brings to it.'[10] In many ways, Milton scholarship is still indebted to and building on the work of Rajan's first book, though with much more specific contextualization and a more interactive model of the author-reader relationship and of reading practices. From the start of his publishing career, Rajan in fact argued that the purpose of locating Milton's work in the seventeenth century is not to estrange it or enclose it in a seventeenth-century cocoon (as current Milton scholarship often seems inclined to do) but to establish the distance necessary for a dialogue with our own time. Changes in the contemporary reading climate will change the character of that dialogue, and will also transform our perception of the seventeenth century, however conscientiously that century is folded into its own thought and language. In our day, the label 'early modern' is used to reinforce the connection with the contemporary, but having been portentously announced, that connection is now in danger of being ignored. Making Milton matter must be something with which the Milton community finds itself incessantly concerned. Milton scholarship enjoys the advantage of being involved with an author who is at home in any climate and whose ongoing relevance is unquestionable and always changing.

In the heyday of the New Criticism, which concentrated on the self-contained literary work, Arnold Stein and Joseph Summers became the leading exemplars.[11] Rajan's 1970 study, *The Lofty Rhyme: A Study of Milton's Major Poetry*, is a product of this age, though his book was more concerned with archival scholarship than were the studies of Stein and Summers. Rajan's investigation of the significance of the 'pinnacle' in a seventeenth-century context, for example, transformed our reading of *Paradise Regained*.[12] In general, *The Lofty Rhyme* examined all of Milton's major poetry, attempting to establish the whole body of Milton's work as a reading context for each of its constituents. Rajan's constant preoccupation and experimentation with Milton is also evident in two of the three other books he has published, namely *The Form of the Unfinished* and *Under Western Eyes*. A Duke University Press reader of the latter book aptly observed that 'Milton is everywhere its ur-text and pretext' as befits 'one of the twentieth-century's leading Miltonists.'

The open-ended narrative of Milton studies presented in *Milton and the Climates of Reading* unfolds in the interrogative criticism written by Rajan over the course of his illustrious career, with an emphasis on the new sites of exploration he offers for current and future Miltonists and literary historians and critics generally. Rajan's early works establish a necessary framework for mapping the mental quest that serves simultaneously as a history of and judgment on Milton criticism. That journey is progressive and self-reflexive, one that advances and inevitably jettisons some of its own narrative. The recent journey involves an engagement with various contemporary approaches, including postcolonialism, to which Milton's works readily lend themselves, as evidenced in chapters that constitute the second half of this volume. Rajan has also participated in refining feminist criticism in his investigations, and the nature of that contribution is outlined in chapter 4, 'Milton Encompassed.' Interventions on controversies that have erupted in Milton scholarship, including the contested relationship of the *Christian Doctrine* and *Paradise Lost*, are presented in chapters 2 and 7, which need in turn to be read in relation to Rajan's study of these texts in chapter 2 of *'Paradise Lost' and the Seventeenth Century Reader*. Rajan has steadily maintained the position he advanced at that time, and the two essays printed here elaborate on the initial argument. While not having addressed questions about Milton's republicanism specifically, Rajan's essays on Milton and imperialism raise the question of how the republican and the imperial (not always the imperialist) are brought together in Milton's writings. Given his interpretative preferences, it is likely that he would once again read the engagement as agonistic rather than antagonistic.

Milton and the Climates of Reading opens with 'Osiris and Urania' (1979) – a transitional essay in Rajan's oeuvre. It represents the beginning of Rajan's questioning and ultimate renouncement of the New Criticism's 'will-to-order.' As an analysis of Paradise Lost, 'Osiris and Urania' demonstrates how contrasting yet interrelated view points presented in the epic are drawn together by Raphael's prevarications in the preamble to his narrative of the war in heaven that commences in book 5. Rajan investigates the manner in which competing perspectives emerge as accomplishments of Milton's verse, the complexity of which can sustain them. Indeed poetry arises simultaneously out of the Osiris principle of the remembering of the torn body of truth and the Urania principles of vision, illumination, and inspiration. 'The historical and the visionary, the continuous and the discontinuous, language as discovery and language as betrayal, are coordinates to which Milton's poetry responds and which remain with us in literary history', Rajan declares in a cogent statement on the nature of Miltonic verse and of poetry generally (chapter 1, p. 30).

The best criticism too is a composite creation, as evidenced in different ways throughout various studies by Rajan, including 'Browne and Milton: The Divided and the Distinguished' (1982); 'Paradise Lost: The Uncertain Epic' (1983); The Form of the Unfinished: English Poetics from Spenser to Pound (1985); 'Milton, Eliot, and the Language of Representation' (1992); and Under Western Eyes: India from Milton to Macaulay (1999). The earliest of these works, 'Browne and Milton: The Divided and the Distinguished,' offers, for example, a comparison of the careers, politics, and philosophies of these two prose writers (one admittedly writing with his left hand). At the outset, it seems that the divided and distinguished worlds inhabited by the two men are incapable of being related. Yet the critic, that great amphibian, is invited to bridge these worlds, and he can best do so by charting the different tenancies by two writers of the common ground that they not infrequently share. Turning to the poetry, 'Paradise Lost: The Uncertain Epic' enacts that contest in the composite genres of Milton's poem and in its language, which Rajan then makes representative of much larger issues than genre or language. This essay (not included here), which appeared in a special issue of Milton Studies, was juxtaposed with a contribution by Barbara Lewalski who read the various genres of Paradise Lost as exemplifying the poem's capacity to blend multiplicity into unity.[13] Rajan, in contrast, interpreted Paradise

Lost as exhibiting a struggle between two primary genres that resist the possibility of closure because the struggle is coextensive with a question mark that continues to hang over human history. Fittingly, both essays won the Milton Society of America award for the best article of the year.

Chapter 2, 'The Poetics of Heresy,' likewise locates the competing interests described above in Milton's major epic, which is judged to be 'bristling with heresies.' Milton's various heretical views, Rajan demonstrates, are interrelated and central to the statement made by *Paradise Lost* as a poem that 'understands itself by virtue of its difference with itself.' The inclusion of heresies is not designed to provide *sotto voce* compliance with Milton's *Christian Doctrine*, which is too often reduced to a gloss on *Paradise Lost*, as evidenced, for example, in Maurice Kelley's study.[14] Rather the heresies are in the epic because it requires them. 'Surprised by a Strange Language: Defamiliarizing *Paradise Lost*' (chapter 3), advances the argument about the contentious nature of Milton's writing by foregrounding the struggle in the poem's language and then making it representative of much larger issues than language or genre. In fact, in this essay, Rajan turns his back on the 'unifying imperative' of Milton studies, a term he invented for this imperative and which refers to the commitment to a rigid coherence made over many years by many Milton scholars including himself. Importantly, Rajan proves that the assault on the will-to-order is conditioned by Milton himself and not simply imposed upon the verse: 'Milton teaches us [the politics of reading] because of the issue-laden nature of his work and because a poem such as *Paradise Lost* is read internally in many different ways which interrogate and yet articulate the poem' (chapter 4, p. 66). The essay takes up the question of how Milton has been represented in the past and it inscribes the previous record, though by writing across it rather than turning against it. Here the problematics of Milton are admitted more readily.

Accordingly, Rajan reads Milton as a voice of resistance, responding to the world and not just registering it, and making a fresh intervention in a field that strenuously resisted change. The 'fresh intervention' that constitutes a new politics of reading also entails a self-reassessment. C.A. Patrides astutely observed in a tribute to Rajan:

> To deem the creator of literature and the critic of literature as one – to accept, that is to say, that 'wholeness' appertains to Rajan no less than to the poets and prose writers he favours – requires discrimination lest the principle at work is confused with the inflexible, the static, the fixed. Rajan

might have been counselling his own reader when he said that the reader
of Yeats 'must decline to see the later poetry as a disowning of the earlier
and he must also be reluctant to see it as the mere reformation of what has
already been said, the throwing away of an embroidered cloak.' One might
indeed propose that the operative experience is not 'mere reformation'
but repentance, in line with Rajan's observation in the seminal essay on
'The Overwhelming Question' that 'One test of a critic is his power to
repent.'[15]

What Rajan refers to as the 'self-realization of the individual talent'
(chapter 1, p. 31) involves a confrontation with 'the mind's ideological
kingdoms,' which 'can be doubly dangerous because of the actions they
promote under the semblance of true intellectual authority' (chapter 6,
p. 105). In Milton's own native tongue, 'Higher Argument' will fail 'if all
be mine, / Not Hers who brings it nightly to my Ear' (*PL* 9.41, 46–7).
Rajan's abandonment of the unifying imperative in the 1980s removed a
weight that was becoming burdensome. It also brought Milton into
a different climate of reading in which the work, though propelled by a
will to cohere, was perhaps at its most revealing and enlightening in its
stubborn resistance to the implementation of that will. All of Rajan's
work after 'Surprised by a Strange Language,' including his studies of
Milton's engagement with imperialisms, builds on the findings of that
essay. 'Surprised by a Strange Language' serves, therefore, as a watershed, though, as I have shown, earlier essays can be seen as moving
steadily to the line that marks the watershed. Indeed from his study of
the seventeenth-century reader to his work on the postcolonial and
Asian reader, Rajan's scholarship in true epic fashion circles back on
itself while opening up new directions in Milton studies. 'Milton Encompassed' (chapter 4) usefully offers an overview of fifty years of Milton's
scholarship and served in its initial version as the impetus for the compo-
sition of *Milton and the Climates of Reading.* The essay underlines the
capacity of Milton's work to connect itself to and even to critique the
changing concerns and the politics of reading of that period, a practice
that Rajan applies as well to all of his critical endeavours.

A rereading of the acts of criticism and creation extends to the poetic
representation of the divine creation. Chapter 7 reminds us that the
Genesis story in book 3 of *Paradise Lost* has been all but ignored by
Milton scholars, and that scholars often write as if only the book 7
account existed. Or they seem uninterested in bringing out the differences between them. At one level, this neglect is understandable since
Uriel's 'excited reminiscence'[16] in book 3 occupies only twelve lines

whereas Raphael's orchestrated narration takes several hundred. But Uriel's eyewitness account ('I saw' *PL* 3.708) comes first and Uriel precedes Raphael in the order of ranking of Cherubim. Raphael's account is shaped to fit a pedagogic purpose, whereas Uriel's aim is to provide information to a 'stripling Cherub' (*PL* 3.636) who addresses him as the 'Interpreter' of God's 'great authentic will' (*PL* 3.656). In such circumstances the book 3 account deserves more attention, particularly as its view of order as latent in chaos rather than alien to it is more in line with the *Christian Doctrine* than the book 7 narrative. Book 3 is also more in keeping with the science of the day than is the memorably imperial statement of book 7.

Milton Today

The critical engagement with imperialist discourses marks a new direction in the narrative of Milton studies and Rajan's own contributions to the field. Many years earlier, Northrop Frye determined that 'Rajan is not a politically-minded critic, but of course his work has also its social aspect ... Mr. Patrides ... points to the two novels, more particularly *The Dark Dancer*, as being concerned with the conflicts of Eastern and Western social attitudes during a revolutionary time. It is clear that the revolutionary ferment in India has played some role in focussing Rajan's awareness of and sympathy with the revolutionary career of Milton.'[17] In retrospect, however, it is apparent that 'putting the politics back into Milton'[18] was a move that Rajan anticipated, if not one in which he participated all along. Most recently Rajan has reminded us that it was in fact during Milton's lifetime that the first stages of England's empire-building history took place; and by the Restoration period in the 1660s, England dominated as a colonial power. In our own day, we have witnessed the gradual disintegration of that empire, involving, among other forms of resistance, India's declaration of independence in 1947.

In the year of independence, Rajan anticipated and eloquently articulated the postcolonial theories of the now late Edward Said published thirty years hence in *Orientalisms*, in the article 'India and the English Mystics' (1947), a critical assessment of England's response to India within political, religious, and cultural (philosophic and literary) contexts. Blinded by an imperial vision, England has been both 'tyrannically arrogant' and 'benevolently paternal' in its construction and treatment of India. 'Under the conditions of British rule in India,' Rajan explained, 'neither Englishmen nor Indians have respected each other enough for understanding or even thought it particularly important to explain themselves in the other side's terminology.' The failure to recognize the dynamics of the self-other relationship amounts to a failure at self-awareness. A hierarchal model must, therefore, give way to dialogue and understanding, a task that belongs ultimately to the poet whose 'gift of comprehension [must be] allied to the scholarship and imaginative insight for complete penetration into another nation's heritage.'[19]

Formed long ago, Rajan's views on cultural appropriation have in fact remained consistent. Moreover, he has taken up the challenge and carried out the mandate outlined in his 1947 article: to study the imaginative literature of both cultures in establishing a dialogic relationship as well as a sense of understanding between them. While Rajan's research has frequently taken him outside of the seventeenth-century literary canon, his scholarship on Milton has certainly been informed and transformed by postcolonialism. The complex entanglements between empire and literature are, for example, exhibited in *Paradise Lost* – a poem about imperialism, as Rajan demonstrates in chapter 5, the earliest of his postcolonial studies of the 1990s, 'Banyan Trees and Fig Leaves: Some Thoughts on Milton's India' (1995/9). The epic voice in *Paradise Lost* is the voice of the imperial imagination, of sumptuous orchestration, of metaphorical opulence, the encyclopaedic, outreaching, all-encompassing voice, that of the unifying imperative. No one articulates this voice more resplendently than Milton; and no one struggles against it more insistently. The epic, as Rajan maintains, displays at once a concern for the destiny of England as an empire and the correspondingly ambivalent responses to imperialism inherent in English culture. The creation of an empire requires the designation of an antagonist or an 'other' whose cultural difference becomes essentialized, demonized, and orientalized. *Paradise Lost* participates in reinforcing the association of India with the infernal, but Milton's portrayal of India also reminds us that it was seen as a mysterious, alluring land – a prized imperial possession. In the epic, the garden of Eden – located where the Ganges had its beginnings – is identified with India as a paradise and as the site of original sin. The complications in the representation of the East are concentrated in the poem's description of the banyan tree, which Milton transplants into Indian soils. Appearing in the book 9 account of the fall of Adam and Eve, the tree lends itself to suggestive readings that betray early modern attitudes about imperialism and indicate the place of Milton's thoughts on India in that cultural context.

In this compelling climate of reading, Rajan demonstrated the importance of engaging with conventions of thought offered by postcolonial

scholars. The questioning of boundaries necessitates the examination of
the nuances of domination and of sites of imperial subjugation. The
results include Rajan's study of the appropriation of India and his
production of *Milton and the Imperial Vision*, which reaches out to Asia
and the Far East, as well the New World. 'The Imperial Temptation'
(chapter 6) shows that the strong relationship between epic and empire
is dismantled in *Paradise Regained* – a poem both antiimperial and antiepic.
The poem, moreover, exposes the most dangerous form of imperialism
by announcing 'that no external empire can set us free from the empire
already established within us.' From 'the subjected side of the colonial
divide,' *Paradise Regained* and its companion piece 'tell us that we are all
subjected, including those who claim the independence of dominance.
All of us are others to the divine will. Finding our way back into selfhood
involves more than a change or even a transformation of power relationships. We have no alternative but to reconceive ourselves.'[20] Such a
reconception involves the invention of alternative interpretive perspectives. 'Milton and Camões: Reinventing the Old Man' (chapter 8) goes
even further, paying attention not only to the varieties of imperial
closure but also to the adequacy of the formats we use to analyse them.
Presented from the position of an Asian, Miltonic reader, Rajan refash-
ions and reinvigorates the Old Man in Camões's *The Lusiads* – the
quintessential poem of the early modern moment – while also revitaliz-
ing the seventeenth-century reader and Rajan's initial work on this
subject.

Rajan's sensitivity to the deeply responsive nature of Milton's thinking
to his time is also evidenced in his final and most recent essay included
in this volume, 'Warfaring and Wayfaring: Milton and the Globalization
of Tolerance' (2004). Toleration in Milton's Europe was predominantly
a religious problem confined to Christianity. Toleration today must
extend not only to different religions but to racial and ethnic differences
and to varying cultural and civilizational formations. Can Milton's engagement with this issue serve as a beginning (in Said's sense) for
extensions which his time never envisaged? In searching for a beginning
for the concept of globalizing toleration in Milton's work, the essay
examines the negotiation in *Areopagitica* of the notions of 'warfaring'
and 'wayfaring,' and invites a reconception of the differences between
them and between the early modern and contemporary worlds. The
study of difference becomes a lesson in dynamics and in 'brotherly
dissimilitudes that are not vastly disproportionall' – the terms and conditions for toleration.[21]

In retrospect it might seem pretentious to say that Rajan has brought Milton into different reading climates by becoming himself a citizen of those climates. All scholars are unavoidably citizens of whatever climate they are in. The point is that Milton is not merely accessible but *responsive* to the ways of reading characteristic of each climate. Much Milton scholarship is indifferent or even alien to contemporary climates, preferring the maximum possible local contextualization of Milton's works in their own time. Awareness of the complexities of interactive reading and of the highly specific 'situatedness' makes these studies far more sophisticated than Rajan's first book published nearly sixty-five years ago. But the power and passion of Milton's search for understanding and the ways in which it continues to educate us become forgotten and are indeed rendered anachronistic by this commitment of scholarship.

The unifying imperative and the one right reading limit Milton's responsiveness to climates other than his own. Joseph Wittreich maintains that 'the truths of poetry are plural not singular,' and they resist encapsulation by any one voice in a poem;[22] nor are they restricted to one historical climate. In our day as in Milton's, poetry is a provocation to mental fight, spiritual adventure, and political engagement. Such approaches to reading Milton, Rajan amply demonstrates, allow the stresses and strains in the poet's work to be differently assessed from diverse reading locations. More than ever, Milton addresses 'climates' impatient with boundaries. Thus the reevaluation of this poet-revolutionary establishes an enduring dialogue not only with the world that Milton inhabited but also with our own time.

> Thought for tomorrow:
> The left hand writes the world. The right hand writes the dream. It is supposed to be the other way around but Milton has it this way because in the end, the dream will write the world. (correspondence with B. Rajan, September 2003)

NOTES

The second epigraph to this Introduction, from *The Dark Dancer*, is quoted in C.A. Patrides's (unpublished) essay. J.R. (Tim) Struthers kindly supplied me with Northrop Frye's 'A Tribute to Balachandra Rajan,' originally intended for a volume, tentatively titled 'The Providence of Style: Essays in Honour of

Balachandra Rajan,' edited by J.R. (Tim) Struthers and E.J. Devereux. The 'Tribute' has now been published in *Northrop Frye on Milton and Blake.*

1 In a period in which, according to John Rumrich, 'intense impatience with the status quo [has] pervaded [North] American culture especially in the academy,' scholarship on Milton has seldom shown any discontent with itself (Rumrich, 'Uninventing Milton,' 249). As Mary Nyquist and Margaret W. Ferguson observe, Milton 'continues to enjoy the status of the most monumentally unified author in the canon' (Preface, *Re-membering Milton: Essays on the Texts and Traditions,* xii). Leah S. Marcus, John P. Rumrich, and Stephen B. Dobranski have recently challenged the unifying imperative of Miltonists, as have Joseph Wittreich, Peter C. Herman, and Jeffrey Shoulson. See Marcus, *Unediting the Renaissance: Shakespeare, Marlowe, Milton*; Rumrich, *Milton Unbound: Controversy and Reinterpretation*; Dobranksi, 'Samson and the Omissa' and *Milton, Authorship, and the Book Trade*; Wittreich, *Shifting Contexts: Reinterpreting Samson Agonistes*; Shoulson, *Milton and the Rabbis: Hebraism, Hellenism, and Christianity*; and Herman's study on the protocols of Milton criticism, *Destabilizing Milton: 'Paradise Lost' and the Poetics of Incertitude.* See also Elizabeth Sauer for a critical response to 'the strong tendency in Milton studies to resist textual indeterminacy and difference' ('The Politics of Performance in the Inner Theater: *Samson Agonistes* as Closet Drama,' 204).

2 Bibliographies of Milton criticism engaged with various theoretical approaches are supplied in chapter 4 of this book.On this subject, see also Patterson, *Reading between the Lines,* 244–52 and Kolbrener, *Milton's Warring Angels: A Study of Critical Engagements.*

3 Wittreich, Preface, *Shifting Contexts,* xi.

4 Wittreich, '"He Ever was a Dissenter": Milton's Transgressive Maneuvers in *Paradise Lost,*' 36.

5 Fish, *How Milton Works,* 14, 5. In the Introduction, '"Normal" Interpretation and the Protocols of Milton Criticism,' Peter C. Herman in *Destabilizing Milton* critiques the interpretive community of Miltonists identified by Fish as advancing a unifying imperative.

6 Fish, 'Why Milton Matters,' Milton Society of America, 2002 Modern Language Association Convention, New York, NY. Fish has since then published his paper as 'Why Milton Matters; or Against Historicism.'

7 The phrase is derived from Phyllis Webb's verses, 'Oh, I have wept for some new convulsion / to tear together this world and his,' to convey the dynamic relationship between heterogeneous concepts that have been yoked together (Webb, 'Marvell's Garden,' ll. 34–5).

 8 Milton, 'On the Morning of Christ's Nativity,' 122; see also chapter 7, note 12 of this book.
 9 Matar, Correspondence with E. Sauer, 2002.
10 Rajan, *'Paradise Lost' and the Seventeenth Century Reader*, 17.
11 Stein, *Answerable Style*; Summers, *The Muses Method: An Introduction to 'Paradise Lost.'*
12 Rajan, *The Lofty Rhyme: A Study of Milton's Major Poetry*, 125.
13 Lewalski, 'The Genres of *Paradise Lost*: Literary Genre as a Means of Accommodation.'
14 Kelley, *This Great Argument: A Study of Milton's 'De Doctrina Christiana' as a Gloss upon 'Paradise Lost.'*
15 Patrides, 'The Nature of Inconclusiveness: The Achievement of Balachandra Rajan.' Patrides quotes from Yeats, *A Critical Introduction*, 9; and Rajan, 'The Overwhelming Question.'
16 *The Poems of John Milton*, 605n. Cited hereafter in the volume as *Poems*, edited by Carey and Fowler (1968).
17 Frye, 'A Tribute to Balachandra Rajan.'
18 Norbrook, 'The True Republican: Putting the Politics Back into Milton,' 4.
19 Rajan, 'India and the English Mystics,' 902.
20 Rajan and Sauer, Introduction to *Milton and the Imperial Vision*, 22.
21 Milton, *Areopagitica*, *CPW*, 2:555.
22 Wittreich, 'Why Milton Matters,' 34.

1 Osiris and Urania

Headnote

This essay first appeared in *Milton Studies* 13 (1979): 221–35. Poetry, Rajan argues, is written in the space between two coordinates – the 'Osiris' principle of the search and the 'Urania' principle of vision. The coordinates can offer themselves to each other or can contest each other, and Rajan explores both of these possibilities. In a publication that appeared three years later, 'Milton, Humanism, and the Concept of Piety' (in *Poetic Traditions of the English Renaissance* [1982]), Rajan observed that the contested space lies between the Christian/visionary and the humanist/historical and is focused on the hyphen that both bridges and divides these terms. Milton's work maps out this space. The map and the way in which its locations are transferred to literature matter more than any specific position on it.

Building on this discussion of Milton's resistance to binaries, 'Milton and the Images of Truth' (in *The Form of the Unfinished* [1985]) studies the principle of the search as closing up truth to truth and as moving to the final form through successive approximations. At the end of time, the coordinates will coincide. History remains the recognition of a space of divergence which those who are committed to the search must struggle to overcome. Rajan finds the theory of successive approximations with each stage ratified by an enlightened consensus as persuasive in its eloquence, but visionary rather than historical. In an era less dedicated to absolutes than the seventeenth century, the search has to be seen as consisting not of a step-by-step advance but of a succession of changes in the climates of understanding, each with its own enablements and constraints.

Reading climates are to be distinguished from the politics of reading. Climates can admit the Urania principle but recent scholarship on Milton (see chapter 4 of this volume) pays virtually no attention to that principle. The current scholarly disposition treats all reading as political, including those resolutely literary readings which ask us to leave politics in the classroom en route to the literary seminar. All understanding is emergent and poets who claim special access to the transcendent are either drowning in hubris or playing with tired conventions.

Much has been written on the prophetic strain and on the line of vision in poetry (see, for example, Wittreich's *Visionary Poetics: Milton's Tradition and His Legacy*). It is important to remember Milton's modest definition of the prophet in the *Christian Doctrine* as differing in degree rather than in kind from other seekers. Deeper and more enlightened understandings are the result not of special access but of a stronger and more persistent endeavour to understand. That understanding offers itself to the human project at whatever stage the project has reached its history. Since the project changes its definition (and agenda) according to its evolving awareness of itself, it is best regarded as a series of reinventions. We learn from what has happened but we do not necessarily advance from it. There are also occasions when we simply refuse to learn.

When Raphael expounds the scale of nature to Adam he assures him of the possibility of body working up to spirit in the movement of creative change in paradise. That possibility is linked to a condition:

> If ye be found obedient, and retain
> Unalterably firm his love entire
> Whose progeny you are.   (*PL* 5.501–3)

Adam expresses some surprise at the possibility of disobedience and of deserting that love which he is counselled to 'retain' in unalterable firmness. Raphael then advises him that God made him perfect rather than immutable, that obedience lies within the area of free choice, and that there have already been certain cases of disobedience. Adam, whose 'constant thoughts' continue to assure him of his commitment to love and obedience, now asks to hear 'The full relation, which must needs be strange' (*PL* 5.556). Raphael then begins his account of the battle in heaven, prefacing it by the following words:

High matter thou injoins't me, O prime of men,
Sad task and hard, for how shall I relate
To human sense th' invisible exploits
Of warring Spirits; how without remorse
The ruin of so many glorious once
And perfet while they stood; how last unfold
The secrets of another World, perhaps
Not lawful to reveal? yet for thy good
This is dispens't, and what surmounts the reach
Of human sense, I shall delineate so,
By lik'ning spiritual to corporal forms,
As may express them best, though what if Earth
Be but the shadow of Heav'n and things therein,
Each to other like, more than on Earth is thought?   (*PL* 5.563–76)

These lines do not overwhelm one by their poetic power, and comment upon them has been less than lavish. Merritt Hughes and Alastair Fowler, following Thomas Newton, cite the beginning of Aeneas's narration to Dido in connection with Raphael's opening phrases. But it is the reference to earth as the shadow of heaven which has attracted the bulk of comment. Fowler's citation is of *Republic*, book 10. Hughes refers us to the *Timaeus* and to Plato's 'doctrine of the universe as formed on a divine and eternal model,' a doctrine evoked explicitly by Milton in 7.555–7. Cicero's interpretation of Plato, which Hughes also quotes, implies that 'the world which we see is a simulacrum of an eternal one.' Jon S. Lawry, whose book on Milton bears the title *The Shadow of Heaven*, suggests that Raphael's lines contain 'an anagogic myth for the existence and meaning of all man's spiritual experience and contemplation ... man's individual experience can be seen within the stories of election, fall and creation.'[1] The shadow here becomes a shadowing forth.

One does not need to read the passage very searchingly to become aware of the prevarications in it. Raphael first points to the difficulty of making the 'invisible' accessible to 'human sense.' He wonders about the extent to which it is lawful to 'unfold / The secrets of another world.' The doctrine of forbidden knowledge touched on here is touched on more emphatically in 8.167–78. Nevertheless Raphael undertakes to delineate what surmounts the reach of human sense by likening spiritual forms to those corporeal forms which express them best. So far the weight of misgiving is sufficient to suggest that the 'likenings' may be less than satisfactory and that their pertinence may be restricted to the injunctions they are designed to exemplify. But then Raphael turns the other way by suggesting not simply that earth may be the 'simulacrum' of heaven but also that the likeness between earth and heaven may be greater than terrestrial experience might suggest. It is true that the suggestion ends with a question mark but we need to ask ourselves about the weight of this device. In particular as we look back on Adam's education so far, we need to remember that the final possibility is firmly supported by Raphael's previous description of the scale of nature and more specifically by his account of intuitive and discursive reason as differing in degree rather than in kind and as being the dominant rather than the exclusive characteristic of angels and men respectively.

The simplest explanation will be offered first and for the sake of comfort we shall call it generic. All storytellers indulge in standard flourishes. The task is always hard and language is always inadequate to the event. Nevertheless the task will be undertaken, and as the storyteller commits himself to his enterprise, he begins to think that he may do better at it than his initial cautions suggested. So he poses that possibility, undercutting it prudently by a rhetorical question mark.

Such an explanation is acceptable as far as it goes but few students of Milton will feel that it goes far enough. We can expect the initiating gestures to be in the right style; but we also expect them to direct our attention to something beyond the gestures. Perhaps at this stage we can take up the view that Raphael is something of a fumbler and ask ourselves whether his prevarications put us on notice about his future fumbling. More charitably we can look at the dramatic situation. Raphael has been asked to bring on discourse (5.233), and his remark about previous disobedience brings it on with a rapidity that finds him unprepared. His reaction is typical of beings other than angels – to say as much as possible while giving away as little as he can. He is uncertain about the extent of his mandate. He wonders if his tactics have not committed him to more disclosure than is really necessary. So he puts it to Adam that the account will be metaphorical, while remaining carefully ambiguous about the eventual status of his metaphors.

In this essay it is proposed to investigate what can be done with a bolder explanation. The suggestion offered is that Raphael's statement is poised between two views of the structure of reality and that these views can be related to and perhaps originate in two views of the nature of language and the possibility of poetry. Both views have substantial roots in Milton's thought. Raphael does not attempt to reconcile them because their reconciliation can only be achieved by the poetic act and may indeed be said to constitute a primary endeavour of that act. The poetic act in turn can be thought of as the mimesis of a larger creative enterprise, a human and historical undertaking for which poetry provides an imaginative model.

Raphael speaks to Adam but he also speaks to an audience which has read Revelation and which is conscious, as Adam cannot be, of links between the Resurrection and the third day of battle.[2] In venturing upon a poem within a poem his difficulties can be representative as well as peculiar to his own task. When he remembers Virgil, that may be a refreshing reminder that angelic problems with language are not very different from human difficulties and that earth even in this sense can be the shadow of heaven. It is also a shadow in the more tragic sense that history on earth repeats history in heaven. It does not seem imprudent to suggest that Raphael is counselling us as well as instructing Adam and that what he says in beginning his poem may have an instructive relationship to what Milton says in beginning and proceeding with the larger poem within which Raphael stands.

Raphael's closing words relate themselves, as we have indicated, to the chain of being which he has already expounded and to that analogical universe in which the chain is a crucial structural component. In a world arranged as metaphor reflected in metaphor, poetry as a metaphor-seeking act becomes an education in the nature of reality. Language invites our confidence in its power of finding. The web of correspondence and the reenactment of structures are assurances of continuity, of our capacity to arrive at 'the knowledge of God and things invisible' by an 'orderly conning over the visible and inferior creature' (*Of Education*, CPW 2:368–9). These are Milton's words but Adam's are not very different when he speaks of ascending step by step to God 'In contemplation of created things' (*PL* 5.511; see 5.507–12). Even in the invocation that begins book 3, the natural world is described as one of the entrances not simply of knowledge, but of wisdom, an entrance 'quite shut out' (50) by the deprivation of blindness. In *A Mask Presented at Ludlow Castle*, Raphael's promise of body working up to spirit is anticipated by the Elder Brother when he speaks of the unpolluted temple of the mind turning by degrees to the soul's essence (461–2). The spiritual marriage of Cupid and Psyche further strengthens our awareness of continuity by liberating rather than repudiating the physical marriage of Venus and Adonis. It is from the higher union that Youth and Joy are born in a fully creative response to natural plenitude. If bearing these and other examples in mind, we return to the nuances of Raphael's wording, the line 'Each to

other like, more than on earth is thought' takes on additional significance. We are almost being advised that the human imagination per-
ceives a discontinuity greater than the structure of reality warrants.

Continuity, discerned in the ladder of creation, is placed before us in a
kind of ontological space. But Milton's universe is not static, as more
than one Milton scholar has rightly insisted. The figure of the dance,
repeatedly used, celebrates the balance of discipline and energy, order
consummated in motion rather than memorialized in stillness. But even
the dance remains a figure of pattern. Body working up to spirit, on the
other hand, is a figure of process advising us that creative change is part
of the perfection of paradise. Michael's sombre exposition of history
may seem an unlikely place to look for a renewal of Raphael's promise.
Yet Michael in explaining how the law yields to the Gospel does point to
a prospective evolution:

> From shadowy Types to Truth, from Flesh to Spirit
> From imposition of Strict Laws, to free
> Acceptance of large Grace.   (*PL* 12.303–5)

The double remembrance of Raphael's phrases in the first line clearly
and firmly relates the prelapsarian to the postlapsarian promise. The
shadow is a means of finding the light, not a betrayal of the light's
nature. We move forward step by step in the continuities of self-renewal
as we might have done in a better world where perfecting rather than
renewing could be seen as the objective. 'Light after light well us'd they
shall attain / And to the end persisting, safe arrive' (*PL* 3.196–7) is
another version of this measured progress. If earth is the shadow of
heaven, the fallen world can be the shadow of paradise and language can
be as music is for Thomas Browne, 'a Hieroglyphicall and shadowed
lesson of the whole world.'[3] Even Michael's statement about progress
from the imposition of laws to the free acceptance of grace looks back to
Raphael's statement about upward evolution 'in bounds / Proportion'd
to each kind' (*PL* 5.478–9). As the kind advances itself, the bounds
change their nature. This transposition into historical time of a movement delineated in ontological space is of some importance in Milton's
view of the making of order and of the relationship between pattern and
process. It also answers to the needs of a poem which can often strive to
be both pattern and process, sequential as well as an escape from
sequence, discovery at the level of experience and implementation from
the cosmic perspective.

A poem can be thought of as an eloquent affirmation of what is known or as a controlled experiment of the imagination in which turbulence is allowed to rage against the endeavours of order so that order can be made more significant by what it subdues. We can also think of a poem as an act of making and finding in which the structure of order is brought into being by the evolving consciousness rather than displayed to us, or tested and maintained under assault. When finding-making involves the recovery of a previous order catastrophically lost, knowledge both in the poem and in the larger undertakings of which it is a model will appear as both discovery and remembrance. A striking affirmation of this principle is the likening in *Areopagitica* of the state of truth to the torn body of Osiris. I have discussed this central and decisive image on a previous occasion,[4] but it is necessary to point out again how the body of truth is recovered fragment by fragment in an individual and collective effort of identification; how the process of recovery will not be completed until the Second Coming; how in an effort of seeking which is coextensive with time and by which creative action in time is therefore characterized, we move forward in a self-advancing endeavour, closing up truth to truth; and how finally, the finished form will be homogeneal and proportional like that Unity of Being which Yeats repeatedly compares to a perfectly proportioned human body.[5] The image can be considered against the background of disputes on religious toleration in the 1640s, which is perhaps to do it less than justice. It can be read more fundamentally as an account of history as a possibly creative enterprise, a magnification of that making-seeking act which is inherent in individual and in collective self-renewal. But the affinities between Osiris and Orpheus suggest that we can also be reading an account of how a poem grows, of how it discovers pattern in its processes, of how it shapes its own history and achieves its fulfilment. The image is not irrelevant as a preface to *Paradise Lost*, and that it should be pertinent is not surprising. If poetry provides us with pleasurable instruction it is not simply in a narrowly didactic sense.

We will return again to the image of Osiris and indeed it is difficult not to be made aware repeatedly of its place in the network of Milton's thought. For the moment, it is sufficient to note that the weight of implication of the image is that the unknown is not the unknowable. What we find is a trustworthy testimony to the nature of what we have yet to find. The movement of restoration mirrors the movement up the scale of nature, with each step on the ladder the shadow of the next step. The search for truth is therefore not simply consonant with Raphael's closing suggestion but is the translation of that suggestion into the creative effort of history.

We have concentrated so far on the final remarks in Raphael's preamble. We have now to remember that the preamble as a whole is poised between two possibilities. To invoke Plato, as Raphael does, is to remind us that there is more than one strand in the Platonic inheritance. If earth is the shadow of heaven, the body is also the dungeon of the soul. These images have their Christian counterparts. The firmament can display the glory of its maker, and the book of nature can be one of the texts of wisdom. But the world can also be an inn where we lodge, or better still, a hospital in which we die.[6] The world can be a perilous flood in resistance to which the true church affirms its identity, a place of darkness from which one can only be delivered by the divine rescue or the two-handed engine. Babylon and Jerusalem stand in an opposition that demands of us that we declare our true citizenship. Reality is other than actuality.

There is a strain in our imagination that takes the transcendent to lie inviolably beyond the reach of human sense, known by its unlikeness rather than its likeness to the ordinary world of our perceiving. The shadow is not an intimation but a deformity. This strain is strengthened by the Reformation insistence on the inward and transforming nature of the experience of relationship with the divine. Justification by faith calls for a crushing sense of the distance between man and God, a distance which can only be bridged by an irresistible force of remaking that lies essentially beyond human capability. John Donne's *Holy Sonnets* are taut with the sense of this distance. The visible cannot guide us across this chasm to the nature of the invisible. We know the invisible only as it chooses to manifest itself – when the thunder speaks, or the siege of the city is silenced.

It is possible to locate these two ways of seeing on two sides of a crisis so that the acute sense of discontinuity is the necessary preface to renewal and the strengthening sense of continuity is the evidence that renewal has begun. But even on this assumption the mixed nature of the human battleground means that each way of seeing will continue to haunt the other. William Butler Yeats tells us that 'Natural and supernatural' are wed 'with the selfsame ring.' He also tells us that 'A starlit or a moonlit dome disdains / All that man is, / All mere complexities.'[7] He does not choose between these propositions. Rather he celebrates the world that is brought into being between them, the push and the pull of contrary understandings in the systole and diastole of the imagination. Milton is less a poet of celebration than of impassioned and reverberating comment. But for him, too, discontinuity has its fascinations, less persistent and characteristic than those of continuity, but sufficient to ensure that the main way of seeing is not unqualified.

The temptation of Athens in *Paradise Regained* can be read as an important statement of discontinuity. One of its effects is to establish a cleavage between knowledge and wisdom so considerable that the former is incapable of leading to the latter and possession of the latter makes the former superfluous. What we know is significant only in so far as it is sanctified by a source of transformation beyond the knower and the known. In *Samson* too the prison house of alienation and blindness does not suggest the kind of tranquilly ordered universe in which the divine presence can be approached through contemplation of created things. Yet these distancing recognitions are embedded in poems of self-making which whether in their calm clarity or their tormented advances take us back to the legend of Osiris. If what we know cannot always lead us to what we know not, what we know not can and does guide us in the forward movement from what we know.

Milton's fascination with discontinuity is perhaps at its richest in the invocations to *Paradise Lost*. Raphael's preface, we can recall, is poised between language as discovery and language as betrayal, between a world in which metaphors give access to reality and a world in which reality can only be compromised by whatever metaphors are chosen to manifest it. Both propositions can·be offered to the poet as caution and as encouragement, and in the struggle to achieve definition both propositions will find roots in the language-experience. Since for the poet the language-experience engages the reality-experience and may be a main means of entry into that experience, the formative force of these propositions can be all the more telling.

Poets are not reluctant to draw attention to the difficulty of their task, and Raphael in doing so is following a well-worn tradition. As the poet in the invocation to book 1 of *Paradise Lost* prepares to attempt the unattempted and to wing his way above the classical accomplishment, the strenuous undertakings help in defining the magnitude of the assistance that is needed. Parnassus gives way to Mount Sinai and Sion hill, and the springs of Helicon to the brook of Siloa. The Heavenly Muse becomes the Muse which inspired the Shepherd by whom the chosen seed was taught. Aspiration, verging upon arrogance, dominates the poem up to this point. The muse is called on to 'sing' (*PL* 1.6), and her 'aid' (*PL* 1.13) is invoked in what is felt as a partnership rather than a yielding.

The 'And' which begins the seventeenth line coming after the taut pride of 'things unattempted yet' (*PL* 1.17) inherits this momentum and seems designed syntactically to initiate no more than an afterthought. It leads us, of course, into the heart of the invocation. The wings descend now instead of ascending, and the wings are those of the muse and not the poet. The boundary of invocation is pushed back further by the effort of self-humbling. A special force is necessary to bridge the distance between the unprecedented task and the frail agent. The spirit which brooded over the creation must now be importuned to brood over what might otherwise be the chaos of the poem. 'Thou from the first / Wast present' (*PL* 1.19–20) makes specific the thrusting to the above and before, to a power beyond the creation that is nevertheless the source of all creativeness. That power cannot be reached. It can only be implored to descend so that the upright heart of the singer can be its temple. The creative dependence thus sought is the narrow yet encompassing ground of man's being, affirmed unshakably by Christ as he stands upon the pinnacle. But the dependence is also an admission of discontinuity, urging the necessity of the descent from above rather than the possibility of the ascent from below. To say this is not to minimize the movement of self-making which qualifies one for the descent so that the assisting response from above becomes the consummation rather than the annulment of an effort already undertaken.

Light, in the invocation to the third book, is first the offspring of heaven and then the firstborn of the offspring. It is a coeternal beam of the eternal, an unapproachable radiance that God has inhabited from eternity, an effluence of essence, an ethereal stream springing from an unknowable fountain. The tentative delineations, superseded before they are fully evolved, keep the mind in movement round a still centre. It is as if the mind can only know this centre by the way in which the centre moves the mind. Raphael's difficulties in likening spiritual to 'corporal' things are lived out by the reachings of the verse. But the inadequacies of metaphor are not felt as defeat. The successive discardings are fitted into the flowing movement, suggesting the harmony rather than the strife of elusive possibilities. One can think of the arresting angularities in which Donne might have embodied a similar effort of definition. The sense of discontinuity is also qualified by the gradations in the invocation as a whole between celestial and physical light and by the ascent from the nonbeing of darkness to the ultimate being of uncorrupted light that is demanded of the poem at this stage in its journey.

Two invocations by the poet himself have preceded Raphael's statement in book 5 about the difficulties of angels in composing heroic poetry. Hubris in these invocations has been followed by humbling. The winged assault of language on the ultimate has been succeeded by the recognition that the ultimate is knowable only as it chooses to disclose itself. Though the light is the source of all singing, there is a presumption in singing of the light. 'The secrets of another World, perhaps / Not lawful to reveal' (*PL* 5.569–70) on the circumference of which Raphael treads with proper caution, have already been put before us by a poet who has told us far more than Raphael will tell Adam. One of the consequences of language as discovery is the discovery of language as betrayal. And betrayal is not simply the staining of vision by metaphor. The poet, like Adam, solicits his thoughts with 'matters hid' nominally because of the nature of his subject but conceivably because of the nature of poetry itself. Retribution can follow the penetration into inviolate places. As we proceed from the illumining of the mind's darkness (*PL* 1.22–3), through the irradiation of a mind surrounded by 'everduring dark' (3.45–55), to the poet in darkness and encompassed by dangers (7.27), the muse evolves as both instructor and protector, shielding the poet both from a hostile world and from the purity of the unmediated vision. Metaphor may be a betrayal; it is also the thin screen of a necessary safeguarding.

We are aware in the invocations of a parallel creative dependence – the dependence of man upon that divine principle which is the ground and origin of his being, and of the poem upon that ultimate muse which it invokes and by which it is instructed and governed. If the analogy is to hold firm and the poet be mimetic in this fundamental sense, the ultimate muse must be joined as closely as possible to the divine nature. In the invocation to book 7, Milton calls upon Urania as the muse of Christian poetry; but since Urania is one of the classical muses he calls upon the meaning, not the name. She is 'Heav'nly born' (*PL* 7.7) as light is in the first line of book 3. The ultimate muse was in being before the hills appeared and even before the fountain of divine creativeness was set in motion. Beyond and before generation as we conceive of it, she conversed with Eternal Wisdom and played with her in the presence of the Father. The eighth chapter of Proverbs, which is the basis of the imagery, does not provide Wisdom with a sister, and it is the sister, not Wisdom, who is Milton's muse. A Rabbinical commentary to which Harris Fletcher has drawn our attention endows Wisdom with a sister, Understanding,[8] but while Urania may be Understanding in so far as she converses with Wisdom, she is more than that by virtue of her play. We do not need to succumb to Denis Saurat's Kabbalistic interpretation[9] to accept the implied view of poetry as an act of comprehension *and* as a performance, a relationship strengthened by the subsequent reference to 'Celestial Song' (*PL* 7.12). 'Instruct me, for Thou know'st' is among Milton's earlier requests (*PL* 1.19). Utterance is not possible without knowledge and perhaps one should add that knowledge is not possible without obedience. 'Instruct' carries more than one meaning, and one of the meanings invites us to contrast the safeguarding obedience of the singer with the disobedience of which he seeks to sing. The act of poetry is the indivisible coming into being of knowledge and eloquence on the basis of the creative humbling of the self. In invoking the ultimate muse, this indivisibility is being recognized, but the source of song and the justification for its nature are also being pushed back as far as is metaphysically possible.[10]

Urania is called on for her version of the divine rescue, saving the committed poet from the perils and recklessness of the language-adventure. The fate of Orpheus is sufficient warning, as is the example of Bellerophon (*PL* 7.17–39). (Percy Bysshe Shelley proceeds further when even Urania fails to save John Keats.)[11] Distance between the singer and the source is necessarily part of the design of supplication. The muse must be placed away from time and from motion, must stand as light in opposition to darkness, if the inspired and instructed act of poetry is to reengage the human with the divine. To put it more brusquely, the perception of discontinuity may be needed in order to validate the finding of continuity. Milton's poetry is distinguished by its full response to both of these necessities, by the firm proportioning and interrelating of both the transcendental and historical loyalties. If his muse is Urania, the poem he writes is dedicated to Osiris. We can possibly go further and suggest that the poem itself with its searching of experience, its internal consolidations, and its step-by-step gatherings, imitates the bringing together of the torn body of truth.

Milton is not the only or even the first writer to pay his respects and pay them simultaneously to the Osiris principle of the search and the Urania principle of vision. The work of other writers falls between these coordinates, and it can even be argued that the strong and simultaneous presence of both principles, the impossibility of accepting one to the exclusion of the other, constitutes not a fundamental frustration, as might be expected, but a basic and shaping source of poetic energy. Writers must find their own ways of responding to these coordinates, of taking tenancy of the space of relationship. But Milton's articulations

have an inclusive and a formative force. I make this point because one of
the purposes of the kind of distinction that I have sought to adumbrate is
to suggest a line of continuity in English poetry and to indicate how the
work of the writer discussed registers an advance along that line and
makes forward movement from its own achievement possible. Books
with titles like *Milton and the English Mind* and more resoundingly *John
Milton, Englishman* do not achieve this placing.[12] Johnson warned us long
ago that readers opening *Paradise Lost* would find themselves surprised
by a new language.[13] Many still feel that however accurately this language
may answer to the necessities and way of life of the poem, it still remains
distant from what is unhelpfully called the run of English speech. Ben
Jonson can write a song to Celia and critics felicitate him on having
brought Catullus into the English countryside. Milton can ask the nymphs
where they were when the waters closed over the head of Lycidas:

> Where were ye Nymphs when the remorseless deep
> Clos'd o'er the head of your lov'd *Lycidas?*
> For neither were ye playing on the steep,
> Where your old *Bards*, the famous *Druids*, lie,
> Nor on the shaggy top of *Mona* high,
> Nor yet where *Deva* spreads her wizard stream. (50–5)

No one, to the best of my knowledge, has ever commended Milton for
bringing Theocritus into the Welsh countryside. It may be argued in
defence of this reluctance that Milton's effort is in a direction different
from Jonson's, that he is moving his landscape back into the distance of
universality while Jonson is bringing his inherited subject and gestures
forward into the particularities of English life. If such a view were offered
and admitted it would make the ensuing discussion more sophisticated,
but it would not make the direction of Milton's effort un-English. Still
less would it justify the contention that Milton's language, far from
standing within the continuities of English poetry, was responsible for a
great digression of some 250 years which was circumvented only in our
century. This view is much less influential than it was; but preoccupation
with it whether in maintaining it or defeating it obscures the recognition
that the true history of poetry lies in its continuities of concern, in the
dominant fascinations to which poetry in search of a meaning addresses
itself, and in the explorations through which it moves in search of an
answer, or a form of containment.

When paradise is destroyed in the eleventh book of *Paradise Lost* – or more correctly, converted into an 'Island salt and bare' (834) – we are brought to a crucial point not only in the history of the poem, but also in the history of the genre. In the poem the destruction means that the way back can hereafter only be the way forward and that given the working of body up to spirit which the poem suggests to us through its own develop-ment, the true paradise must hereafter lie within. In the genre, the destruction points to the end of the long poem of exterior action and the beginning of the heroic poem of consciousness. The point is made because the very nature of a poem of consciousness makes it likely that it will be written in the presence of Osiris and Urania.

The historical and the visionary, the continuous and the discontinu-ous, language as discovery and language as betrayal, are coordinates to which Milton's poetry responds and which remain with us in literary history. Milton's sometimes overwhelming skill in the uses of the past makes it natural to look back at cultural history through the concentra-tions and refractions of his poems. It is less easy to look forward along the ways in which a poem ought to open. Perfection is petrifying, adding to the burden of the past the crushing marmoreal weight of final accom-plishment. One test of achievement is that it extinguishes the genre. If, disregarding these persuasions, we decide to look forward rather than back from Milton's accomplishment, we can ask ourselves to what extent the relationship between Urania and Osiris is reformulated in the mar-riage of Jerusalem and Albion. Is it accidental that one of the opening lines of the *Prelude* echoes one of the closing lines of *Paradise Lost*, or that Wordsworth's declaration of belief in man comes at the same structural point in his poem as the creation of man does in Milton's epic? Is it merely coincidental that the ascent of Snowdon takes place at the same point as the ascent of the highest hill of paradise from which Adam discerns the sombre lessons of history? Are we being no more than fanciful in linking the Urania-Osiris relationship, the discontinuous and the continuous, to the Simplon experience and the Snowdon experi-ence or to what Professor Ferry defines as the mystic and the sacramental views of nature?[14] To the question of who killed John Keats, Middleton Murry's unambiguous and resounding answer is 'Milton.'[15] Neverthe-less, as we read *The Fall of Hyperion*, we can ask ourselves to what extent the dialogue of the evolving consciousness that takes place between the poet and Moneta has its antecedents in the processes of self-knowing and self-making that are enacted in *Lycidas* and in *Paradise Regained*. To what extent do 'The Dialogue of Self and Soul' and the other battle-grounds which Yeats arranges for himself renew the confrontations of the Osiris-Urania relationship, the commitment to time and the hunger for the timeless? Let us look at the poet whose disavowal of Milton has been so influential in forming the critical climate of the earlier part of our century. Do not the heap of broken images which the speaker in *The Waste Land* begins, and the fragments which he finally shores against his ruins, put us in memory of a familiar Milton image? Can we not see the step-by-step advance of Eliot's oeuvre as the putting together of the structure of truth, with each poem finding and forming the basis which makes the forward movement of the next poem possible? Can we say that in the still point and in the point of intersection we find Eliot's version of the presence of Urania and that in the return to the 'life of significant soil' we find his version of the commitment to Osiris? Is the movement in *Four Quartets* from language as betrayal to language as fulfilment not evocative of earlier distinctions that this essay has sought to draw? I pose these questions not to suggest that Milton's successors pay tribute to him by their imitation of him – such language defines and therefore ought to dismiss the idea of a present that is no more than the servile rerendering of the past – but rather to suggest that even in the finding of a signature, in the self-realization of the individual talent, there remains present a continuing metaphysical language. That language may be more important than the stylistic gestures the emulation of which is usually taken as the main evidence of the extent of Milton's presence. As we explore the language more fully we will come to understand better the place that Milton occupies in the continuities of English poetry. We will also understand how the place is creative.

NOTES

1 *Poems*, edited by Carey and Fowler (1968), 711n; Hughes, *John Milton, Complete Poems and Major Prose*, 315n; Lawry, *The Shadow of Heaven: Matter and Stance in Milton's Poetry*, 199–200.

2 See Hunter, 'The Center of *Paradise Lost*,' 32–4, and 'Milton on the Exaltation of the Son: The War in Heaven in *Paradise Lost*,' 227, for an account of these links. See also Martz, *The Paradise Within*, 124. The earliest recognition of this relationship seems to be by Greenwood as recorded in Newton's 1749 edition of *Paradise Lost*. See *Milton 1732–1801: The Critical Heritage*,159.

3 Browne, *Religio Medici*, 2.9. George Steiner's application of the thought to 'the speech of a community' (*After Babel: Aspects of Language and Translation*, 465) is an attractive extension.

4 Rajan, 'The Cunning Resemblance,' 36–7.

5 I have discussed some of Yeats's more striking statements of this idea in 'W.B. Yeats and the Unity of Being,' 150–61.

6 Browne, *Religio Medici*, p. 95, 2.11.

7 Yeats, 'Ribh Denounces Patrick,' p. 556, l. 4, and 'Byzantium,' p. 497, ll. 5–7 in *The Variorum Edition of the Poems of W. B. Yeats*.

8 Fletcher, *Milton's Rabbinical Readings*, 111.

9 Saurat, *Milton: Man and Thinker*, 132, 291–2.

10 The progressive, 'pushing back' is made apparent when we consider 1.19–22, which associates the muse with the creation, as superseded by 3.7–11, which invokes a light that existed before the creation. The fountain and stream imagery in which light is invoked is then superseded in its turn by 7.8: 'Before the Hills appear'd, or Fountain flow'd.'

11 Shelley's Urania 'chained to Time' (*Adonais*, 234) differs from Milton's Urania who is insistently presented as prior to generation. In terms of *PL* 7.5, and its context, one might say that Shelley is calling upon the name and not the meaning. A transcendental muse presents difficulties to any poet who finds himself committed to the ultimacy within. Perhaps the continuity of naming is intended to suggest that no muse, however fundamentally conceived, can protect the poet from his own creativeness.

12 Hutchinson, *Milton and the English Mind*; Hanford, *John Milton, Englishman*.

13 Johnson, *Life of Milton*, in *Milton 1732–1801: The Critical Heritage*, 308.

14 Hartman, *Wordsworth's Poetry, 1787–1814*, 66–7; Ferry, *The Limits of Mortality: An Essay on Wordsworth's Major Poems*, 16–50.

15 Murry, *Keats and Shakespeare; A Study of Keats' Poetic Life from 1816 to 1820*, 191–3.

2 The Poetics of Heresy

Headnote

This essay (heretofore unpublished) is based on a paper read at a special session convened by Stanley Fish at the 1980 Modern Language Association Convention, Houston, Texas. A fuller version was read at a one-day conference at McMaster University, Hamilton, Ontario in 1981. Other participants included Louis Martz and John Steadman.

Rajan's view of the relationship between *Paradise Lost* and the *Treatise on Christian Doctrine* was first laid down in *'Paradise Lost' and the Seventeenth Century Reader*. His position has not changed in substance though his awareness of the complex and entangled relationship between the two texts has grown. As the present chapter shows, treating the *Christian Doctrine* as a gloss on *Paradise Lost* – to use a now notorious phrase coined by Maurice Kelley – impoverishes the relationship between the two texts. The *Treatise's* principal heresies are not simply present in *Paradise Lost*; they are taken into its imaginative world. The two works are conceived in different realms and the differences between them are substantially more than differences of presentation. A poem is embedded in the world. The *Treatise* is an act of reading in which right reading must be sought with piety and vigilance. *Paradise Lost* on the other hand is an act of writing seeking to render what is read into the frustrations of history and into the 'fury and the mire of human veins.'

The passionate foregrounding of human self-determination, notwithstanding its potentially tragic cost, is striking in *Paradise Lost*. The imaginative commitment which anchors the principle in the poem is absent from the *Treatise's* more analytical tone. Surrendering the creation to the hazard of free will is a crucial act of which God is the strenuous

Olympian advocate whose choice of agency is not without its overtones of anxiety. By embedding free will in the creation and the consumer ethos in the Fall (see chapter 8), Milton lays a foundation for understanding which shapes the diverse structures that time and place build on it.

If we read *Paradise Lost* in relation to the commonplaces of its time, we can be forgiven for seeing Milton as a compulsive conformist, a man who says nothing unless seventeen people have said it. Christopher Hill's *Milton and the English Revolution* closes the door firmly against this inclination. Beyond that it raises the possibility that dissent might comprise the mainstream of the time's religious thinking with conformity little more than a refuge from its torments.

Dissent had its unintended beginnings when the transparent text was set in opposition to the avoidance of obscurantist exegetes. Milton could be contemptuous of 'Ancient Fathers' except when they were intelligent enough to agree with him.[1] In contrast to their complicating rhetoric (in which Milton himself was a notable participant), the Scriptures could be heard protesting 'their own plainness and perspicuity.' The Gospel was a 'mirror of Diamond' able to 'dazle and pierce' the 'misty ey balls' of those anxious to turn away from the truth. In a particularly jubilant paradox the Gospel's apparent frailty, the 'mighty weaknes' of its gentle teachings, would be able to 'throw down' the 'weak mightines' of human reasoning in its voluable arrogance (*CPW* 1:566, 569–70, 827).

As the self-evident truth became increasingly disputed and the transparent text increasingly opaque, the struggle to read rightly was licensed in the hope that an enlightened consensus would emerge from diversity's ferments. The 'homogeneal and proportional' form of truth was placed on a horizon always imaginable but forever receding. Milton's *Treatise on Christian Doctrine* needs to be read in this context. It is not a final statement but a contribution to a discussion probably waning in energy as Milton composed his compendious intervention. In a conversation no longer eager to 'subdivide and mince' itself 'almost into Atomes'[2] Milton's integrated assault upon the theological status quo might have stimulated a further movement towards the homogeneal form of truth. The world lacked a consistently heretical compendium of divinity that reinvented Christianity from the ground up and that could offer a frame for radical rethinking. Any such possibility was aborted by the Restoration.

Swept to the margin by a great event of the wrong nature, the *Treatise* made its appearance in print only in the second generation of the Romantic era. By then Keats, Shelley, and Byron were dead, and Milton's revolutionary individualism caused little more than minor ripples of interest.[3]

Hill points to several sects that held two or three heresies in common with Milton. No sect seems to have espoused all of his heresies. He was a church of one claiming to be closer than any to the true church.[4] It can be argued that he was led to this splendid isolation by nothing more than scrupulous loyalty to the text of the Bible.[5] But, as we have seen, other people who considered themselves equally loyal to that text came to conclusions about it which were wholly dissimilar from Milton's. Even when the mind is apprenticed to a text it is sensitized by its own self-understanding to read that text in one way rather than in another. We have to ask what is made possible and in particular what imaginative consequences are launched in the mind of a poet by reading the text in the way that Milton did.

In discussing Milton's heresies, Mary Ann Radzinowicz tells us that 'every one of [them] ... asserts the brotherhood of man, the community, the equality and the godlike potentiality of man.'[6] According to Christopher Hill, Milton's heresies 'point in two directions – towards individual freedom for man, and towards the goodness of matter' (285). I am not in disagreement with the general import of these statements though I find it difficult to fit Milton's mortalism into either characterization. Moreover while Milton may tell us emphatically in the *Treatise* that first matter is intrinsically good and the productive stock of every subsequent good and while Raphael may confirm this proposition in his description of the Scale of Nature, the chaos of *Paradise Lost* presents us with a picture that is strikingly different. These complications suggest that while Milton's heresies may form a structure with strongly creative poetic consequences, that structure may not be one of straightforward convergence in one or even two directions. The discovery need not depress us; with a mind as obstinately literary as Milton's we can expect the aesthetics of heresy to share in the complexities that define a literary work.

Despite William Riley Parker's more optimistic view of Milton's prospects after 1660 I agree with Christopher Hill that the poet was fortunate not to be hanged, drawn, and quartered following the Restoration.[7] Sir Henry Vane, for whom Milton composed a sonnet, went to the block even though he had not supported the king's execution. Milton not only supported it but defended it with an enthusiasm 'Of which all Europe talks from side to side' (Sonnet 22, l. 12). In the circumstances it was desirable for a poet already briefly taken into custody to be tactful about his heresies and the *Treatise on Christian Doctrine* does indeed suggest that in times of danger it is not essential to declaim one's convictions from the housetops. *Paradise Lost* is circumspect about Milton's doctrinal position. It would be foolish to argue that the circumspection was not influenced by the desire to avoid unpleasant consequences; but it is also necessary to recognize that Milton respected that 'grand masterpiece,' 'decorum,' and that the decorum of an epic poem does not invite the parading of individualistic beliefs. There is, however, one heresy about which *Paradise Lost* is unable to be circumspect. The poem is resolutely Arminian. In fact it gives Arminianism the highest possible doctrinal status by making it one of the subjects of God the Father's summit speech. The speech is dense with scriptural references but significantly in the passage on free will, God is citing Milton rather than the Bible. Underlining could scarcely be more emphatic.

Arminianism in the first half of the seventeenth century was a heresy of both the left and the right. Its bivalent nature should be a warning against drawing political inferences too readily from religious positions. Arminians of the Dutch persuasion according to Robert Baillie, writing in 1641, were 'much inclined after Vorstius and Socinus.' On the other hand British Arminians were 'hot and inflamed after the abominations of Rome.'[8] The anonymous author of *The Arminian Nunnery*, a book about Little Gidding also published in 1641, was excoriating Arminianism of the right and would have relished Marvell's later views on nunneries. His title must have struck him as a witty inflation of insult. Clearly in the Romish world of the Restoration, Arminianism, which by then had ceased to be a heresy, was an excellent matter about which to be candid.[9] Candour might also have the advantage of distracting attention from other deviations which were anathema to the right. I trust that no one will believe that Milton was frank about his Arminianism for this reason. He underlined it because his epic demanded it. No other poem directs itself so powerfully from the infinite theatre to the infinitesimal nucleus, or brings to the central act of choice so comprehensive a pressure of convergence. Man's responsibility lies at the heart of Milton's world and responsibility would be meaningless without that freedom which is its condition and can be its cosmic cost. The Fall all but obliterates our propensity to creativeness; but the will in every individual no matter how deeply infected, must remain capable (assisted perhaps by prevenient grace)[10] of turning to the good and progressively reestablishing its relationship with it. Such a potentiality cannot be selective. It must be universal, a necessary element in the structure of the self. Yet there is a difference and it is clearly a crucial difference between a universal possibility and a selective inevitability.[11] Instead of irresistible grace bestowed on a few and withheld from all others, we have an alliance voluntarily chosen and capable at any point of being dissolved. Instead of the irreversible march towards salvation we have a step-by-step progress in which every step is necessary for the next step and failure is possible with every step that we take. History is no more than the record of collective acts of self-making or self-destructiveness. The future lies open before the human community as it does within the individual. The glory of Milton's world is in its uncertainty, in its preferring tragedy to determinism. It is art and not machinery. Even the supreme poet may be in dialogue with his oeuvre.

Milton's view of history is post-Augustinian, but with a crucial difference: it is Augustinianism wrapped round an Arminian centre. For a brief period Milton seems to have subscribed to what might be termed the 'elect nation' view of history. When events made such a view untenable the natural course was to fall back on the traditional rendering of the true church's view of itself. Milton's originality lies in his accepting this rendering and the model of the divine drama which it suggests, while altering the status of the agent, so that the drama becomes potentially open-ended. Because free choice is so steadfastly at the core of Milton's world the paradise within can be something more than a retreat to the interior. The creative possibilities of history are steadily maintained by Michael at every significant stage in his sombre chronicle. The step-by-step advance through which the image of God in man is reconstructed is written larger in that step-by-step understanding through which a community working together, as in *Areopagitica*, reconstitutes the body of truth in the structure of society. Michael firmly sculptures the nature of that society in a decisive differentiation of the world under the gospel from the world under the law – a differentiation which, as much as his views on free will, is part of the integrity of Milton's thought. We can indeed progress from the shadow to the substance but the progress must be earned; the earning calls for universally offered grace, for an alliance between the divine and the human into which each individual can freely enter and for a collective order which is the outcome of accumulated acts of self-formation. Not all of these propositions are Arminian, but in Milton's time it would have been difficult to proceed to them without an endorsement of Arminian doctrine.

Milton's anti-Trinitarianism is discussed more extensively than his

Arminianism, but the discussion is mainly concerned with accurate label-
ling (the contending alternatives are Arian and Subordinationist) and
the diligent charting of affiliations.[12] Little is said about how anti-
Trinitarianism works in *Paradise Lost* or of the narrative and structural
dispositions that make anti-Trinitarianism almost impossible to avoid.
The divine principle must be Satan's antagonist and eventual conqueror
in the theatre of history. Since God can scarcely be a combatant in a
drama of which he is the producer, some degree of dissociation within
the godhead is necessary. The dissociation maintains legislative power in
God while investing executive authority in the Son. This fictional separation, combined with Milton's use, at crucial moments, of biblical texts to
which he gave unorthodox interpretations, seems to have been sufficient to keep suspicion at bay. But the purpose of the poem is to instruct
the reader, not to soothe the suspicious heart. We are instructed in the
first place by a humanizing of the godhead which places man in an
experiential relation with the divine, thus providing not only access but a
language of access of which the poem can be the instrumentality. We are
instructed in the second place via the approach of the divine to the
human, of the continuity between Christ's perfect sonship and the
presence of the divine image in ourselves. Continuity, as expounded by
Raphael in his presentation of the Scale of Nature, is an important
structural principle in Milton's universe. A monist as committed to
continuity as Milton must take steps that will reduce imaginatively not
simply the ontological but also the psychic distance that might otherwise
separate man from God.

Milton's most unusual heresy, the *creation ex deo*, joins his anti-
Trinitarianism in reducing the distance between the human and the
divine. It is apparent that the scale of nature as a figure of continuity is
more easily sustained if we believe that all things are of God, though the
scale is of course confidently expounded by those committed to a *creation ex nihilo*. The scale can accommodate discontinuity if we argue that
the invisible world while essentially unknowable, corresponds sufficiently
to the visible world for the visible world to serve as its figure of access. We
are invited to a metaphorical understanding but one in which the tenor
can only be discerned by the extent of its disclosure through the vehicle.
Another way of accommodating discontinuity is that adopted by Thomas
Browne who posits a series of increasing distances between the steps or
links in the scale, culminating presumably in the infinite distance between the creator and the highest of his creation (*Religio* p. 44, 1.33).
Most of those who orate upon the scale miss this elegant solution since

they are not aware of a problem to be resolved. Raphael, in his language, treats the differences in the scale consistently as differences of degree which permit the natural evolution of the lower into the higher. The scale is however presented less as a declaration of the goodness of matter than as a statement of order and of the integral dependence of order on the divine will.[13]

In the antithetical world of *Paradise Lost* first matter is definitely not seen as intrinsically good. It is 'Outrageous as a Sea, dark, wasteful, wild' (*PL* 7.212), and these are the adjectives used of hell (*PL* 1.60). The stilling of the conflict within it does not liberate its natural creativity. Vital virtue and vital warmth must be 'infused' into it and that which is 'adverse to life' (*PL* 7.239) must be purged away. Structure and form are foreign to chaos which is comprehensively suicidal in its frantic but also perfectly self-cancelling energies. Spenser like Milton contrasts the 'hate-full darkenesse' and 'deepe horrore' of 'eternall *Chaos*' with those 'fruit-full progenyes' for which it provides the 'substances.'[14] But Spenser's chaos is imaginatively presented as prior to form rather than hostile to it. Its relationship to nature is not uncooperative. In *Paradise Lost* on the other hand chaos must be transformed rather than formed by the 'Almighty Maker' and not by nature. The creator must 'ordain' the constituents of chaos as 'His dark materials to create more Worlds.' The poetics of heresy are particularly interesting here (*PL* 2.915–16). The statement of the *creation ex deo* in *Paradise Lost* is scarcely discernible in itself and is brief, muted and restricted in its consequences even when read in the light of the *Treatise on Christian Doctrine*. Finally, the an-nouncement that God creates by putting forth his goodness into an infinity from which he had withdrawn, which is prominent and perplex-ing in *Paradise Lost*, is not even to be found in the *Treatise*. It occurs at a crucial point in the epic in order to make us aware of how history echoes the creation in God's repeated putting forth of his goodness. Fortu-nately for the human race, freedom of choice does not have as its consequence a policy of cosmic *laissez faire*. Michael in 11.335–8 clearly has God's words in mind. Even more important, Christ in *Paradise Regained* unambiguously states that the showing forth of God's goodness rather than the proclamation of his glory was the 'prime end' of the creation (3.122–6). The strong and almost exclusive identification of goodness with God's creative will and the deemphasizing of the potenti-ality for goodness in matter are not wholly in consonance with the *Treatise*. They do not, for example, harmonize fully with the statements that first matter was 'adorned and digested into order by the hand of

God' and that 'it merely received embellishment from the accession of forms.' It should be apparent that Milton knows when to make concessions to the higher imaginative priority which he assigns to his antithetical universe.

As has been shown, both Milton's anti-Trinitarianism and his belief in the *creation ex deo* diminish the discontinuity between man and God, though the latter heresy operates within constraints. Milton's antinomianism also brings the human closer to the divine but, characteristically, it does so by increasing the distance between man fallen and man redeemed. In an antithetical universe the contrast must be dramatized between a world responding to supernal grace and a world given over to its inherent sinfulness. Michael singles out this particular contrary as crucial to Adam's understanding of history.

Law, as Michael points out, can identify sin but not remove it. Its constant rebuking of human nature, its unceasing exposure of our inherent destructiveness, force us into realizing our incapacity to reform ourselves and so persuade us to seek salvation in Christ. The modern remedy is to elect a more permissive government. In a world less self-indulgent than ours the turn towards creativeness which could make possible the attainment of society under the gospel was intended to maintain continuity with the ideal character of society under the law. The law was not abolished but regenerate Christians were set free from its bondage. It became a declaration of the structure of the self rather than a specification to which the self must conform. Milton's dissociation of the two societies suggests that the politics of a regained paradise can be fundamentally different from politics as we know it. A structure of deterrence may not simply be replaced by an equivalent structure of selfhood in which previous constraints become paths to self-realization. The structure itself may be altered in ways which the fallen mind cannot predict.

Antinomianism carried to its absurdity results in a sanctified licentiousness in which the saints can do no wrong because they are saints. When it stops sufficiently short of that point it underlines the hope of revolutionary change in history, putting it to us that the shared regenerateness of transformed individuals can form the basis of a transformed society in which the forces of cohesion and consent will be quite other than in the societies with which we are familiar. Michael's presentation of history is largely tragic. Given the time's disillusionments, there could be no other response; but in an antithetical world there must also be a creative promise which man's free choice can translate into actuality.

Mortalism, possibly the century's most fashionable heresy, is a heresy sympathetic to monism. If the soul is not substantially different from the body but simply a different organization of the same substance it seems reasonable that it should die when the body dies. There are ways to avoid this conclusion even if one is a monist. Different organizations of the same substance can have different characteristics and indeed an entity in which the humours are in perfect balance is traditionally not subject to mutability and decay.

Milton does not seek the avoidances of mortalism that are possible for a monist. He also refrains from emphasizing the proposition that the soul, being of the same substance as the body, must die when the body dies. His argument is rather that since the whole man sinned, the whole man must suffer death and that the soul, as the principal offender, can scarcely presume to escape the overall punishment. Moreover the soul is the breath of life and the body lives only because the soul animates it. Death, to mean anything, must require the death of the soul. The argument is ferociously plausible. It is to be found partially in *Paradise Lost* but Adam advances it in a highly distraught soliloquy which is scarcely the place for the statement of central doctrines. Indeed Adam prefaces the argument by expressing the fear that death may not be total and may involve only the body. The mortalist possibility is entertained as a reassurance. It is succeeded by the fear that the annihilation for which Adam hopes may not be compatible with God's eternal wrath. If the heresy has literary consequences, they are not to be found in this confusion.

To identify the literary consequences it is important to remember that the universe of *Paradise Lost* is powerfully homocentric in its spatial and temporal dispositions, that it 'zeroes-in' on a centre of human freedom. Arminianism is vital to the poem because it preserves the possibility of free choice even at a fallen centre. The importance of free choice even when it entails that perilous balance which in book 3.99 is maintained on the fulcrum of the line's caesura, is affirmed with significant strenuousness by God the Father on that one major occasion when he quotes Milton rather than the Bible. Freedom is part of the perfection of the species, human and angelic, and that perfection must be permitted to exist even if its consequence is the exposure of the cosmos to tragedy. The gift is measured by the cost of the gift. If we remain mindful of this context we can see that mortalism raises the cost far beyond normal views of the Atonement. When Christ says 'Account mee man' (*PL* 3.238), he undertakes to suffer more than the death of the body. 'The soul even of Christ,' Milton tells us, 'was for a short time subject unto death on account of our sins.' 'Just' for 'unjust' pronounced by God and repeated to Adam by Michael is a deep affirmation of the nature of love's inequity (*PL* 3.214–16; 12.293–5). What the Atonement means is made evident by what it involves.

If we now look at Milton's heresies in conjunction with each other we find them reducing the distance between man and God,[15] increasing the distance between the fallen and the redeemed, subduing themselves where necessary to allow the construction of an antithetical universe, contributing to the creation of a perilous centre of free choice for that universe and underlining the importance of that centre by increasing the price which must be paid to sustain it. It is no accident that in drawing this outline, we are specifying some of the primary characteristics of *Paradise Lost*. Milton may have arrived at his beliefs for other than literary reasons. But in a literary mind the beliefs were likely to have a literary aftermath. It would be an exaggeration to say that Milton could not have written *Paradise Lost* without his helpful heresies since with the exception of Arminianism, none of the heresies is an essential part of the deep life of the poem. Nevertheless it can be argued that the heresies predisposed Milton to see certain shaping forces in the poem more clearly than he otherwise would have seen them. We can also argue and perhaps it is time to argue that thinking about the poem in relation to the political and historical events that nourished it predisposed Milton to certain doctrinal understandings.

In looking at the presence of heresy in the poem we must recognize the careful restrictions placed upon that presence. The Arminianism is necessary and therefore explicit. But the anti-Trinitarianism can be treated as a fictional arrangement rather than as a statement of beliefs. When we first see the Son he is engaged in dialogue with the Father. It can scarcely be argued that the dramatic distinctions which make the dialogue possible correspond to real dissociations in the nature of the Godhead. Nevertheless, as a result of these distinctions, the Son's subordinate status is imaginatively legitimized from the moment of his entry into the poem. As for the other heresies, our detection of the *creation ex deo* depends on one word in an otherwise impeccable exposition of the Scale of Nature and that one word, 'proceed,' has connotations which attach it to a relatively respectable stream of Neoplatonic thought. Our detection of Milton's mortalism depends on our treating as authentic a possibility confusedly entertained by Adam that is sandwiched between two other quite different possibilities. The other main mortalist text, Christ's 'All that of me can die,' can be read as a moving preparedness to submit to total death when it is read in conjunction with the *Treatise on Christian Doctrine.* A reader not educated by the *Treatise* might have noted that Christ does not say, 'All of me then shall die' as Adam does in a time of mental perplexity.[16] As for Milton's fifth heresy, the proposition that the entire Mosaic Law was abolished by the Gospel, we have to admit that *Paradise Lost* nowhere says this, though what Michael says is entirely compatible with such a belief.

We need to recognize that the way in which the poem faces the public differs from the way in which it faces the author. This essay has been concerned with the inward face since that is the face to which the poet speaks and from which he can learn. Indisputably, the poet writes the poem but major poems sometimes rewrite their authors. The making of the self in a fictive world engaged as *Paradise Lost* is with both an historical and a transcendental actuality, involves discoveries about the nature of making to which the author and the oeuvre must be adjusted. We must also remind ourselves that Milton does not adopt his heresies because of a passion for unusual beliefs. He arrives at them because they are the most accurate possible reading of a text which governs all other forms of understanding. The imaginative shapes that text sustains will always have a special authenticity and its accommodation of the frustration or even the outrage of events will always convey a 'peace of thought' not attainable from other translations of experience. Milton's poem is written for a contemporary audience in a language as universal as possible, in the sense that it is accessible to more than one reading of the primary and initiating text. The public face is the externally settled result of the negotiations between the author and the autonomy progressively claimed by his own poem. On the other hand the inner face is formed out of a reading of the Bible which the author must hope will one day become the reading that is generally accepted. As the poem takes hold, its persuasive energies, notwithstanding its external compliances, will come to substantiate the justice of such a reading. In this sense, the inner face looks to the future, to the audience of true readers of the true text. Yet as the poem itself makes sadly evident, history may never provide that redeemed consensus.

NOTES

1 Milton, *Of Prelatical Episcopacy, CPW* 1:626; Argument to *PL,* book 1.
2 Browne, *Religio Medici,* p. 13. 1.8. Browne made this prophecy when the wars

of Truth were beginning. Also see Rajan, 'Browne and Milton: The Divided and the Distinguished' (1982).

3 Thomas Babington Macaulay's *Essay on Milton* was written to mark the disinterment of the *Treatise* from the Public Record Office. It seems unperturbed by its disclosures.

4 Maximum convergence according to Hill was between Milton and the Muggletonians (*Milton and the English Revolution*, 111–12). Hill's book charts the contemporary diffusion of the heresies Milton espoused. Their historical lineage is examined by C.A. Patrides in *Milton and the Christian Tradition*.

5 Maurice Kelley estimates that something like 7000 proof texts are cited in the *Treatise* (*This Great Argument: A Study of Milton's 'De Doctrina Christiana' as a Gloss upon 'Paradise Lost,'* 216).

6 Radzinowicz, *Toward 'Samson Agonistes,'* 315.

7 Parker, *Milton: A Biography*, 1:567–76; Hill, *Milton and the English Revolution*, 207–10, 235.

8 See Davies, 'Arminianism versus Puritanism in England c. 1620–50,' for the association of Arminianism with the religious right. On Anglo-Dutch Arminianism, see Colie, *Light and Enlightenment*, 1–21.

9 Hill notes this possibility in *Milton and the English Revolution*, 277.

10 'Prevenient grace' is not mentioned in the *Treatise* though it is crucial in the tenth book of *Paradise Lost*. *PL* 3.231 can be read as implying it.

11 Hill observes that 'the great leap is from predestination to universalism in theology' (273). *PL* 3.183–5 affirms this universalism, though a residual Calvinism also seems to inhabit these lines. Further investigation shows that this was a possibility concurred in by Arminians. See Rajan, *The Lofty Rhyme: A Study of Milton's Major Poetry* (1970), 166–7n.

12 Important contributions include Kelley, *This Great Argument*; 'Milton's Arianism Again Reconsidered'; 'Milton and the Trinity'; Patrides, *Milton and the Christian Tradition*; 'An Open Letter on the Yale Edition of *De Doctrina Christiana*'; Hunter, Patrides, and Adamson, *Bright Essence: Studies in Milton's Theology*. See also chapter 7 of *Milton and the Climates of Reading*.

13 Jeffersonian Democrats should feel encouraged by this cosmic precedent. However, the division of powers is criss-crossed by the Justice / Mercy and Law / Love relationships. We are contemplating an interplay within the godhead rather than the structure of checks and balances appertaining to an imperfect dispensation.

14 Spenser, *The Faerie Queene*, 3.6.36.9

15 *PL* 3.313–14: 'Therefore thy Humiliation shall exalt / With thee thy Manhood also to this Throne' seems to reduce this distance even more than the *Treatise*. The *Treatise* merely says that Christ's exaltation applies to his human

nature by virtue of its accession (*CPW* 6:443). It does not specify the extent of this accession and certainly does not place it on a par with the exaltation of Christ's divine nature to the throne of God.

16 *Paradise Lost* 3.245–9; 10.790–2. Milton's language in the third book is closer to the Authorized Version than to the proof-texts offered in the *Treatise*.

3 Surprised by a Strange Language: Defamiliarizing *Paradise Lost*

Headnote

An earlier version of this hitherto unpublished essay was read as the annual address to Milton Society of America as a plenary paper at the 1985 Modern Language Association Convention, Chicago, Illinois, and to the Association of College and University Teachers of English in 1986, Winnipeg, Manitoba. In *The Form of the Unfinished* (1985) Rajan identified the 'unifying imperative' as a shaping force in interpreting Milton's work. This essay is his most sustained reconsideration of that imperative. As Rajan concedes, he himself contributed strongly to the imperative in *The Lofty Rhyme* (1970) and in 'To Which Is Added *Samson Agonistes*' (1973), both of which apply the principle to the whole oeuvre and not merely to single works. *'Paradise Lost' and the Seventeenth Century Reader* (1947) is more open to the idea that the poem has its fault lines. *The Lofty Rhyme* in complying with the unifying imperative, combines close attention to the text with the historical situating of that attention. It endeavours to reduce difficulties in the poem to problems of interpretation rather than to inherent fault lines.

In '*Paradise Lost*: The Uncertain Epic' (printed with revisions in *The Form of the Unfinished*), *Paradise Lost* is examined as a poem struggling to find itself between the competing claims of tragedy and epic. Both genres are implanted in human nature and human history is the result of the contest between them. The poem is inconclusive because the struggle within itself mirrors a larger struggle with an uncertain outcome.

'Surprised by a Strange Language' carries the contest between genres broached in 'The Uncertain Epic' into a much fuller examination of the deeply contested nature of *Paradise Lost*. The unifying will is recognized as having a strong and persistent presence in the poem, but it is no longer a controlling presence. If the poem falls short of totalization, that falling short is not a noble failure or a disaster courted by a recklessness of which the poet is repeatedly aware in his invocations (see 'Osiris and Urania,' chapter 1 of this volume). The poem's eloquence and the enduring nature of that eloquence arise from deep-seated differences within itself, differences that can be carried forward into a dialogue with any reading future.

This chapter can be read as registering and uncovering in Milton's work the turn towards poststructuralism in the climate of reading. It does considerably more than that. By dismantling the unifying imperative and by recognizing *Paradise Lost* as deeply self-contesting, it opens the way to the postcolonial turn in the critical climate (reflected in chapters 5 and 6) and to the engagement with globalism (reflected in chapters 8 and 9). If *Paradise Lost* is comprehensively controlled by its unifying imperative so that the contesting elements in it are either assimilated or marginalized, postcolonial and feminist readings of it can be little more than resistances to its arrogance. A dialogue with the poem rather than acceptance or rejection of its *diktat* is only possible when the poem has more than one voice.

In the poem's 'great argument' with itself the reader is not a combatant or referee. He is a participant whose place in the poem will be determined by his own location. That location will necessarily be responsive to the climate in which the reader meets the poem.

Several years ago Dennis Burden published a book entitled *The Logical Epic*. Ernest Sirluck followed with a study entitled *Paradise Lost: A Deliberate Epic*. In reviewing the latter work (anonymously) for the *Times Literary Supplement*, I suggested that reason had had its say and that emotion might be given its opportunity, especially in view of Milton's remark that poetry differed from rhetoric in being less subtle and fine but more simple, sensuous, and passionate.[1] In 1983 I myself published an article entitled '*Paradise Lost*: The Uncertain Epic.' The purpose was not to suggest that the naming game could be carried on indefinitely or that the poem humiliates characterization, as the exuberance of Byron's *Don Juan* mocks it.[2] The aim was rather to indicate that more than one name could be found because *Paradise Lost* was a poem seeking to name itself, a poem open to competing claims on its identity as is the fate of man in

Milton's symbolic cosmos. In acknowledging and indeed underlining an element of indeterminacy in *Paradise Lost*, my suggestion tried to identify a watershed. On one side we have an Olympian poem, a created totality which, like the creation, answers a great idea or, less monumentally, a poem which attains finality by surmounting its own obstacles, including that most insidious of obstacles, the resident subversiveness of the satanic voice. On the other side we have a poem of self-discovery, a poem sufficiently stern with itself to reflect on and jettison some of its own history, a poem which pursues its meaning in the continually changing engagement between an obdurate world and the creative endeavour, a poem which understands itself by virtue of its difference with itself. Milton is heavily committed to the dialogue form. My suggestion is that *Paradise Lost* is a poem that is dialogic as well as extensively cast in dialogue. It is also a poem of the vast design, magisterially expounded. Its fascination lies in its troubled occupation of territory on both sides of the watershed.

To consider *Paradise Lost* anew we must divest it of some of the surroundings within which we habitually view it. As the last reward of consummated scholarship (to characterize Mark Pattison's remarks upon *Lycidas*)[3] it calls on us to read it in a manner which justifies the English Honours program. It is a central statement of the seventeenth-century mind, the window through which we look at Protestant Christendom. It is not simply a poem of the mainstream but a poem which prescribes the nature of the mainstream. In writing itself it writes the history and even some of the future of literature. As the best-known commentary on Genesis it overlays Genesis to such an extent that the sacred text must be read in the secular shadow. We need to remind ourselves that this decisively central document was written on the margin of a paradigm shift, on the brink of an epistemic fissure. Milton's poem responds to these possibilities by resolutely looking backwards, by claiming the future out of its own obsolescence. It is natural to think of *Paradise Lost* as a supremely representative poem of its time. We need to think of it also as a poem against its time. If we remind ourselves that it was published seven years after the Restoration when Dryden's reputation was at its height we may be able to recognize more readily the poem's loneliness, its status as an outcrop of another era. Ironically, the man needs the moment in the alliance of forces which Matthew Arnold identifies but it is the frustration not the power of the moment that kindles the energy of the poem, the driving momentum of its quest for permanence. A life-long nonconformist writes a poem of estrangement, of implacable otherness, defiant even in its versification. His function is to tell the tale of the tribe to a tribe that refuses to listen. He is a contributor to the art of exile and to the looming proposition that there is no art but in exile.

Three assumptions have hitherto entered strongly into the reading of *Paradise Lost* – that it is a unified poem; that it is a poem of consensus; and that it is a poem of the inheritance rather than of the author.[4] The assumptions are sufficiently interrelated for each of them to invoke the presence of the others. An epic is a poem of consensus. Pound is right in observing that the satirist can stand aloof from his time but that the writer of *epos* must voice the general heart.[5] A poem of the inheritance seeks to be a poem of the intertextual consensus, establishing itself as a locus of organization in the flow of literature. The epic, because of its compendiousness, is most likely to occupy this position in relation to which lesser works are located and around which they circle in their planetary wheelings. It should be evident that to occupy this position of privilege an epic has to be comprehensively unified; a central status among poems and an authority to prescribe the order of their relationships can scarcely be claimed by a work which is itself unsatisfactorily centred. Each assumption supports the others in this triangle, marking out a space which accommodates only the genre, the world view, the public voice, and the communal understanding. There is no room for the deviances of personality, for sectarian thought, for eclectic philosophies, and for the self-interrogations of a work of literature that speaks to itself when it should speak for its epoch.

This structure of assumptions needs to be and is slowly being questioned. We might ask what consensus means in the dissidence of dissent when the torn body of the true church is being put together and the house of God is being built from many timbers and diverse quarries. Unification can be more impressive when several genres are made contributory to the unified genre of totality as Barbara Lewalski has persuasively shown us.[6] Nevertheless we might ask what unity means when totality is deferred and when the space of deferral is laid open not only to the coalescing truth, but equally to its tragic fragmentation. The poem may then be in the insecure position of claiming in its form the very finality which it places at the receding horizon of its argument. Lastly, a poem of the inheritance is less firmly founded when the fulfilment of that inheritance is a claim made by the imagination, a claim that must continuously be exposed to the force of subversion inherent in the actual.

As has been indicated, these assumptions are being nudged into instability but they still stand firm in the minds of most Milton scholars. Within them, *Paradise Lost* is read as a poem assimilated to its announcements about itself in a manner which should gladden the heart of E.D. Hirsch. If its accomplishment seems to diverge from its intention it is because the reader is incorrectly situated in literary history. Alternatively, he is to be surprised by sin. Divergences in the poem are the means by which its rhetorical strategies are to be carried out, or dissensions which the poem designedly offers in order that it may mediate them into unity, or the results of insufficient preparation in hierarchic thought or Ramist logic. Milton scholarship remains notably reluctant to acknowledge the existence of real and continuing differences in *Paradise Lost* which form the dialogic basis of the poem as well as the heterogeneity it persistently struggles to unify. The epic is not read as nonproblematic, since that view would slight the many difficulties which the poem seems as concerned to precipitate as to avoid. *Paradise Lost* is read instead as overcoming or at least containing its problems, as being able to take command of itself even while agreeing to question and threaten itself. The alternative to the totalization it achieves imperiously against its own resistance is implicitly taken to be chaos – a proposition supported by the poem's cosmic dispositions, the *either-or* of its antithetical universe. The unifying imperative in reading *Paradise Lost* is pervasive and particularly difficult to disown because it responds to the unifying energy of a poem more militantly organized than any other [poem] in the language.

To defamiliarize *Paradise Lost* it is necessary to set aside the dominance of the unifying imperative and to recognize that a text as inclusive and complex as Milton's is entitled to some autonomies in the name of its own richness. It is entitled to surprise intention. The result will not be a poem in disarray, a series of schisms papered over by the grand style, but a poem that cannot avoid the dialogic even in its determined drive to univocality. That progress is made all the more compulsive precisely because *Paradise Lost* is a poem against its time, written at the margin and written out of exile. If it is to stabilize its own precariousness it can only do so by countering the abandonment of the real which it everywhere contemplates, by insisting on a pattern which no desertion can efface. There can be little room for delay in this embattled urgency, for Herbert's benign reconciliations of the labyrinthine with the linear, or for Penelope's web of deferral in *The Faerie Queene* weaving errancy into purposiveness. Milton lives in a universe under assault, a universe with no time for *aporia*, with chaos beating on the walls of its fragile containment. No adequate reading of *Paradise Lost* can fail to respect the power and perseverance of its will to order. The nuance offered here is only a matter of arguing that the poem is not merely the implementation but also the education of that will.

The unifying momentum of *Paradise Lost* is strengthened by an anti-thetical structure which seeks not the reconciliation of both terms in the antithesis, but the dismissal of the false one. A contrast with Spenser's structure of differences will make the starkness of Milton's oppositions clearer. *The Faerie Queene* offers us epic versus romance, purposiveness versus errancy, spatial form versus narrative flow, organization versus proliferation, and more modernistically, oeuvre versus text. Its narrative prolixity, making full use of the opportunities provided by the romance form, seems to offer an analogue to textual behaviour as it is discerned by contemporary critical theorists. In the Spenserian schematization, the differentiated terms are meant to engage not eliminate each other and the poem is poised on the line of their engagement. Neither family of terms *demands* privileged treatment, though traditional Spenserians have given primacy in practice to the first group and poststructuralists would prefer to give primacy to the second. The Miltonic oppositions include good versus evil, light versus darkness, destruction versus creation and Christ versus Satan. For Spenser the poem of finality will be a harmony blending the voices of difference to which his own poem has generously responded. For Milton the true poem will celebrate a world from which the false poem has been decisively erased. We could conclude that Spenser provides us with a dialectic of difference and that Milton urges upon us a dialectic of negation. This conclusion is immensely plausible. The question is whether we can carry it to the point of making *Paradise Lost* a monolithic epic, a poem in which none of the incorporated elements can resist or deflect the drive to totalization.

To initiate the counterstatement we could argue that the relationship between reason and passion, so important in human and psychological terms, is not a relationship of exclusion. *Areopagitica* tells us that passions 'rightly temper'd are the very ingredients of vertu' (*CPW* 2:527); *Samson Agonistes* that the passions are not to be suppressed but rather 'reduce[d] ... to just measure' (Preface to *SA*, *Poems*, 549); and *The Reason of Church Government* that the affections are not to be dispensed with but 'set ... in right tune' (*CPW* 1:816–17). The right tuning involves each constituent keeping its place and finding its meaning in the overall harmony. The relationships are hierarchically structured but they are relationships of contributory elements which require each other to achieve the judicious balance. The engagement between tragedy and epic, the two primary genres of Milton's poem, is more complex but it is also not a relationship of exclusion. If tragedy is the cost of epic, the weight of woe which *Paradise Lost* confronts, the epic envelopment is the promise which, while it remains in being, makes tragedy endurable. Neither genre can exist in its purity in the mixed and entangled world of the human. Both are implicated in the precarious centre which is man, 'self-ballanc't' (*PL* 7.242) as the earth is in the creation, 'sufficient to have stood though free to fall' (*PL* 3.99) with the rival genres seeming to compose a see-saw, pivoted on the fulcrum of the line's caesura. Having said this we should not ignore what is obvious, namely that Milton's interweaving of tragedy and epic is more sombre-hued and disturbing than the interweaving of design and errancy in *The Faerie Queene*. At the end of time we will contemplate not the richness of the pattern, but the extent of the stain that will inevitably mar history. Nevertheless the stain will be part of the fabric.

The engagement of genres in *Paradise Lost* points to a poem that is open to some degree, that can move in more than one way within a closed structure of argument. The question then raised is whether there is a contest of principles that takes advantage of the formal uncertainty brought about by the contest of genres. As is well known, *Paradise Lost* relies more than once on narrative juxtapositions designed to work in conjunction with the dismissive orientations of the poem. Examples might be the infernal and celestial councils in the second and third book, the hymn to light at the opening of the third book set against Satan's address to the sun at the opening of the fourth, and the victory in heaven in the sixth book followed by the creation in the seventh. Another crucial juxtaposition is between the principle of self-determination announced by God in the third book and the hierarchic principle embodied by Adam and Eve in the fourth. This juxtaposition has gone unnoticed because it is not a contribution to the poem's dismissive framework as is the juxtaposition of icon and idol represented by the two councils or the double manifestation of the light represented by the victory in heaven and the creation. It may be helpful to look more closely at the engagement of the two principles.

God's announcement of the principle of self-determination gives it the highest possible authority, particularly because the entire celestial assembly is made witness to the cosmic cost which is paid before them to keep the principle in being. It is hard to find a precedent for the colloquy between the Father and the Son in which the cost is dramatized and accepted. The device can be treated as necessary to establish a relationship between the infernal and celestial councils in which parody is prior to the truth and the anti-quest of Satan prior to the creative-sacrificial journey. Tragedy and epic are involved in each other at the highest level and the principle of freedom lives at the heart of both. These are important benefits of the structure Milton adopts but the main purpose of the innovation is surely to maximize the importance of the ' principle of self-determination by the momentous circumstances that are made to surround it and by the way in which it is identified as the hinge of the poem's action. Finally, though the Bible is quoted ninety-nine times in the first three hundred lines of the third book of *Paradise Lost*, it is significantly absent from the lines in which God expounds the nature of angelic and human freedom. The divine voice has been appropriated in order to carry a Miltonic message. The audacity of the appropriation is further testimony to the importance of the message.

The hierarchic principle is ushered into the fourth book by the narrative voice which may be less ultimate than the voice of God the Father but is paradoxically, the sponsor of that voice. We are first told that the image of God is manifest in both Adam and Eve and that this image includes 'Truth, Wisdom [and] Sanctitude' in the context of 'filial freedom' (*PL* 4.293–4). 'True autority in men' flows from these attributes and it is not clear that 'men' is a synonym for humanity (*PL* 4.295). In fact later in the passage, Adam's 'Hyacinthine Locks' are associated with 'absolute rule' and Eve's 'unadorned golden tresses' with 'subjection' (*PL* 4.301, 305–8). The restrictive effect of 'men' mediates a differentiation in which Adam is identified with 'contemplation [and] valour' and Eve with 'softness' and 'sweet, attractive grace' (*PL* 4.297–8). Then follows 'Hee for God only, Shee for God in him' (*PL* 4.299). The hierarchic individuation rests not altogether securely on the authority of St Paul's Epistle to the Corinthians, already alluded to seven lines earlier. The passage seems to move uncomfortably between the two versions of the creation in the Book of Genesis, offering the more progressive version only to retreat from it into a hierarchic structuring of two levels of manifestation of the divine image. A little later it is Satan who sees the 'Divine resemblance' manifest in both Adam and Eve, without commenting on the superiority of one manifestation to the other (*PL* 4.364). Satan is not the most reliable of interpreters but he is supported by Adam's addressing of Eve as 'Daughter of God and Man,' a periphrasis which is surely more than ritually courteous (*PL* 4.660). In fact the phrase clearly echoes God's naming of the Son after his exaltation as 'Son both of God and Man' (*PL* 3.316).

The wavering narrative voice and Adam's upholding of the less progressive part of it leave only Eve's voice available for appropriation by the hierarchic principle. The forthcoming commitment is not very subtly introduced by Eve's account of her origin in which a guiding voice undertakes to lead her from absorption in her own reflection to him 'whose image thou art' (*PL* 4.472). It is now not God but Adam whom she primarily images. The story ends with Eve's 'sweet attractive grace' (*PL* 4.298) excelled by the 'manly grace' of Adam and by the 'wisdom' which once 'shone' in her countenance manifest apparently exclusively in her consort (*PL* 4.490).

The appropriation of the feminine voice to justify its own hierarchic subordination now comes to a climax in Eve's hymn:

My Author and Disposer, what thou bidd'st
Unargu'd I obey; so God ordains,
God is thy Law, thou mine: to know no more
Is woman's happiest knowledge and her praise.   (*PL* 4.635–8)

The rhetorical lavishness is formally licensed by the elaborately ceremonial character of Eve's utterance. Nevertheless it is not simply hyperbolically in excess of the facts as an earlier authorial intervention has defined them. It is also contrary to the facts. First, Adam is not Eve's author. She was formed of his substance but formed by the divine hand. Second the hierarchic principle was traditionally justified in the name of responsible government. It cannot be invoked to place Eve at Adam's disposal. 'Man over men / He made not Lord' is Adam's firm judgment in the twelfth book of God's order as it applies to Nimrod's tyranny. If we feel that the gender restricts the application the next two lines make the scope of the conviction evident: 'Such title to himself / Reserving, human left from human free' (*PL* 12.70–1).

Third, unargued obedience is a strange proposition for the author of *Areopagitica* to advocate. If we are not to believe in the truth simply because the Assembly says so but only after our own powers of reason have tested it, we also cannot believe in the alleged truth simply because it happens to be affirmed by one's spouse. Adam himself as is made clear in the eighth book seeks not unargued obedience, but conversation to help or give solace to his defects. God recognizes Adam's need and responds to it by creating Eve. His decree in this matter, as the poem states it, thus diverges notably from Eve's view of her status. Since Eve's view in its turn has behind it the implicit authority of a guiding voice, the poem can be read as prolonging an initial vacillation which, as we shall see, is too much part of its nature to be resolved or erased. Mary Wollstonecraft first noticed this particular divergence but not the unexpected roles assigned to Eve and Adam as its coauthors.[7] Finally, there is no point in writing a work of literature justifying the ways of God for those whose commitment is to unargued obedience. The overstatement of the hierarchic principle and the appropriation of the feminine voice for this purpose put the poem into contention with itself and that contention is evident in the very nature of Eve, who is both the celebrant of cosmic order and the claimant to that dangerous autonomy by which the principles of order will be undermined. Because the fissure identified by this dual allegiance is so deeply embedded in the poem the conclusion should not be that the situation could have been avoided if the author's tactics had been less overbearing. The passage merits attention not as an error in planning, but as an indication of the poem's uneasiness in preparing to confront the impending collision of two principles, both of which are indivisibly part of its nature. This is not the only fault line in the poem although it is probably the most conspicuous. Other rifts can be congregated around the main rift. The poem seeks knowledge for instance and yet is about the presumption of seeking knowledge. It is a hymn to cosmic conformity written by a powerfully nonconformist intelligence, an extraordinary exercise in symbolic self-alienation. It thus needs to be on its guard against itself. Its anxieties about its status can be thought of as strengthened because so much of what it seeks to sing about is located in domains that lie outside the boundaries of its speech. It must continually strive to be exterior, anterior, and transcendent to the stubbornly constraining world out of which it is written. Mediated to us through the voice of God and by the tongues of angels it is also called on to enclose and govern the enunciations to which it makes itself subject. It must clothe with poetic authority the very sources which endow it with that authority.[8]

It is therefore understandable that the poem should strengthen the linkages of order as it moves to a crisis in which the structures that it values so highly must be exposed to a potential disruptiveness that it has also enshrined in the principle of free choice. But the understanding concedes that the poet is not a remote and lofty intelligence standing invulnerably apart from the work which he inscribes. He is implicated in the poem and some of his security measures may have to be read as defences against himself. The view that the real subject of *Paradise Lost* is the Miltonic personality – a view urged over fifty years ago by Saurat and Tillyard – is excessively simplified but no longer without foundation after Kerrigan's remarkable book.[9] It is easier now to suggest that the author and the work involve each other in their respective dynamics of self-formation and that to explore either is to examine both. Yet such a suggestion would run counter to decades of new critical urgings which seek either to erase the author from the poem or to insist that the authorial self is relevant only in so far as it exists as a 'literary' complex within the poem's boundaries. Genre scholarship and history-of-ideas scholarship have also helped to make the poem nearly anonymous by emphasizing its external relationships with such impersonal forces as decorum, convention, and the codified expectations of the literary-cultural inheritance. Even the idea of an author has become suspect in current critical theory. Yet if we restrict ourselves to prudently postulating no more than a force of inscription, we can still argue that the force is in dialogue with the potential work that it enters and that it both forms and must consent to be formed by. The dialogue will not be untroubled but when the inscribing complex is identified with the voice of certainty, it is a reassuring impoverishment of the poem to conclude that the result is indeed unproblematic. It is more difficult but also more rewarding to read the poem as complicating its claims even if the ways in which it does so call for restraint and delicacy in judgment. The poem cannot be wholly one with its claims. On the other hand it cannot overthrow them. It is engaged to them and not separated from them. The richness of the poem arises from the depth and scope of the engagement and from the importance of the claims themselves.

The commitments of *Paradise Lost* are not only important but divergent. There may be only one shape of order to which self-determination can finally subscribe but that shape can be identified only by departure from it, as a sign is known through its relationship with other signs. A text of order in which no difference from order can be entertained may not be a text which consciousness can write. Milton is not unaware of this difficulty. Evil into the mind of God or man can come and go as long as apples are not actually eaten. But the view that the Fall took place when the conception became the actuality and that all could have been well until the rash hand reached forth is too simple a view of Milton's catastrophe. It suggests a sequence of potentially dangerous but rectifiable inclinations that proceed to a point where rectification is impossible. The truth is that much that happens in Paradise is capable of being put to creative use and not simply capable of being held short of destructiveness. The Fall takes place at a dividing line that too deeply involves the making of the self for ambivalence to be any longer possible.

These thoughts have a bearing on the separation scene, examinations of which now lie around us thick as autumnal leaves.[10] The range of possibilities can be briefly reviewed. We can regard the separation as unfortunate and responsibility for bringing it about can then be assigned to either Eve, Adam, or the mystifications of divine disposal. Alternatively we can regard the separation as ambivalent since it increases the risk of catastrophe but also increases the significance of virtue when it is maintained successfully under conditions of greater risk. The greater risk must fall short of foolhardiness but the phrase 'sufficient to have stood' (*PL* 3.99) implies sufficiency to stand alone and does not exclude Eve from the scope of that sufficiency. If the separation is not unfortunate it can still be argued that the predispositions it displays – Eve's insistence on self-determination and Adam's too easy relinquishment of his hierarchic responsibilities – seem likely to lead to unfortunate consequences. On the other hand it can be argued that 'self-esteem grounded on just and right' (*PL* 8.572) is all that Eve claims and all that Adam concedes. Finally we can argue that the separation, regardless of its nature, is inevitable, not narratively but philosophically, since there is a level of self-understanding at which all of us must arrive and at which responsibility can no longer be shared. This is the deep content of self-determination but to urge it is to place it in potential contention with a hierarchic structure writ large in the cosmos as the most fundamental shape of order it can manifest. The scene resists characterization because of these deep-seated divergences. It is obliged to hesitate before itself. Indeed we can go further and say the poem should be suspect if it did not break down at some point in this way. The hierarchic principle and the principle of self-determination must come into confrontation with each other and the poem must be unable to arbitrate that confrontation since both principles are equally important in its life. Moreover, it is a consistent Miltonic understanding that those primal acts of choice by which the self is constituted or undone must be undertaken by the self in its solitude. We can find this understanding at work in every temptation scene that Milton wrote. The separation is therefore a necessity in the poem's staging; but it gains force because the impossibility of coming to a judgment upon it is a necessity in the poem's deeper statement.

In the debate that initiates the separation, unargued obedience is an

automatic casualty simply because a debate is taking place. More inter-
estingly, it is made a casualty by the very voice which had spoken so
ardently in its favour. A difference begins to open between the reality of
that voice and its appropriation – between naive obedience to a hierarchic order and that armed loyalty which Milton has endorsed from *A
Mask* onwards. Moreover, to recognize Eve's earlier conformity as containing an element of appropriation is to see the order within which that
conformity is situated as ceremonial and potentially obsolescent – the
protective fiction of a poem which must now turn to the stern truth
about itself. This is not the only occasion on which the poem rebukes its
poetry. Indeed we can argue that some of the effects of *Paradise Lost* arise
from a contrast between the literary and the real which enables the
poem to treat some of its cherished assumptions as 'literary' and as
therefore 'fictive' within its larger fiction. In this sense the poem must
say farewell to an internal as well as an historical past. It must prepare
itself to meet its own desolation. It too stands on the margin of a
paradigm shift.

The shifts which the poem mediates (or seeks to situate on its own
uncertainties) include the transitions from a Ptolemaic to a Newtonian
universe, from a world of metaphor to a world of fact, from a feudal to a
bourgeois society, from the lofty rhyme to the middle style in poetry,
from the heroic poem to the poem of consciousness, and from the
narrative poem to the novel. It is tempting to argue that these shifts are
treated as historical figurations of the most radical shift conceivable, that
of the Fall. They can certainly be made to take their places in relation to
the Fall and their alignment on either side of the partitioning event adds
considerably to the poem's strength of engagement with the secular
world it endeavours to translate. But since the shifts are neither obviously nor exclusively changes for the worse, the ambiguous relationships
between them inhabit the central fissure, undermining any simplistic
reading of the Fall as a catastrophic transformation that the regaining of
Paradise must totally reverse.

Eve's decision is the point of entry into these tragic but not wholly
uncreative opportunities, opening the world of Paradise to the wound
and the redeemed potential of its freedom by divesting it of every
safeguard except that of right reason, unrelaxingly vigilant. Adam's 'Go;
for thy stay not free, absents thee more' speaks for an order not simply
upheld but nourished and animated by fully tested adherence to its
principles (*PL* 9.372). His acknowledgment echoes God's 'Not free, what
proof could they have giv'n sincere / Of true alleagiance?' (*PL* 3.103–4).

The poem is haunted by the tensions between the necessity and the cost of self-determination, between an order to which it is committed and the endangering of that order by a principle which it is also pledged to support and, enveloping all, by the pain of an omniscience which must refrain from preventing what it is called on to foresee. In listening to the cross-play of these voices, the orchestration of its own dissensions, the poem can make and modify agreements with itself. It is not able to make peace with itself. If it could do so it would be less moving as a poem.

The world is different when Eve departs not only from Adam's side but from a previous declaration. It is a changed Eve who says, 'Both have sinned, but thou / Against God only, I against God and thee' (10.930–1), gently correcting the narrative voice of the fourth book with that momentous replacement of the preposition 'in' by the conjunction 'and.' In these circumstances 'Both' is a significant introductory admission. One of the gains of a fallen world may be partnership, though Christ's judgment of Eve seems to decree otherwise. Nevertheless the fallen are in too perilous a state to refuse to learn from each other and it is obvious that at least in matters of the spirit, a repentant wife cannot submit to an unrepentant husband. The joint repentance which ends book 10 and which is the outcome of mutual counsel and supportiveness is a model which is hard to find inferior to the relationship of Eve and Adam in the fourth book. It makes it clear that the ceremony of innocence is over. In the unfolding of the poem's knowledge of itself the fourth book now becomes the memorializing of a literariness which the poem must learn to relinquish even though it can never cease to desire it. The physical destruction of Paradise in the eleventh book simply sets the seal on that relinquishment.

Eve's final dream develops her changed relationship with Adam. Michael claims to have 'calm'd' her with 'gentle Dreams' (*PL* 12.595) These portend good but only in a general sense since Adam is instructed to share with Eve his knowledge of 'The great deliverance by her Seed to come' (*PL* 12.599). He is to do so 'at season fit' but he finds Eve already aware of the 'deliverance' and Michael's solaces seem to have been overlaid by a higher dream from a superior source (*PL* 12.600). 'God is also in sleep' may be Eve's way of advising Adam that there are other ways to knowledge than instruction by archangels (*PL* 12.611). In telling Adam that she regards him as 'all things under heav'n' she points out implicitly that she stands under the same heaven which is the author and disposer of them both (*PL* 12.618). Diane McColley, in her consideration of Adam and Eve's entrance in the fourth book wonders whether

'Shee for God in him' excludes 'he for God in her.'[11] It probably does for most readers given the momentum of the language, but at this point it probably does not.

If Eve knows imaginatively what Adam learns by discourse, her participation in the divine image is more than a matter of 'sweet attractive grace.' The hand in hand gesture that closes the poem does not revive an earlier relationship. Rather it supplants it in a way that the choreography of the final scene should make clear. As most readers realize by now, despite Milton's illustrators, the expulsion is unique because it is not an expulsion. Adam and Eve are escorted out of Paradise. Michael takes them both by the hand and those who believe that the right hand is superior will find no mention of whether Eve or Adam held it. He leads them down the cliff to the 'subjected Plain' and then 'disappear[s]' leaving Adam and Eve to join hands across the space of mediation (12.640). The repetition of 'them,' 'they,' and 'their' four times in the last five lines gently confirms the persistence of companionship. The singular pronoun is never used as it is in the differentiations of Adam's and Eve's entrance.

This account of the Adam-Eve relationship shows it as subject to dialogic pressures rather than as an ideal and perfected structure that was catastrophically lost and that future effort must strive to reinstate. The fall mediates a transition from a world that is hierarchically controlled to a more open exchange of understandings in which right action is the product of joint effort. It cannot be said that this relationship is inferior to the preceding one. If fallen, it is also more responsive to the realities of a world 'in the midst whereof God has placed us unavoidably.' Since its reconversion into hierarchic form is not an objective that can be seriously supported, the moral is that the end is not the beginning but rather the transmuted outcome of everything that separates it from the beginning. The beginning belongs to a past world, like the fading world-picture within which the poem is written or the opulences of language that the poem progressively discards. The beginning is not the future and it is deceptive to install it as the future by suggesting that the garden was a place of change, that the 'entrance' relationship was capable of development and that this development is to be projected into the relationship's future retrieval. Development and fulfilment are words that attach themselves to the flowering of latent possibilities, leaving the originating structure intact. We are concerned with the alteration of those possibilities by the force of events, events which are not simply narrative but changes in the poem's perception of itself. Eve is more important than any other agent in *Paradise Lost* in bringing about . these changes and in moving the poetics of *Paradise Lost* from a hierarchic dominance of idea over text towards a dialogic relationship between jointly creative energies. In retrospect it can be no accident that Eve, created for conversation, is herself the fulfilment of a conversation between Adam and his maker for which Milton scholarship has so far found little precedent. As the first-born of dialogue she has a crucial part to play in opening up and making productive those silences which the poem's commitment to its cosmos would otherwise invoke.

Julia Kristeva, in supporting Mikhail Bakhtin, assigns epic discourse along with the discourses of science and history to the realm of the monological. In this realm she tells us the dialogue inherent in all discourse is smothered by a prohibitive, a censorship, such that that discourse refuses to turn back upon itself, to enter into dialogue with itself. This is not a characterization which should be made to encompass *Paradise Lost*.[12] Nevertheless we can see how it is provoked by *Paradise Lost*, how it seems to be called for by a poem concerned not to scrutinize the authority it claims from the foundational nature of its statement but rather to affirm that authority irresistibly, gathering the known world into its investigative sweep. The dialogic pressure in *Paradise Lost* arises not from local resistances which the poem, in its self-empowerment, can set before itself in order to master but more subversively, in the inner nature of the very coherence the poem seeks to expound. That coherence, as has already been underlined, is based on two principles posited as ideally coincident but placed before us as historically divergent. In seeking to go further we might even say that history as we know it is not possible without that divergence and that the reassimilation of the two principles to each other is the *telos* by which the traditional dream of history is sustained. The consequence is that to narrate the Fall convincingly the poem must bear witness to rather than smother the fissure within its own originating assumptions and must authorize its own fall out of the monologic. It is assisted in doing so by the extraordinary range of interpretative voices which it assembles in order to discuss itself. These voices, formally endowed with authority (and in God's case apparently with supreme authority), destabilize the potentially monological function of the narrative voice and disseminate through their interplay the prospect of a centre which the poem nevertheless, resolutely continues to maintain at the horizon of its imaginative reach. The result is not Carnivalesque or Menippean as it is in the view of the dialogic put forward by Bakhtin. It offers us rather the profound self-recognition of a work of the mind on origins and destiny that is at the twin roots of its genesis irreversibly gathered into yet led away from itself.

If the poem's propositional nucleus is potentially dialogic and if its central engagement of primary genres as well as its only human relationship is also subject to dialogic stresses, we are looking at a work that is much more open, much more the chronicle of its own self-making than previous readings of it tend to suggest. We are also looking at a troubled poem and to say this is not to offer the prospect that the poem can be read as triumphing over its troubles, as failing nobly against overwhelming odds or as falling to pieces as a result of its miscalculations. It is time for the act of reading to divest itself of these implicit scenarios, the naive fables of a poem's poetics. To say that the poem's richness arises out of differences within itself, differences that it has to respond to rather than manipulate, may be only to lay the foundation for another fable, superior to those it displaces only in being more sophisticated and more likely to appeal to contemporary interests. Nevertheless the fable is untried enough and speaks to the poem with sufficient persistence for its consequences to deserve exploration.

Reading assumptions are more difficult to identify than the tragic, epic and farcical fables already discussed since they involve propositions about the nature of poetry rather than about individual poems. Among the assumptions we must resist taking for granted are those of the impersonal poet writing the public poem and of the artist standing apart from his creation. The aim is not necessarily to discard these assumptions. It is rather to estimate more judiciously the stresses to which they are subject, to ascertain how public poems might form themselves in a period of dissent, how a poetic voice is to remain impersonal in exile, and how the tale of the tribe is to be told from the isolation and precariousness of the margin. Finally, we need to ask how the artist is to stand apart from a creation which may be his principal solace, his main means of conversation, the other whose hand he holds, as he walks out of the eastern gate of an Eden that had frustratingly failed to materialize in history and which remains symbolically obliterated even in the imagination's world. Paradise is the first inscription on a palimpsest, the trace that haunts tomorrow from which tomorrow must know itself to be different. To write a poem doctrinal and exemplary to a nation in such circumstances may be to write it for fit audience though few. To write a public poem may be to write a personal one. To chart the progress of the soul may be to submit the self to continuing modification by the very movement it undertakes to expound. To be a representative thinker, an unsurpassable craftsman of consensus, a writer whose organizing capability brings the genres of literature to their fulfilment and integration, may also be to compose a work bristling with heresies, a work perceived as problematic in its genre and uncertain as to its hero from the moment that Dryden raised these questions. It is necessary to read this poem yet once more.

NOTES

1 [Rajan], 'The Higher Heroism,' *Times Literary Supplement* (3 Feb. 1968), 134.
2 For Don Juan's resistance to characterization, see Rajan, *The Form of the Unfinished*, 177 ff.
3 Pattison, *Milton*, 29–31.
4 John Carey observed that Milton has been made the 'preserve of orthodoxy himself' (*Milton*, 7).
5 Pound, *The Spirit of Romance*, 216.
6 Lewalski, *'Paradise Lost' and the Rhetoric of Literary Forms.*
7 Wollstonecraft, *A Vindication of the Rights of Woman.*
8 This last difficulty is discussed by Guillory, *Poetic Authority: Spenser, Milton and Literary History.*
9 Saurat, *Milton, Man and Thinker*; Tillyard, *Milton*; Kerrigan, *The Sacred Complex: On the Psychogenesis of 'Paradise Lost.'*
10 Examinations of the separation scene include Low, 'The Parting in the Garden in *Paradise Lost*'; McColley, 'Free Will and Obedience in the Separation Scene of *Paradise Lost*'; Safer, '"Sufficient to Have Stood": Eve's Responsibility in Book IX'; Revard, 'Eve and the Doctrine of Responsibility in *Paradise Lost*'; Reichert, '"Against His Better Knowledge": A Case for Adam'; Nyquist, 'Reading the Fall: Discourse and Drama in *Paradise Lost*'; and Bennett, 'Milton's Antinomanism and the Separation Scene in *Paradise Lost.*'
11 McColley, *Milton's Eve*, 40–3.
12 Bakhtin, *The Dialogic Imagination*; Kristeva, *Desire in Language: A Semiotic Approach to Literature and Art*, 64–91.

4 Milton Encompassed

Headnote

An earlier version of this essay was read at the 1997 Modern Language
Association Convention, Toronto, Ontario, in the session 'Milton Studies and Critical Practice 1947–1997,' which served as the venue for the
conception of *Milton and the Climates of Reading*. Rajan's conference
address was first published as 'Milton Encompassed,' *Milton Quarterly*
32.3 (1998): 86–9. This overview of the main contours in a half-century of
Milton scholarship included here is a sequel to the compendious survey
undertaken by Rajan in the first chapter of *'Paradise Lost' and the Seventeenth
Century Reader* (1947), published exactly fifty years before this essay was
prepared. Since then, Milton scholarship has passed through a succession
of reading climates, all strongly inflected by the politics of reading. Feminist, republican, and postcolonial approaches to Milton are branches of
the same trunk. As 'Milton Encompassed' shows, even the controversy on
the authorship of the *Treatise on Christian Doctrine* is hardly an innocent
scholarly development. Two different views of Milton are involved, which,
as Rajan argues herein, are interrelated rather than oppositional.

While not an exhaustive survey of Milton scholarship since the publication of Rajan's first book, 'Milton Encompassed' thoughtfully attends
to some of the shaping trends of that scholarship. Much of the best in
Milton scholarship is not apprenticed to these trends and is also not
methodologically self-conscious. Nevertheless, methodological self-consciousness is part of today's climate; and responsiveness to that climate is
crucial if we are to bring Milton into the current moment.

My qualification as a respondent is that I have been in the Milton
business for fifty years and have lived through some of the coalescences

that Professor Labriola has outlined.[1] I cannot say that I have single-handedly engineered these coalescences and I also cannot point with confidence to any collectivity that may have engineered them. There is a lesson to be learned from this inability and perhaps the lesson can be more sharply defined by glancing at a critical moment in the scholarship of another period.

In 1971 M.H. Abrams published *Natural Supernaturalism*, the distinguished climax of a long commitment to the exploration of Romantic poetics. In the same year Paul de Man published *Blindness and Insight*. These two works marked a watershed so decisive that it was almost a razor's edge. The sharp revisionary turn marked by the watershed led to a remarkably productive decade which domesticated French theory on this continent by giving it both a literary site and a New England habitation.

In Milton scholarship the poststructuralist infiltration lasted for much less than a decade. It was mild as well as brief. It left behind a book by Rapaport, an essay or two by Goldberg, and a slim volume by Catherine Belsey with gentle poststructuralist accents.[2] The new historicism which followed was restricted in its newness. It was prepared to treat literary sites as conflicted rather than consensual, and it made its salutations to the interdisciplinary by contextualizing literary works in relation to the political and religious thinking of their day. It had been engaged in this practice for thirty years before awakening to its avant-garde possibilities. Milton scholarship did not proceed beyond this cautious contextualization which was scarcely avoidable, given the nature of Milton's work. In particular, it shied away from the idea of cultural poetics and even today the prospect of imperialism as a cultural genre – a natural development of cultural poetics – is treated as a reckless generalization, unscholarly rather than premature.

Milton scholarship is the work of the Milton community rather than of individuals or of groups. Its guild character safeguards the quality of its workmanship; but it also makes it assimilative rather than methodologically adventurous. It seeks to reorient itself rather than to move itself to another location. The fixed foot of the compass stabilizes the world of Milton scholarship while the errant foot takes what is possible into that world's circumference.

If we proceed with a conceit which is Donne's as much as Milton's we can translate the fixed foot as the authorial presence and the just circumference as drawn and redrawn by the politics of reading. The politics of reading are prominent in Elizabeth Sauer's presentation and the concept of the postcolonial reader takes the hermeneutic spiral to a point in alignment with that seventeenth-century reader whom I tentatively invented fifty years ago. Both readers of course have to be emblems of reading communities characterized by moderate varieties and *Areopagitican* brotherly or sisterly dissimilitudes, but communities nevertheless, drawn together in dialogue rather than segregated by their differences. The postcolonial community in particular will be impoverished if its brotherly dissimilitudes do not embrace readers from the East as well as from the West. It must be genuinely global rather than a global endeavour with the fixed foot of the compass Western-centred.

We do not simply apply the politics of reading to Milton. Milton teaches us those politics because of the issue-laden nature of his work and because a poem such as *Paradise Lost* is read internally in many different ways which interrogate and yet articulate the poem. Within the poem the politics of reading are dynamic. Outside the poem they are dynamic too with the just circumference continually redrawn by the fresh intervention that the poem makes and by the changing nature of a response which has itself partly constructed the intervention.

The politics of reading question boundaries. They enlarge the just circumference by drawing attention to its injustices, by problematizing the once transparent work, so that its world can contain more without ceasing to be a world. As Sharon Achinstein indicates, the politics of reading may have had their beginnings in the interregnum proliferation of tract literature.[3] The seventeenth century was fiercely concerned and one might even say dominated by the problem of how to interpret sacred texts, but as the art (or imperatives) of reading evolved, ways of reading the Bible have elided themselves into ways of construing the canon.

The feminist interrogation of the unjust circumference was strongly begun by Christine Froula[4] and carried further by scholars such as Mary Nyquist.[5] It gained its initial momentum by perceiving a Milton adversarial to its politics. Since then it has been productively complicated in ways that invite us into *Paradise Lost* more fully, but which also make it difficult to align the poem along a single straightforward patriarchal axis.[6]

The postcolonial questioning of boundaries goes beyond the feminist interrogation in arguing that there can be no just circumference, that the outside must always be reached for by the inside if it is not to become the prisoner of its mystique. Exploring Milton's place in the imperial continuity gives this proposition historical depth by examining seventeenth-century uncertainties as to where the just circumference might be and on what principles the compass is to draw it. This rapidly emerging trend in Milton scholarship has gathered strength from complementary studies by David Quint and Martin Evans, one concerned with filiation and the other with affiliation, to use a distinction made by Edward Said.[7] Both coordinates invite considerably more exploration if the terrain between them is to be adequately mapped.[8] Sites other than the New World and works other than *Paradise Lost* have to be taken into account in determining the contours of this terrain. And though Milton scholarship is methodologically cautious, it may be less than wise in declining any engagement with the conventions of thought of postcolonial scholars.

The argument that there can be no just circumference questions the legitimacy of containment. It is doubtful if we can take the politics of reading Milton this far when not simply the divine creation, but its answering echo in the scribe's poetics, depend on containment passionately sought, on limitedness as a principle of order which must somehow be reconciled with inclusiveness. But to take the politics of reading any distance is to discover a Milton who is neither imperialist, nor anti-imperialist, nor an intermediate, ambivalent figure stumbling falteringly along an overdetermined road. Milton works within a discourse of conflicting parameters, a discourse that is theologically secessionist yet secularly imperial, that must walk a tightrope between dissent and obedience, frayed slowly by its own internal stresses. He brings to this conflict his familiar will to coherence. Some of us have become Miltonists because we share some of that will with him. The will falls short of assimilating everything it encounters. We are educated not only by what it does but by what it cannot do or cannot see as needing to be done.

We have looked at the roaming foot of the compass as it maps the receding and dissolving line which the politics of reading call on it to trace. It is time to turn now to the fixed foot of the authorial presence. It seems profoundly unnecessary to say that Milton scholarship is Milton-centred but when a scholarly effort amounting almost to an industry is dedicated decade after decade to a single author, it must be influenced in its character by that dedication. The single author moreover is anything but self-effacing. Romantic writers were correct in noting Milton's refusal to disappear into his work and in contrasting that refusal with Shakespeare's invisibility.

Overdetermination tends to substitute the conflicted site for the uncertain author. Milton, far from being in hiding, is obstinately active on the site. It is hard to conceal him in a fold in language. In fact he folded language with such vigour that English poetry, according to T.S. Eliot, took two and half centuries to recover from the trauma of the fold. The

Babylonish dialect Milton created ought to be less harsh and barbarous in a multivocal world than it was in the sensitive ears of Dr Johnson. But it also entrenches in the language itself the Roman strain within English imperial discourse. Milton specializes in these bivalencies. He is a principal voice in the articulation of imperial discourse and also a principal voice in its dismantling. His work straddles the apparently unnegotiable watershed between resolute dissent and the totalizing will. The spectacular surrender in book 3 of *Paradise Lost* of the entire divine poem to the hazards of agency surely says something about an author determined to do battle with himself.

The Miltonic self is indeed embattled and the controversy on *The Treatise on Christian Doctrine*, which Professor Rumrich has looked at as an important coalescence in Milton scholarship, is a contemporary recognition of this embattlement.[9] Behind the conjecture that Milton may not have written the *Treatise* and the indeterminacy about Milton's share in its authorship arrived at by a team of researchers whose meticulous work is nevertheless legitimately questioned by Rumrich, lies the recognition that the *Treatise* is an identity sign of major importance. It points to a Milton who was a militant nonconformist, a lively member of a robust fringe group, a man central to the character of English thought, the sponsor of a concatenation of heresies which made him a member of a church of one, unless of course the real author of the *Treatise* is admitted to that lonely Everest. On the other hand, we have in *Paradise Lost* a poet of the mainstream who has been read increasingly as constituting the nature of the mainstream. The tension, subversive or creative, between the establishment icon and the defiant dissenter is not unknown to previous readers of Milton. The Romantics made it internal to *Paradise Lost*. Because of the radically divergent agendas it supports, the contrast continues to invigorate Milton criticism.

William B. Hunter's way out of the paradoxical relationship between the two Miltons is to suggest that the author of the *Treatise* may not have been Milton. This is an evolution from Arthur Sewell's view, now apparently obsolete, that the *Treatise* and the epic were written at different times rather than by different persons.[10] Others before Hunter, most notably Maurice Kelley, have treated the differences between the *Treatise* and *Paradise Lost* as differences of presentation, modal rather than substantial, so that in effect, the *Treatise* writes the poem.[11] Despite my well-known addiction to poetry, I do not propose to reverse this proposition by arguing that the poem writes the *Treatise*. I wish to argue instead that the two are constitutive of each other.

The natural consequence of this proposition is that the choice we are called upon to make is not between one Milton and another. Both Miltons are necessary and have to be placed in contestation in the *agon* of his identity. As we study this *agon* we find ourselves brought back to that other major trend in Milton scholarship which Professors Labriola and Sauer have illuminated. Far from being autonomous, the two coalescences we have examined today are linked, as the self and the world are linked, and as the two legs of the compass are joined. The *agon* of self is not the sealed repository of a struggle limited to the imagination, which can issue only in an aesthetic catharsis. It is both nourished by, and in its turn sustains, the disseminations of that founding paradox on which English imperial discourse is engineered and by which it is inevitably fragmented. That paradox, as I have pointed out, lies in the self-annulling relationship between an England that is theologically secessionist and an England that is secularly imperial. Dissent and obedience, the interrogating passion and the totalizing will thus become constituents not only of the Miltonic identity, but of that crisis in national self-formation in which that identity finds its responsibilities and roots.

If the circumference of Milton scholarship is able to take in nearly all that our current preoccupations call for, it is because so much of the circumference is already at the centre. That fact sustains the integrity of Milton scholarship, preventing the politics of reading from sliding into wilfulness, or from finding a Milton antipathetic to those politics. There is almost always a connection and often a critique enabling us to learn from and not simply make the connection.

I cannot let this occasion pass without expressing my gratitude to the Milton community in which I have participated for fifty years. Working in this community has been for me a steady source of intellectual happiness. I have had my disagreements with its members but the disagreements have never been less than courteous. Spenser put justice and courtesy together in the last two complete books of *The Faerie Queene*. The Milton community has shown me the purpose of this conjunction.

NOTES

1 The 1998 essay printed here is revised, updated, and extended through the inclusion of notes. The original essay is prefaced by an Editor's Note, describing the special session in which Rajan presented his address as one

'devoted to changes in critical perspectives on Milton's work since the publication of Professor Rajan's landmark *"Paradise Lost" and the Seventeenth Century Reader* in 1947.' The presentations consisted of Albert C. Labriola's 'Chaos and Creation in Milton Studies,' John P. Rumrich's 'Reinventing Milton,' and Elizabeth Sauer's 'Milton Studies and the Post-colonial Reader.'

2 Rapaport, *Milton and the Postmodern*; see, for example, Goldberg, 'Dating Milton'; Belsey, *John Milton: Language, Gender and Power.*

3 Achinstein, *Milton and the Revolutionary Reader.* Some of the ramifications of the politics of reading are explored in *Books and Readers in Early Modern England: Material Studies*, published after this essay was printed. Page 237n1 lists important contributions to the topic.

4 Froula, 'When Eve Reads Milton: Undoing the Canonical Economy.'

5 Nyquist's essays include: 'The Father's Word/Satan's Wrath'; 'The Genesis of Gendered Subjectivity'; 'Gynesis, Genesis, Exegesis, and the Formation of Milton's Eve'; and 'Reading the Fall: Discourse and Drama in *Paradise Lost.*'

6 For an overview of this subject to 1986, see Shullenberger, 'Wresting with the Angel: *Paradise Lost* and Feminist Criticism.' See also Wittreich, *Feminist Milton.* The following are among the significant post-1987 contributions: *Milton and Gender*, ed. Gimelli Martin; Grossman, 'The Rhetoric of Feminine Priority in *Paradise Lost*'; Swiss, 'Repairing Androgyny: Eve's Tears in *Paradise Lost*'; Chaplin, '"One Flesh, One Heart, One Soul": Renaissance Friendship and Miltonic Marriage'; and Polydorou, 'Gender and Spiritual Equality in Marriage: A Dialogic Reading of Rachel Speght and John Milton.'

   Gender differences in *Paradise Lost* are presented not only along the Adam-Eve axis but also along the Father-Son axis, the classical-Christian heroism axis, and the Poet-Muse axis. These play into each other in a manner which makes it simplistic to isolate any single orientation.

7 Quint, *Epic and Empire: Politics and Generic Form from Virgil to Milton*; Evans, *Milton's Imperial Epic: 'Paradise Lost' and the Discourse of Colonialism*; Said, *The World, the Text and the Critic*, 16–24, passim.

8 Some of the mapping takes place in *Milton and the Imperial Vision*, published after this essay was prepared. Pages 323–4n4 of that book list significant studies of the topic. Studies of Milton's republicanism are less likely to be embarrassing than studies of his imperialism, and have prospered accordingly: Worden, 'Milton's Republicanism and the Tyranny of Heaven'; von Maltzahn, *Milton's 'History of Britain': Republican Historiography in the English Revolution*; Patterson, *Reading Between the Lines*, 211–75; *Milton and Republicanism*; Mueller, 'Contextualizing Milton's Nascent Republicanism'; Norbrook, 'The True Republican: Putting the Politics Back into Milton'; and *Writing the*

English Republic: Poetry, Rhetoric and Politics; Kolbrener, *Milton's Warring Angels: A Study of Critical Engagements*; Skinner, *Liberty Before Liberalism*. The engagement (or contest) between republicanism and imperialism has not been sufficiently examined. We can treat both as aspects of nationhood. If we do so, we are arguing for a complex and shifting perception of national identity in which priorities are desirable but not clear.

9 The controversy was initiated by William B. Hunter in a paper read to the International Milton Symposium at Vancouver, British Columbia, in 1991 and published as 'The Provenance of the *Christian Doctrine*.' Earlier discussions of the issue include Campbell, '*De Doctrina Christiana*: Its Structural Principles and Its Unfinished State,' answered by Kelley, 'On the State of Milton's *De Doctrina Christiana*.' The growth of the controversy since Hunter's article is evident in Lewalski and Shawcross, 'Forum: Milton's *Christian Doctrine*'; Hunter, 'The Provenance of the *Christian Doctrine*: Addenda from the Bishop of Salisbury'; and Hill, 'Professor William B. Hunter, Bishop Burgess, and John Milton.' Also see Kelley, 'The Provenance of John Milton's *Christian Doctrine*: A Reply to William B. Hunter'; Sellin, 'John Milton's *Paradise Lost* and *De Doctrina Christiana* on Predestination'; 'The Reference to John Milton's *Tetrachordon* in *De Doctrina Christiana*'; and 'Further Responses'; Campbell et al., 'Final Report on the Provenance of *De Doctrina Christiana*'; Fallon, '"Elect Above the Rest": Theology as Self-representation in Milton'; 'Milton's Arminianism and the Authorship of *De doctrina Christiana*'; Hunter, *Visitation Unimplor'd: Milton and the Authorship of 'De Doctrina Christiana*'; Lewalski, 'Milton and *De Doctrina Christiana*: Evidences of Authorship'; Rumrich, 'Milton's Arianism: Why It Matters'; Hunter, 'Responses'; Donnelly, 'The Telos of Genres: *Paradise Lost* and *De Doctrina Christiana*'; Lieb's award-winning '*De Doctrina Christiana* and the Question of Authorship'; and Fish, *How Milton Works*, 15–19. Also see chapter 2 of this book, 'The Poetics of Heresy,' and chapter 7, 'The Two Creations.'

10 Sewell, *A Study in Milton's 'Christian Doctrine.'*

11 Kelley, *This Great Argument: A Study of Milton's 'De Doctrina Christiana' as a Gloss upon 'Paradise Lost.'*

5 Banyan Trees and Fig Leaves: Some Thoughts on Milton's India

Headnote

Rajan's earliest postcolonial reading of Milton was published as 'Banyan Trees and Fig Leaves: Some Thoughts on Milton's India' in *Of Poetry and Politics: New Essays on Milton and His World*, edited by P.G. Stanwood (1995), and then revised for inclusion in *Under Western Eyes: India from Milton to Macaulay* (1999).

The self-contesting nature of *Paradise Lost*, established at length in chapter 3, results in multiple representations of India, which in their entanglement with each other reflect imperialist perceptions that are correspondingly entangled. The maximum degree of entanglement is displayed in the banyan tree image. The tree is suggestively located in 'Malabar or Deccan,' the site of the first Western presence (Portuguese) on Indian soil.

Paradise Lost may not be imperialist but it is imperial in its deportment and in its consolidating energies. Its shaping presence in imperialist perceptions of India is brought out at length in Rajan's *Under Western Eyes*. Milton's earlier work reinforces many of those perceptions but as the present chapter and chapters 6 and 8 indicate, it also provides a critique of them, focused tellingly on the consumer ethos and its consequences for the future of our world.

Scholarship on Milton's India is not voluminous, and the student in search of understanding cannot proceed very far beyond the Milton encyclopedia article on the subject. The general disposition is to treat the handful of references to India as unrelated excursions into the exotic, part of an encyclopedic epic's obligation to be encyclopedic even in its naming of places. If the references are taken together, their most conspicuous characteristic is that nearly all of them occur in infernal or postlapsarian contexts. They can then be regarded as collectively proposing the satanization of the Orient in a way becoming familiar to Milton's time. Milton's contemporaries were not unanimous on this matter.[1] Commercial relations with the East were strengthening, and it was hard to argue that the devil and his associates were the only possible source of supply for commodities that European nations wanted. The biblical imagination was less entangled in these niceties. Egypt was an abomination, and anything east of it was likely to be worse.

The first book of *Paradise Lost* is indeed heavily laden with pejorative references to the Orient. Both the catalogue of false gods and the building of Pandemonium provide rich opportunities for moral invective. The opportunities, although seized with characteristic energy, remain sufficiently routine for J.B. Broadbent to observe directly that 'the oriental similes place the building as a citadel of barbaric despotism.'[2] It is to be noted that Babylon forms the eastern limit of these similes, almost as if the true heart of darkness has been set apart for deeper castigation. Nevertheless, Pandemonium is not totally oriental. Its facade reflects the Mediterranean world, with Doric pillars that may be designed to remind us of the colonnade that Gian Bernini built for St Peter's. The bee was the emblem of Pope Urban VIII, who consecrated St Peter's, and Milton duly provides us with a bee simile that deflates the fallen angels and embroils the papacy in oriental viciousness. We are now in the outer chamber of Pandemonium, and a reference to pygmies beyond 'the *Indian* Mount' (*PL* 1.781) helps us to fix Pandemonium's location in the poem's imaginative space. The reference to 'Faery Elves' that follows confirms the location.[3] It remembers Shakespeare's *Midsummer Night's Dream* (2.1), where dissension in the fairy realm, sufficient to upset the seasonal order, arises over a young boy given to Titania by an Indian queen who is Titania's votaress (2.1.121–37). Spenser goes further in *The Faerie Queene*, claiming dominion over India for the world of Faerie (2.10.72). The claim can become more than fanciful in view of Queen Elizabeth's Faerie ancestry.

Pandemonium itself is hierarchically organized, with class distinctions cementing the imperial display. Its great hall is for the democratic multitude, who must contract themselves to cope with the hall's limited seating facilities. 'Far within' is the council chamber for the 'secret conclave' of the power elite, who are provided with 'golden seats' and can maintain without compromise 'thir own dimensions like themselves' (*PL* 1.790–7). The first book ends poised on these lines, and as we turn the page, the imagination opens the doors to the interior:

> High on a Throne of Royal State, which far
> Outshone the wealth of *Ormus* and of *Ind*,
> Or where the gorgeous East with richest hand
> Showers on her Kings *Barbaric* Pearl and Gold,
> Satan exalted sat, by merit rais'd
> To that bad eminence.   (*PL* 2.1–6)

Ormuz was once the emporium of the Orient, and Marvell's deluded voyagers to the Bermudas dream appropriately of 'jewels more rich than Ormuz shows.' By the time Milton wrote *Paradise Lost*, this legendary splendour was becoming a thing of the past. Ormuz's fortunes declined after its capture from the Portuguese in 1622 by an Iranian expedition with British naval support. Described in *The Lusiads* as a barren mountain of salt (10.41.1–2), important only as a marketplace for Eastern riches, it became in Milton's poem that 'island salt and bare' to which Paradise was eventually reduced.[4] On the other hand, the wealth of Ind was very much a matter of the present and was commented on by every traveller to India, including English emissaries such as Sir Thomas Roe and Sir Richard Hawkins. Their interest in the peoples and cultures of India seems marginal in comparison with their zeal in making inventories, but evangelical fervour can erupt revealingly through the assiduous stocktaking. Thus Thomas Coryat, having first described the Hindus along expected lines as a 'gentle people,' describes them almost immediately afterward as 'brutish ethnicks,' as displaying 'superstition and impiety most abominable in the highest degree,' and as 'aliens from Christ and the common-wealth of Israel.'[5]

In these circumstances, the 'Throne of Royal State' that Satan occupies and that outshines the wealth of Ind could point specifically to the Peacock Throne as the most conspicuous embodiment of that wealth. Since 1634, when Shah Jehan moved the Mughal capital to Delhi, the throne had stood in the Hall of Public Audience, a structure 600 feet long and 370 feet wide, which might have suggested the outer court of Pandemonium. Jean-Baptiste Tavernier, the French jeweller, had examined the throne in 1665, and although his detailed description was translated only after the second edition of *Paradise Lost* was published, reports about the throne would have been widespread in a London where the East India Company had been in existence for two-thirds of a century. With its pearl-fringed canopy supported by golden pillars, the throne was the epitome of the 'gorgeous east' in its opulence.[6]

When *Paradise Lost* was published, the monarch on the Peacock Throne was Dryden's hero, Aurangzeb. He could be said to have been raised to his eminence by merit, if by merit we mean the successful killing off of every other claimant. History fits the image, but Milton may not have been aware of the fitness. It is tempting to think that he was aware of the inscription, four times repeated in letters of gold, in Shah Jehan's white marble Hall of Private Audience, which corresponds to the council room of Pandemonium. As a comment on Satan's situation, its layered irony must be deemed Miltonic: 'If there be Paradise on earth, it is this, it is this, it is this!'

The direct application is obvious, but the statement becomes more interesting read against the grain, with the triple repetition compounding the force of the 'if.' Paradise can be not native but alien to the earth, won laboriously against the earth's resistance. Shah Jehan built in this way, and his achievement has become identified with one matchless building demonstrating that death is the mother of beauty. The proud hedonism is really not in conflict with another description to be found over the Victory Gate in Akbar's abandoned palace at Fatehpur Sikri: 'The world is a bridge, pass over it, but do not build upon it. He who hopes for an hour may hope for eternity. The world is but an hour; spend it in devotion, the rest is unseen.'[7] Pandemonium has been built, and the two statements put before us both the elation and the vanity of building. The mind is its own place but can only be its own place by installing itself on the Peacock Throne of the self. The throne is in the inner chamber and is thus a statement of identity as well as a public announcement, a tacit disclosure of the weakness to be found in its strength.

So far, the movement to the centre through the precincts of Pandemonium and through a corresponding geography of vainglory and ostentation seems to assign India a decisive place at the heart of the evil empire. The proposition is staged with sufficient persistence to persuade us that no other proposition needs to be made. The moral imagination can be discouragingly simplistic, but Milton is fortunately not a simple writer. In the spice trade simile, which transports Satan on his journey to Asia, he is doing much more than once again presenting India as one of the primary sites of infernality:

As when far off at Sea a Fleet descri'd
Hangs in the Clouds, by *Equinoctial* Winds
Close sailing from *Bengala*, or the Isles
Of *Ternate* and *Tidore*, whence Merchants bring
Their spicy Drugs; they on the Trading Flood
Through the wide *Ethiopian* to the Cape
Ply stemming nightly toward the Pole. So seem'd
Far off the flying Fiend.

(*PL* 2.636–43)

Ternate and Tidore are Spice Islands in the Moluccas, but the phrase is also an alliterative remembrance of *The Lusiads*, and Satan's voyage, the ancestor of all voyages, is being placed in relationship to da Gama's voyage to India, of which Camões's poem is the epic celebration. *The Lusiads*, as we have already seen, celebrates a voyage not simply from Lisbon to Calicut but also from a medieval to an imperial world order. Not without regret, it leaves the previous view and its voices of protest symbolically at its margins. As the defining of an imperial moment, it made its deflationary appearance in the midst of what should have been another imperial moment. Fanshawe's translation of it was published in the year in which Jamaica was captured as a consolation prize in Cromwell's failed Western design.

The failure of the design led to the usual reassessment of what Providence may have had in mind for God's Englishmen. An influential decoding of the divine rebuke was that English expansiveness should hereafter be commercial. England should complete its reformation before dissipating in imperial adventures, an identity that had yet to be bonded into nationhood.

Commerce in such dissociations is always presumed to be innocent of empire. Milton's accomplishment is to have seen with clarity the necessary and potentially Satanic merging of the two realms. In an age uneasily engaged in discriminating the sanctified from the demonic uses of imperialism, Milton moves hesitantly to the proposition that imperialism is itself a form of use and a form of use so profoundly exploitative that its right use is impossible. It is not a proposition Milton can endorse resoundingly. Ireland stands in his way and so does the New World. But to write a poem is to transgress ideologies.

The imperial vision in *The Lusiads* is one in which honour, dominion, glory, and renown go hand in hand with the rich rewards of the spice trade. Milton accepts the integrity of that vision and then uses that integrity to discredit both components. Classical heroism is devalued by

Christian heroism, and the main motive of commerce is discerned as consumerist self-indulgence. Milton's treatment of Camões is indeed heavily revisionary.[8] The old man's voice is heard again, but it is a critiquing, not a protesting, voice. It does not helplessly query the new order. It points instead to an immemorial order that cannot be violated without tearing apart those who violate it. The nature of his poem enables Milton to endow his warning with the weight of ancestral authority. But the warning is also culturally focused. It exposes the rottenness at the core of the consumerist apple.

According to one enthusiastic estimate, da Gama's voyage and Columbus's discovery of the New World were the greatest events in history since the Incarnation. More prosaically, the purpose of da Gama's rounding of the cape was to end the Venetian monopoly of the spice trade and to break the Arab stranglehold on the trade routes by which the 'spicy Drugs' of Asia came to Europe. Milton's realignment can be approached by noting that Bengal was not on the spice trade route and that European trade with Bengal was not in spices. The detour through Bengal may have been made to include within the scope of the simile the East India Company, for which the Bay of Bengal had been a principal theatre of operations ever since the founding of Madras in 1640. But the geographical expansion is also designed to advise us of an expansion in the scope of the term 'spicy Drugs.' As G.V. Scammell, a leading historian of early European imperialism, observes:

> Spice was a vast and ill-defined generic which also embraced perfumes like incense and musk, medicines and drugs (the galingales of China and the aloes of Socotra), dyes, and the exquisite manufactures of the East, ranging from Chinese silk and porcelain to the carpets and tapestries of Persia. To those were added the products, as we shall see, of the Middle East – the glassware for example of Damascus.[9]

The term is in fact a synecdoche for the entire range of conspicuous consumption, and conspicuous consumption had been an issue with Milton ever since 1634, when Comus produced a bizarre ecological argument in its favour.[10] Thrift needed to be part of the Protestant ethic if the middle class was to be instrumental in capital formation. At this point in the poem, 'spicy Drugs' anticipates Adam's and Eve's transgression and the hallucinogenic qualities of the forbidden fruit. The link is invited even though drugs in seventeenth-century usage were not typically hallucinogenic and even though Adam Smith as late as 1776 described tea as a drug.[11] Milton's aim in inviting the link and in departing from his view in the *Treatise on Christian Doctrine* that the forbidden fruit was 'in itself neither good nor evil' (*CPW* 6:352) is to join original sin to all subsequent excesses in consumption ('Greedily she ingorg'd without restraint' [9.791]) and to inscribe the Satanic voyage within subsequent voyages of exploration and commerce as the tainted origin from which they may need to be rescued. In the process, attention shifts from the Orient as a primary site of evil to the Orient as supplier to a clientele who have discovered it and made use of it to pamper the weakness within themselves. It is notable that the fleet described in the simile is en route to Europe, laden with the profits of the spice trade, even though Satan is en route to Asia.[12]

In looking at Milton's similes, we have to pass by their most important characteristic, namely the extraordinary completeness with which the similes translate what they purport to resemble. We have to restrict ourselves to how India is perceived within the translation. It is already clear that there can be more than one perception, depending on the course of action or the religious or moral imperative to which the construction of India is annexed. The next reference to India occurs when Satan alights on the outer shell of the 'pendent world' – an outer shell where limbo is derisively located and that is compared in its desolation to the central Asian plateau:

> As when a Vultur on *Imaus* bred,
> Whose snowy ridge the roving *Tartar* bounds,
> Dislodging from a Region scarce of prey
> To gorge the flesh of Lambs or yeanling Kids
> On Hills where Flocks are fed, flies towards the Springs
> Of *Ganges* or *Hydaspes, Indian* streams;
> But in his way lights on the barren Plains
> Of *Sericana,* where *Chineses* drive
> With Sails and Wind thir cany Waggons light:
> So on this windy Sea of Land, the Fiend
> Walk'd up and down alone bent on his prey.   (*PL* 3.431–41)

The crucial element in this compendious simile is the pun that joins Tartar to Tartarus. Milton did not invent the pun; it is attributed to Pope Innocent IV in response to Tartar invasions that, by 1241, had extended into Hungary and Germany. In further response to those invasions,

Pope Innocent's successor, Pope Alexander IV, issued the following warning to the princes of Christendom:

> There rings in the ears of all, and arouses to vigilant alertness those who are not befuddled by mental torpor, a terrible trumpet of dire forewarning which, corroborated by the evidence of events, proclaims with so unmistakable a sound the wars of universal destruction wherewith the scourge of Heaven's wrath in the hands of the inhuman Tartars, erupting as it were from the secret confines of Hell, oppresses and crushes the earth [so] that it is no longer the task of Christian people to prick up their ears so as to receive surer tidings of these things, as though they were still in doubt, but their need is rather for admonition to take provident action against a peril impending and palpably approaching.[13]

The similarities between the papal bull and Milton's poem, written over four centuries later, do not need to be laboured. Particularly important is the connection between the Tartar invasions and the opening lines of book 4, where the poet wishes that Adam and Eve had been shocked into attention by that 'warning voice,' that 'terrible trumpet,' as the papal bull has it, foretelling the 'wars of universal destruction' envisioned in Revelation 12:7–12. The conspicuous difference is that the pope's concerns are limited to the penetration of Europe by the Tartars. India is not even on the horizon of calamity. In Milton's simile, on the other hand, India is central. It is the destination to which the vulture flies, leaving an inhospitable and barren habitat in search of a more fertile environment where it can 'gorge the flesh of Lambs or yeanling Kids.' It is true that the vulture seeks the sources of the Jhelum (Hydaspes) and the Ganges rather than the plain that those great rivers irrigate and that future invasions of India were to ravage. But its flight, Satan's journey, and the Tartar debauchment into India run related courses, brought together all the more evocatively because the earthly Paradise was reputed to lie where the Ganges had its beginnings. In the opening lines of the seventh canto of *The Lusiads*, for instance, all India is hailed as lying in proximity to this Paradise (see also 4.74). More than one ancient father followed Josephus in making the Ganges one of the rivers of Paradise.[14] Milton, like most of his contemporaries, locates Paradise elsewhere, but his simile remains freighted with these associations.

In linking India to Paradise and the vulture's flight to the Satanic journey, Milton now presents India not as the site of infernality but as its victim. It is a construction reinforced by 'Lambs or yeanling Kids,' which, apart from its religious overtones, cannot but suggest the exposure of inexperience and helplessness to the onslaught of power and cruelty. Tamburlaine sacked Delhi in 1398 and is said to have slaughtered 80,000 of its inhabitants, leaving pyramids of skulls to mark the milestones on the city's highways. The Great Mogul, on the Peacock Throne when Milton wrote his poem, proudly affirmed his descent from the house of Timur. Milton's immediate reference is to the Tartars, but the reference can be extended to all the invasions that the snowy ridge of Imaus could not contain and that erupted into India along a much-travelled route of conquest. We can even read the 'windy Sea of Land,' which so felicitously materializes the indeterminate nature of limbo, as pointing to a windy sea not of land, which was to become the route of further conquests. Milton obviously did not intend to say this, but poems have a life beyond their boundaries.

In the fifth book, Raphael descends to Paradise not to blow 'a terrible trumpet of dire forewarning' but to 'bring on' 'discourse' and thereby instruct Adam and Eve on their place in the order of things. He approaches the Edenic pair through a wilderness of 'flow'ring Odors,' a 'spicy Forest' that invites us to reflect on the misappropriation of the spice trade (5.291–9). Dinner is served, with an international menu on which India is prominently, although vaguely, featured. The emphasis is not on indiscriminate variety but on 'Taste after taste upheld with kindliest change' (5.336). There is no gorging on the flesh of lambs or yeanling kids. The meal is vegetarian, and the three partake of it in order to suffice and not to burden nature (5.451–2).

Commenting on the meal, Alastair Fowler detects a 'grim irony.' Pontus was notorious as a source of poisons, and Punic figs were best known for the threat to Rome that Plutarch made them symbolize.[15] Good things can be directed to evil uses, as is apparent even from the pre- and postlapsarian connotations of words such as 'errant' and 'wanton.' Milton is at pains to advise us that when the right order of things existed, it was eloquent about itself, even in such matters as serving an appropriate meal to a visiting angel. But the right order of things can no longer be presumed to exist pristinely behind the masks of misappropriation. Shifting depictions of India do not necessarily lay bare an essential India that lies beyond and is uncontaminated by the depictions. Representations may unmask previous representations, but they, in turn, may put in place assumptions that need to be unmasked. Milton's multiple constructions of India place strikingly before us the relativity of constructions and their entanglement with one another in a confused amalgam that both represents the texture of imperial discourse and lays its prevarications open to scrutiny. Milton is complicit in some of the prevarications. He is also committed to the scrutiny.

These entanglements have to be borne in mind as we proceed to the proliferations of the banyan tree passage, which, of all Milton's images of India, is the most compelling and also the most evasive (9.1099–1118). Before doing so, we need to consider Satan's activities in the interval between his expulsion from Paradise by Gabriel and his assistants and his second entry for the successful temptation. Satan has circled the earth three times in an east-west and four times in a north-south direction. The purpose of these peregrinations is not merely to survey his kingdom while he awaits another opportunity but also with 'inspection deep' to consider which among the world's creatures might best 'serve his wiles.' His last stop is the 'Land where flows / Ganges and Indus,' and his final choice, 'after long debate,' is 'The Serpent subtlest Beast of all the Field' (9.81–2, 86–7). It is more than arguable that the infernal potentiality of India is once again being underlined and that India as victim or as prime provider of a repast fit for angels has receded into the background.

Satan now enters Paradise but not with his earlier exuberance, when, with 'one slight bound,' he leapt over the garden's protective barrier (4.181). This time he makes his entry via one of the rivers of Paradise, fortunately not the Pison, which was identified with the Ganges, but the Tigris, which shoots into an underground gulf at the foot of Paradise and surfaces as a fountain next to the tree of life. Satan emerges in the rising mist of the fountain 'involv'd' with the primordial fluidity, as if inextricably part of the elemental nature of things (9.69–76).

The choice of India as the last stop before Paradise and of the serpent, with which India is strongly associated, as the fittest vehicle for the original sin might be regarded as appropriate preliminaries to the choice of the banyan tree for the original cover-up. Milton's emphatic dismissal of alternatives seems designed to pave the way for the cumulative infernalization of India. The subtlety and deviousness of which the serpent is the symbol and the comprehensive concealment afforded by the banyan tree are invested in *Paradise Lost* with the authority of origins. These propositions were soon to be engraved in imperial rhetoric as routinely part of India's representation.

Paradise Lost is a scholarly poem, and when Milton, in choosing his tree, waves aside 'that kind for Fruit renown'd' (9.1101), he reminds us of an earlier gesture. In the fourth book, the possibility that Paradise may lie at the summit of Mount Amara, 'under the *Ethiop* Line / By *Nilus* head,' is dismissed. It is, Milton tells us, 'by some suppos'd' (4.281–3). In fact, it is hard to find anyone who confidently upholds this possibility, although every discussion of the location of Paradise raises it. The citation count is extensive, but the acceptance count approaches zero. Milton is very much in the majority here, tilting at a windmill in the robust fashion of scholarship. In the ninth book, on the other hand, he may be in a minority, even though Sir Walter Raleigh, in discussing this possibility, is able to cite more than one precedent.[16]

Reasons for going against the majority view can always be found and are most persuasive when they can be shown to be part of the imaginative logic of the poem. If the choice of the banyan tree is striking, so too is the readiness to make Paradise a site for postlapsarian lust. 'God áttributes to place / No sanctity, if none be thither brought' is Milton's justification for the destruction of Paradise (11.836–7). The desecration of sanctity that Milton's departure from precedent serves to underline deepens the original shame and calls for a more comprehensive cover-up. The connections are plausible, but we still need to argue that an innovation is not justified by referring it to another innovation that need not have been made.

Another view might be that infernalizing India has always been part of the poem's agenda and that the more benign presentations we have explored merely mean that the infernalization is not total. 'The proliferating tree is a tree of error,' John Carey and Alastair Fowler tell us categorically. 'It is an objective correlative of the proliferating sin that will ramify through Adam's and Eve's descendants.'[17] If true, this conclusion is a virulent desacralization of a tree that has always been holy to Indians as both the site and the subject of Upanishadic instruction, a tree that Southey, in a poem not particularly sympathetic to India, approaches with respect as a temple of nature.[18] Moore similarly refers to the 'sacred shade' of those 'holy trees whose smooth columns and spreading roots seem to destine them for natural temples of religion.'[19]

Milton's similes invite straightforward readings by their sustained correspondences between tenor and vehicle. But his language can also circumvent and retreat from the dominant momentum it nourishes. The tree 'spreads her Arms' in an encompassing gesture reminiscent of the crucifixion. The 'Daughters grow / About the Mother Tree' (9.1105–6), and the gesture can be read as bringing together and protecting the human family rather than as bringing about the confusion that John Gerard describes in his *Herball*: 'The first or mother of this wood or desart of trees, is hard to be knowne from the children.'[20] The 'Pillar'd shade' that the daughter trees provide suggests a composed architecture rather than a wilderness of reflections. Yet in putting forward his representation, Milton always seems aware of another representation that may be the normal reading and that the turns of his language are not prepared to reject. The pillared shade also recalls the Doric pillars of Pandemonium, and their 'High overarch'd' formations take us back to the Vallombrosa simile, in which the infernal angels were compared to leaves fallen from the tree of life into the valley of the shadow of death (1.302–4). The '*Etrurian* shades' of the Vallombrosa trees were 'imbow'r[ed]' as they turned in on themselves. The bower of concealment is similar and is in designed contrast to the nuptial bower of book 4, lines 690–708. Yet when Kester Svendsen describes the recesses of the tree as a 'deep interior sanctuary,'[21] he is not proceeding against Milton's language. The tree serves as shelter, although it can also be used for concealment. It permits withdrawal into meditative depths. It also encourages absorption in a narcissistic coma. Its 'echoing Walks' can be self-imprisoning, but they can also prolong the cadences of voices that need to be heard (4.680–5).

The contesting interpretations of itself that the spreading tree puts forward do not debar us from seeing it as a temple of nature, but they encourage us to read its proliferations and decentrations as an expanding assault on hierarchical order. Its leaves are not really as 'broad as *Amazonian* Targe,'[22] and if bodily concealment were the objective, other trees in India would have served the purpose better. But other trees would not have lent themselves to the emblematization delighted in by Renaissance herbalists and compilers of dictionaries. The Amazons are introduced not so that a passing reference can be made to the size of their shields but as a further source of hierarchical disturbance, with which readers of book 5 of *The Faerie Queene* would have been familiar. They go well with the role reversal that has been prominent in Milton's version of the Fall and with the feminization of the tree, which, blessed exclusively with daughters, compounds by its generative wantonness the destabilization of structure and design.

As we trace the echoing walks of this particular passage, many of the echoes lead us back through the history of the poem into occasions or images of the infernal. The lines are all the more disturbing because the tree's natural attributes lend themselves so easily to demonic appropriation. In addition, Milton compounds the discommoding effect by making gestures towards scientific accuracy, reminding us that the Fall was history to him even though it may be mythology to us. 'Columbus found the American so girt,' he tells us decisively. Primitive societies are closer to the source, and the characteristics of the source can be discerned more clearly in them.[23] The land that was mistaken for India justifies its erroneous identification by indicating how the resources of the true India were used. The banyan tree is 'at this day to *Indians* known.' Any official of the East India Company could inspect it and verify that there was no better way for Adam and Eve to cope with the sudden problem of their nakedness.

It is against the passage's traversals of itself and the received interpretations it accepts and circumvents that we need to consider the figure of the herdsman. Fowler is less than tactful in arguing that 'the Indian herdsman is put in because he is primitive and pagan.'[24] He is put in to point out to us that, although his responsibilities are far more limited than those of the faithful herdsman in *Lycidas*, he observes these responsibilities, unlike the corrupt clergy whom Milton excoriates and unlike Adam and Eve at this moment. He 'tends his pasturing Herds,' and if he seeks the protection of the tree and cuts loopholes through the 'thickest shade' of its foliage, it is not to conceal himself but to perform his task more efficiently and with less likelihood of being incapacitated by sunstroke.

Other revealing images offer themselves as we contemplate the figure of the herdsman. Adam and Eve, like him, are hidden in the tree's recesses, but it is the flock that is now hidden, not the shepherd. The shepherd seeks refuge from the heat of the sun's rays. Adam and Eve seek refuge from the 'blaze / Insufferably bright' (9.1083–4) of the Son's presence. The Son is the shepherd, offering a protection symbolized by the tree's outstretched arms, which the guilty pair unknowingly invoke in using that very tree to avoid the Son's gaze. Milton's lines in their dense entanglements work powerfully to persuade us that appropriation is not simply a matter of channeling the properties of the tree to infernal uses. The tree is reinvented by the perspective in which it is installed. And the perspective cannot be said to be optional. It is largely responsible for inventing those who use it.

The final reference to India is in the panorama of the world's empires that Adam sees from the highest hill of Paradise. The *Aeneid*, book 6, is being remembered, with Milton's typical distancing from that seminal text. The vision is seen from a hill and not foretold in the underworld; it is concerned with all empires, not one; and it turns from those empires to 'nobler sights' (11.411), from the sequence of secular pomp to the meaning of sacred history. Camões, diligently Virgilian in his machinery, is intermediate between Virgil and Milton. Like Virgil, he is concerned with a single nation's imperial destiny. Like Milton, his hero is shown the future from a mountaintop. But it is a future in which empire building is glorified, not questioned. Adam looks at the havoc to which his actions will lead. Vasco da Gama looks at the fulfilment of his mission in a future that is only possible because of his heroic accomplishment. The splendours of the Portuguese empire are elegantly displayed to him gift wrapped in the layers of the Ptolemaic universe (*Lusiads* 10.78–91).

Virgil associates the Roman destiny with ancestral statements of the white man's burden, with bringing justice and the rule of law to barbarians.[25] Camões is less concerned with such refinements and shows us the face of imperialism more candidly. Those who chafe under Portugal's light yoke will be made to pay dearly for their insolence. Ironically, the example chosen is Ormuz, which was to pass out of Portuguese hands forever half a century after Camões published his poem and well before Fanshawe's English translation became available.

The mountaintop prophecy, the panorama of empires, and the roll call of place names form multiple lines of connection between *Paradise Lost* and *The Lusiads*. The connections are enforced by the second of Milton's alliterative remembrances – '*Mombaza,* and *Quiloa,* and *Melind*' (11.399).[26] Melind was da Gama's last port of call before setting off on the final stage of his audacious voyage to India under the helpful guidance of an Indian pilot.[27]

The overlap in the view from the two mountaintops is extensive. One might argue that some attention has been paid to making it extensive. To connect the two poems is to become pointedly aware of the sudden blaze and swift extinction of the Portuguese imperial dream. That recognition finds its way back into Milton's poem as a general comment on the transience of empires. What we see from the mountaintop in the first place is the peripheral turbulence and pandemonium of history, not the inner theatre of clarified engagement where the forces shaping history are exposed.

Much has changed in the descent from Virgil, and Virgil's Rome is among the empires dismissed. From an Iraqi mountaintop, Rome and 'Agra and Lahor of great mogul' (11.391) are approximately equidistant;[28] 'great mogul' designates not simply the dynasty but a diamond of unprecedented size (the Kohinoor) presented to Shah Jehan. Stereotypes of oriental opulence are reinforced, taking us back in one of the poem's many circularities to the wealth of Ind and Satan's throne of royal state. But Rome was also a centre of ostentatious excess, as *Paradise Regained* makes clear, and so far there has been nothing in the poem to suggest that Asia surpasses Rome in moral turpitude. We can even conjecture that if Milton had known of it, the Augustinian inscription at Fatehpur Sikri would have appealed to him more than any Roman text.

The inner theatre of significance, surrounded by an otherwise meaningless periphery of empires, dramatizes the proposition that the only true kingdom is the kingdom of God. The nature of things in their purity does not permit the rule of one people by another: 'Man over men / He made not Lord; such title to himself / Reserving, human left from human free' (*PL* 12.69–71). Unfortunately, we are dealing not with the nature of things but with their fallen nature. In such circumstances, 'Tyranny must be, / Though to the Tyrant thereby no excuse' (12.95–6).

The argument does not condone tyranny, but it does suggest that attempts to overthrow tyranny will only reinscribe it unless they are accompanied by a radical change in the structure of the self. One can accept this as an argument, but it needs to be pointed out in reply that Milton unbalances his critique of dominance by too strong an insistence that subjected peoples deserve their own misfortunes. In the England of a failed revolution, this insistence may have been proper to the poetics of the moment. On a less localized scale, we have to observe that phrases such as 'Tyranny must be' amount to a de facto acquiescence to tyranny. Tyrants are seldom deterred by the observation that their behaviour cannot be excused.

The failed revolution and the need to justify its failure continue to be present in Milton's thought as the temptation of Rome is offered. In *Paradise Regained*, Satan accompanies his offer with the hyperbolic statement that not merely India but also Sumatra and the Malay Peninsula render obedience to '*Rome*'s great Emperor (4.73–6).[29] Christ does not contest this exaggeration. Presumably, he has more important things on his mind. He points out predictably that Romans have earned their fate by their degeneracy. 'Peeling thir Provinces,' already exhausted by lust and rapine, and carried away by the 'insulting vanity' of their triumphs, they are luxury loving, cruel, greedy, and 'from the daily Scene effeminate' (*PR* 4.136–42). That last and climactic epithet, used extensively by the Romans in the denigration of Egypt, was to be much used again in marginalizing India. Originating in Michael's rebuke to Adam (*PL* 11.634), it becomes the final touch in the conqueror's inward enslavement to the other he constructs for his contempt.

Milton's description of Rome's degeneracy is not surprising, but his prelapsarian characterization of the Romans as just, frugal, mild, and temperate (*PR* 4.133–4) seems to invoke Christian rather than classical heroism.[30] The choice of virtues becomes clearer when we turn to the *Second Defence*: 'To be free is precisely the same as to be pious, wise, just, and temperate, careful of one's property, aloof from another's, and thus finally to be magnanimous and brave' (*CPW* 4:684). A parallel between Rome and seventeenth-century England is clearly in the making, and perhaps it is the pursuit of this parallel that leads Milton to observe that the Romans 'conquer'd well, / But govern ill' (*PR* 4.134–5).[31] Government by conquest can never be good government. Human was 'left from human free' by the divine edict, and relationships between peoples based on dominance can never be other than deformed. Difference turned into confusion and conversation into the failure to communicate when the original tower of dominance was built. Milton's language at this point moves away from an egalitarian recognition that his previous language has inscribed. In an age when empires were materializing on the horizon and India was beginning to assume its glittering shape as the most coveted of imperial prizes, he cannot quite say that the pursuit of empires can only be destructive and that no people can 'conquer well.' In addition, his concentration on an inner theatre where the principles of a single wisdom are made manifest by their performance in history reduces other wisdoms to peripheral status. At best, the periphery can only reflect the centre or be the shadowy type to the centre's truth. The design of understanding is potentially imperial. Other designs that are less lofty and humane will sustain themselves on the same geography of privilege.

The appropriation of Milton to this geography of privilege is an important thread in the fabric of this book. His references to India may not be numerous, but his part in India's representation is not merely a matter of six similes that show that he is capable of seeing India in more than one light. *Paradise Lost*, although not imperialist, is imperial as no other poem in the canon is. It is true that the imperial display is consecrated to the pervading and benevolent force of the universal and mild monarchy of heaven, but in the inevitable secularizing of the sacred, other translations of the display must emerge. The centre-circumference dispositions, the hierarchical ordering of the poem's principal and almost only human relationship, the omnific word transforming a cosmic chaos that it is not difficult to displace into political anarchy, and the wilderness set against the ordered garden that must be tended and watched over if it is not to relapse into its origins are all perceptions that play a crucial part in the imperialist statement as an apparently timeless work of the literary canon, symbolically blind to the contingent, finds its way back into the arena of power.

Paradise Lost is the work of a totalizing energy by which dreams of empire cannot but be nourished. That nourishment sustains not merely the rhetoric of imperialism but, more fundamentally, the fictions of self-justification that stabilize that rhetoric and endow it with its necessary dignity. Ironically, the poem's foundations (as distinct from those of the imperialism that appropriated it) include a concept of Christian heroism that can be perceived as leading through *Prometheus Unbound* to the nonviolent strategies that gained India its independence. That fact is not simply to be savoured with relish; it educates us in the extent to which the canon itself, in its sometimes troubled self-awareness, can be instrumental in its own dismantling.[32]

NOTES

1 Dryden's play *Aureng-Zebe*, first performed at Drury Lane on 17 November 1675, the year after the twelve-book edition of *Paradise Lost* was published, seems to offer a different view of the Orient. Appearances can be wittily misleading, as chapter 3 attempts to show.

2 Broadbent, *Some Graver Subject*, 102.

3 India's association with the land of Faerie is picked up in Keats's 'The Cap and Bells or The Jealousies.'

4 See Sims, 'Camoëns' *Lusiads* and Milton's *Paradise Lost*: Satan's Voyage to Eden,' 38–9.

5 Roe, *The Embassy of Sir Thomas Roe to the Court of the Great Mogul 1615–19*. For Hawkins, see *Early Travels in India, 1583–1619*, 70–121; for Coryat, see ibid., 269. A typically lively account of Roe's embassy is provided in Bamber Gascoigne's *The Great Moghuls*, 141–50.

6 The phrase is used by Shakespeare in *Love's Labour's Lost* 4.3.220, although not with the associations with which Milton invests it. Its most famous and possibly final use is in Wordsworth's sonnet on the extinction of the Venetian republic.

7 As translated in Hansen, *The Peacock Throne*, 68.

8 On Milton's revisionary treatment of Camões, see Sims, 'A Greater Than Rome: The Inversion of a Virgilian Symbol from Camões to Milton.'

9 Scammell, *The World Encompassed: The First European Maritime Empires*, 101–2.

10 Milton, *A Mask Presented at Ludlow Castle, Poems*, ll. 705–35.

11 Smith, *The Wealth of Nations*, 235.

12 The view put forward here is consistent with that offered in Sims, 'Camoëns' *Lusiads* and Milton's *Paradise Lost*,' 43–4. See also Quint, *Epic and Empire*, 253–67. Quint rightly observes that 'Milton in keeping with his general criticism of the earlier epic tradition exposes as false the distinction which that tradition draws between martial heroism and mercantile activity' (264).

13 Pope Alexander IV, qtd in Latham, trans., *Marco Polo: The Travels*, 11.

14 See Drew, *India and the Romantic Imagination*, 166. Compare *PL* 9.76–82 and the comment in *Poems*, edited by Carey and Fowler (1968), 86n. Joseph E. Duncan observes that the association of Paradise with India was strongest during the Middle Ages when Prester John was reputed to have established himself in the Far East. With his relocation to Ethiopia, interest in India as the site of Paradise waned (Duncan, *Milton's Earthly Paradise: A Historical Study of Eden*, 76, 195). The most extensive discussion is in Darian, *The Ganges in Myth and History*, 172–82.

15 *Poems*, edited by Carey and Fowler (1968), 695n.

16 Raleigh, *History of the World*, 136–9. In his introduction, Patrides sees Raleigh as a possible source for this passage, but it should be remembered that Raleigh seems to distance himself from the identification he discusses (38).

17 *Poems*, edited by Carey and Fowler (1968), 920n.

18 Southey, *The Curse of Kehama*, in *The Poetical Works*, vol. 8, 13.5.

19 Moore, *Lalla Rookh*, in Godley, editor, *The Poetical Works of Thomas Moore*, 42. In an even more fervent commendation of the banyan tree, Sydney Owenson describes it as 'the most stupendous and beautiful production of the vegetable world' and as a 'symbol of eternity' whose 'great and splendid order the Architect of the universe himself designed.' Defying 'the decay of time, it stands alone and bold, reproducing its own existence and multiplying its own form' (*The Missionary*, 2:9–10). See also the compendious entry in Yule and Burnell, *Hobson-Jobson: A Glossary of Colloquial Anglo-Indian Words and Phrases and of Kindred Terms*, 65–7. Milton's lines on the tree were sufficiently known to be quoted by a Bengali Moslem, Dean Mahomed, in a 1794 account (published in Ireland) of his travels in India and departure from it. See Fisher, *The First Indian Author in English: Dean Mahomed*, 82.

20 Quoted in *Poems*, edited by Carey and Fowler (1968), 920n. Although Renaissance herbalists resemble each other markedly in their descriptions of the banyan tree, Gerard's language here is striking in suggesting the essential similarly between the proliferating wood and the barren desert. Both are places of temptation in Milton's work. Gerard's infernalizing of the tree, which Romantic writers reverse, should be contrasted with Milton's ambivalences. R.R. Cawley in *Milton and the Literature of Travel* cautions us against

searching for single sources of passages in Milton, who usually amalgamates more than one source. Viswanathan, 'Milton and Purchas's Linschoten: An Additional Source for Milton's Indian Figtree,' puts forward a case for this ingredient in the conflation. The case is disputed by McHenry in 'A Milton Herbal,' 69. .

21   Svendsen, *Milton and Science*, 135.

22   Pliny makes the comparison to Amazonian shields, but Raleigh, who claims to have actually seen banyan tress in the New World, disagrees (*History of the World*, 137–9).

23   These crucial lines are as follows: 'Such of late / *Columbus* found th' *American* so girt / With feather'd Cincture, naked else and wild / Among the Trees on Isles and woody Shores' (*PL* 9.1115–18). The 'of late,' which seems to advise us of the up-to-dateness of Milton's scholarship, refers to discoveries that took place 170 years before *Paradise Lost* was published. The distant event is also misperceived. Columbus did not find the American girt at all but clad in 'native Honor,' as Adam and Eve were before taking refuge in the banyan tree. The 'feather'd Cincture' in which Milton chooses to attire the '*American*' refers to much later encounters on the mainland. The confusions of time and place seem to be made with one overriding purpose. If First Nations can be identified with the original shame rather than with the original innocence, their distance from a redeemed Christian state can be made more important than their proximity to the Edenic. Western encounters with the New World were initially beguiled by that proximity. As the need to devalue subjected civilizations took over, the depth of distance inevitably prevailed. Milton seems to provide a micro-enactment of this historical change in perception, as his language passes from a nakedness associated in the fourth book with majesty and innocence to a nakedness now associated with wildness. Paradise can be a 'Wilderness of sweets' and 'Wild above Rule or Art' (5.294–7), but these Edenic connotations are heavily overlaid by the infernal associations that surround wildness in its fallen state. So pressing are these associations that Adam sees the luxuriance of Paradise as a wilderness, even as he decides to partake of the fruit with Eve (9.910).

24   *Poems*, edited by Carey and Fowler (1968), 920n.

25   This is the mandate given by the shade of Anchises to Aeneas in the sixth book of the *Aeneid*. The excellence of others (presumably the Greeks) may lie in astronomy, philosophy, literature, and the fine arts; the Roman accomplishment will be to govern other nations with the firmness and justice those nations are unable to find within themselves.

26   Camões (*The Lusiads* 1.54) mentions Mombasa, Quiloa, and Sofala. Milton

repeats all three names in 11.399–400 and inserts Melind, not simply for the alliterative effect but because Melind was crucial to the outcome of da Gama's voyage. See Tillyard, *The English Epic and Its Background*, 241, and *Bowra, From Virgil to Milton*, 238.

27 Scammell identifies the pilot as Ibn Majid, 'the most distinguished navigator of the time' (*World Encompassed*, 235). Ravenstein, in his edition of the *First Voyage of Vasco da Gama*, identifies the pilot as 'a native of Gujarat' (45–6n). See chapter 8 note 11 for further information.

28 Carey and Fowler do not capitalize 'great mogul' (*Poems*, edited by Carey and Fowler [1968]). Other editions capitalize and underline it. I retain the capitalization elsewhere. In coupling Agra and Lahore, Milton follows early travellers such as William Finch, Thomas Coryat, and Edward Terry, the last of whom describes Agra and Lahore as 'the two choice cities of this Empire.' The tree-lined boulevard connecting the two cities is admired by all (*Early Travels in India*, 155–67, 243–93).

29 *Paradise Regained* in hereafter cited as *PR*. Carey and Fowler note that G.W. Whiting (*Review of English Studies* 13 [1937]: 209–12) has produced evidence to indicate that Taprobane usually meant Sumatra (*Poems*, edited by Carey and Fowler [1968], p. 1139). However, *The Lusiads* (10.107) identifies Taprobane with Sri Lanka. Since Taprobane is mentioned by Milton in conjunction with the Malayan Peninsula ('golden Chersoness'), Sumatra is indicated, particularly since *The Lusiads* (10.124) suggests that Sumatra was once joined to the Malayan Peninsula. 'Indian isle' may seem to suggest Sri Lanka, but Sumatra was part of 'further India,' and 'utmost' would be less effective if Sri Lanka were intended. According to Major, the identification of Taprobane with Sumatra 'was maintained throughout the maps, almost all of them Italian, of the sixteenth century and was continued by Mercator' (*India in the Fifteenth Century*, lxii).

30 Since contemporary Rome was the other of Protestantism, it is fitting that classical Rome in its decadence should provide this other with its ancestry. But Rome's story is also England's and is a clear warning of how the re-formed collective self can slide back into the other if it is wanting in vigilance.

31 Milton may be alluding to the passage in the *Aeneid* discussed in note 25.

32 English imperialist and Protestant poetics are never very far from each other. Barbara Lewalski's *Protestant Poetics and the Seventeenth Century Religious Lyric* has demonstrated how heavily the religious poetics of seventeenth-century England depended on the image of God in the self. Within imperialist poetics the presence of the image confers the right to dominion, but

the right can be argued to be contingent on a standard of behaviour that testifies convincingly to that presence. Gandhi's achievement was to have brought the interrogative pressure of the civil disobedience movement to bear decisively on this moral linchpin, displaying in the process a degree of Christian heroism that the dominant power was requested to find in itself.

6 The Imperial Temptation

Headnote

This essay first appeared in *Milton and the Imperial Vision*, edited by Balachandra Rajan and Elizabeth Sauer (1999). The volume won the Irene Samuel Memorial Award in 2000. Rajan's first essay on *Paradise Regained* appeared in *Th'upright Heart and Pure: Essays on John Milton Commemorating the Tercentenary of the Publication of 'Paradise Lost,'* edited by Amadeus P. Fiore (1967). A revised and enlarged version was reprinted in *The Lofty Rhyme* in 1970. From the beginning, Rajan has been struck by Milton's elaborate and extended treatment of the temptation of the kingdoms in the Son's trial in the desert and in particular by Milton's invention of the temptation of learning. In this essay, Rajan considers the Son's rejection of the world's kingdoms in the antiimperial context to which it naturally lends itself.

The epic has long been regarded as imperialism's literary vehicle, with its allegedly monological character typifying the imperial attitude. David Quint shows how Milton's revisionary treatment of the epic reflects a revisionary understanding of imperialism and in particular of the then current claim that the realms of commerce and empire were distinct. Rajan sees the temptation of the kingdoms in *Paradise Regained* as a critique not simply of imperialism but also of its literary vehicle. To avoid reinstating an unacceptable ideology, the epic decorum must be reinvented. *Paradise Lost* moves towards such a reinvention, but struggles with itself in the endeavour to do so.

Some of the questions raised by this essay are addressed by Homi Bhabha in his Afterword to *Milton and the Imperial Vision* (1999).

I

A poem on the Son of God's temptations presents a singular opportunity for a response to imperialism grounded on a biblical narrative. When the poem is a brief epic, the response can be more sharply focused. When the brief epic is in the form of a debate, the response can become a critique and the critique in its turn can become a scrutiny of principles. When the poem emphasizes and elaborates the temptation of the kingdoms, the area of the meditative combat (to use Louis Martz's felicitous phrase) can become the terrain for a carefully developed antiimperial statement.[1]

Paradise Regained fulfils all these specifications and does so with the quiet insistence characteristic of the poem. Many years earlier in *The Reason of Church Government*, Milton had described the Book of Job as the brief model of an epic. He had done so in outlining a range of possibilities which his roving mind presented to itself 'in the spacious circuits of [its] musing[s]' (*CPW* 1:812–13). The agenda was tentative indeed; but the poet was sufficiently committed to it to give substance over the years to every item in its formidable scope.

Paradise Regained, Milton's brief epic, indicates its lineage by referring to Job seven times. The poem is not about Job because Job, despite his 'strong Sufferance' (*PR* 1.160), cannot be made into an antiimperial voice. The Son can be such a voice and a voice for which one is prepared by the later books of *Paradise Lost*. Christian heroism had superseded classical heroism in the ninth book of Milton's epic, castigating that 'tedious havoc' (*PL* 9.30) which had spread over some of the poem's previous books. The castigation was followed by the famous abandonment of history in the last two books and the retreat to the paradise within. None of these moves could be construed as preludes to the celebration of empire. Scholarship has subsequently reinterpreted the last books, tending to treat them as the heart of the poem rather than as its dangling postscript. They still provide no support for an imperial platform.

The many references to Job implicitly specify the genre of *Paradise Regained* and Barbara Lewalski's classic study amply documents the poem's place in the genre.[2] Nevertheless David Quint's view that *Paradise Regained* and *Paradise Lost* 'effectively create their own new genre' remains important.[3] Milton's treatment of inherited genres is heavily revisionary. The proposition that he stresses the mould but stops short of breaking it may be reassuring to literary conversationists but makes it difficult to do justice to the innovative force of these revisions. In *Paradise Regained*

Milton's revisionary move (and it is a strategy of some brilliance) is to make the temptation an incitement to epic. The resistance to temptation – and it is paradigmatic of all political and moral resistance – is therefore inexorably antiepic.

To achieve this result, the temptation of the kingdoms must be compellingly foregrounded. Milton follows the Luke sequence of temptations, contrary to the consensus of his day. In doing so, he provides us with an account of the first temptation that is almost marginalized by its brevity and with a final temptation on the pinnacle in which brevity compounds the enigmatic impact.

The Book of Matthew, in making the temptation of the kingdoms the final one, juxtaposes the temptation to turn stones into bread with the temptation on the pinnacle. Seventeenth-century commentators in preferring the Matthew order, routinely contrasted the two as temptations to mistrust and to presumption. The pinnacle for them was not a spire but a small terrace on which one could stand safely, or from which one could descend if smitten with vertigo, by a rear staircase. Casting one's self down from the pinnacle was, like turning stones into bread, an attempt to assert sonship by a display of the miraculous. Both were imprudent demands upon the power of God.[4]

With these temptations out of the way, the Son could be subjected in the Matthew sequence to the more expansive and testing temptation of the kingdoms. Milton prefers a climax in which recognition and reversal combine in catastrophe in the best Aristotelian manner. He therefore centralizes what Matthew makes climactic and then makes the climax the dramatic result of Satan's central failure. In doing so he threads his way with a poet's creative confidence among the opportunities offered by each version.

The temptation of the kingdoms is not merely centralized. It is elaborated and extended so as to occupy most of the poem's confrontational space. The initial extension consists of the Epicurean banquet which Satan conjures up for the Son's delectation in the wilderness. Euphemistically described by Carey as 'non-canonical,'[5] the banquet at first seems to have little to do with either epic or empire. We have to remember that wine and women are among the principal rewards of valour, and that they are dwelt on at some length in the ninth book of Camões's epic, *The Lusiads*.[6] The climax of that poem is reached when the future Portuguese empire is displayed to Vasco da Gama from a hilltop similar to the one that Christ is soon to ascend.[7]

Fanshawe's translation of *The Lusiads* was published in 1655, the year in which Jamaica was captured as a consolation prize in Cromwell's Western design. The Lusiadic blending of commerce, religion, and conquest fits the design even if in doing so, it underlines the resemblance between the Cromwellian self and its Iberian other.

Sims's articles on Camões and Milton indicate the extent to which *Paradise Lost* was engaged in a revisionary treatment of *The Lusiads*.[8] One can read this treatment not only as a critique of Camões's poem but also of the imperial program to which the circumstances of publication connected it. We can even argue that Milton's movement from a ten- to a twelve-book structure for his epic was part of an effort to distance himself from Camões.

The banquet in *Paradise Regained* is a further stage in this revisionary removal. Comus's 'curious taste' (*A Mask Presented at Ludlow Castle*, 713) was among the economic incentives for the spice trade. The last two books of *The Lusiads* are obsessively devoted to the profits of that trade in commerce and empire, and the first two books of *Paradise Lost* are inexorable in demonstrating the potentially Satanic nature of those profits. Satan offers a banquet designed to appeal to a more cultivated taste than Comus's. Nevertheless it is an invitation to conspicuous consumption, reproached by the modest yet elegantly varied meal which Eve serves Raphael in Paradise. 'Pompous Delicacies,' the Son's withering rejection of Satan's proffered feast (*PR* 2.390), is critical not only of Satan's tactics but of a current lifestyle and its exploitative results. The Son too can create opportunities for gourmandizing in the wilderness but there is a different hunger with which Satan has nothing to do (*PR* 2.383–9).

Commercial spoils are not the purpose of empire for those committed to heroism, Christian or epic. More serious temptations are needed. Satan's next inquiry relates to glory, the brightest jewel in the heroic crown. The Son's rejoinder that the only glory worth pursuing is service to the greater glory of God poignantly overwrites verses 70 to 76 of *Lycidas* (*PR* 2.46ff.) His response is sufficient to persuade Satan that it is profitless to proceed further in this direction. The appeal has to be to the cause and not the individual.

The cause has already been spelled out in the Son's boyhood dreams of 'victorious deeds' and 'heroic acts,' aspirations which he describes vividly as flaming in his heart. Israel would first be rescued 'from the *Roman* yoke.' The movement of liberation would then reach out to quell 'Brute violence and proud Tyrannic pow'r' wherever it was found to exist (*PR* 1.215–20).

Israel in bondage to Rome in *Paradise Regained*, is in bondage to the Philistines in *Samson Agonistes,* the other poem in the 1671 volume. As Elizabeth Sauer notes, the Philistine dominance is replete with echoes from Restoration England.[9] The relationship between the two works in the 1671 volume has been much discussed and more than one view is desirable. One effect of the juxtaposed servitudes is to foreground biblical Israel as a typological site for the unbinding of the future. That foregrounding acquires the force of contemporaneity when a second Israel lies in bondage to a Philistine monarchy given to Romish practices.

The emphasis on Israel's captivity and on the self-enslavement of Israel's captor, Rome, make *Paradise Regained* doubly a liberation text. In a liberation text, Satan cannot offer empires for cultivating what Said calls the pleasures of imperialism, some of them already put together in the banquet which Christ has disdained.[10] Empires have to be offered instead to implement the Son's emancipatory agenda and to forge a strategic alliance between an idealist Son and a pragmatic Satan that would give Satan a dignified place in the future order of things. Imperial power is to be used to free and protect subjected peoples. Since imperial power has customarily been used for quite the opposite purpose, Satan's offer is paradoxical to say the least. On the other hand, those whose possession of power is unassailable (Satan can promise that much) are free to determine how power is to be employed.

Satan proceeds on the basis that Israel's true king will not wish to reign over a captive Israel. He listens to the Son even if he does not hear much of what the Son says. Secular power responds to Satan in crafting persuasive agendas for dubious designs. Milton asks us to hear the Son more insistently and not commit ourselves, without searching thought, to empires acquired on preemptive or defensive pretexts.

An independent Israel cannot exist between the competing empires of Rome and Parthia. It has to form a strategic alliance with one of them. At this stage, Satan recommends Parthia. It is closer to Israel and has shown itself capable of standing up to Rome. Parthian power was past its zenith at the time of the Son's ordeal in the desert and Satan exaggerates Parthia's military might. That military might is the essence of the offer is apparent from the excessive attention given to Parthian battle tactics. But military might cannot save a people who have surrendered to the other within the self.

The stereotypical imperial relationship is between a dominant self and a subjected other. Edward Said has tended to see the subjected other as totally constructed by the discourse of dominance that contains it, as able to speak only with an allotted voice, as predestinated even in its protests. Homi Bhabha sees the self-other relationship as fundamentally unstable, as subject to spillages and reabsorptions, and as generating an indeterminate third force of hybridity between the polarities it attempts to keep in being.

Both Said's almost Calvinist model and Bhabha's theorizing of the spillage between binaries need to be taken back to the Reformation origins of English imperial discourse. Spillage can be studied more easily in a culture that is close to its founding paradox of being theologically secessionist yet secularly imperial. Since the other is by definition non-conformist, a nonconformist nation will find it difficult to expel the other totally from itself. It must allow dissension from itself and even allow it as an imitation of itself. There is a secret sharing which will result in an illicit reabsorption.

This fallout is predictable but lies well down the road which imperialism will travel. In engaging the seventeenth century, postcolonial theorizing will be mindful of these long-term instabilities; but its more immediate concern should be with the complication of the self-other model by the psychology of fallenness.

The self in falling generates an other that did not previously exist and places itself under that other's imperial control. A psychic relationship is thus set up within the self, which is the reverse of the stereotypical imperial relationship. This inconsistency diminishes in due course to the kind of botheration that vexes only scholars; but in seventeenth-century England, the consciousness of fallenness was always immediate and sometimes overwhelming. Its internal anxieties were registered in its construction of a subjected selfhood struggling against the dominance of the other within itself; but they were also reflected in devising multiple others as reflections or rectifications of its internal instability.

Pre-Christian, anti-Christian, ex-Edenic, Spanish imperial and papal imperial others are among the monstrous shapes on the horizon of the seventeenth-century English self. Ireland combines the worst of all possible worlds in being pre-Christian, anti-Christian, papal and Celtic-Amazonian.[11] Fortunately, she is available for comprehensive cleansing.

Any of these others can be internalized. They all maintain fifth columns in the self. The self must not only deal with these fifth columns but must also emancipate itself from the other to which it is internally subjected. That other, moreover, has a propensity for entering into psychic alliances with the external others by which the self is threatened.

Bhabha's model is more responsive to these complications than Said's, particularly as Bhabha is more adept in recognizing that the outside will always be the inside. Exorcism by othering can give a historical and political shape to demons; but to give them shapes is not to cast them out. Cleansing the self root and branch, or banishing the other to the exotic distances of Asia or the New World, will not free the self from its internal tyranny. In their imperial vehemence these actions may even domesticate rather than eradicate the problem which they export or eject. It follows that acquiring empires in order to overthrow the aims of empire – a temptation Satan consistently offers – is a paradox which should be unconvincing to others besides Christ.

Milton is consistent in arguing that the fallen psyche is to be integrated rather than purified. The other within the self is not to be cast out; it is merely to be deprived of the dominance which gives it its otherness. The perturbations of the mind will be allayed and the affections set 'in right tune' (*CPW* 1:816–17). Pity, fear, and similar emotions will be reduced to just measure. More confidently, *Areopagitica* argues that the 'passions within us' and the 'pleasures round about us' are, if 'rightly temper'd,' 'the very ingredients of vertu' (*CPW* 2:527). One might wish the tempering to be the result of a relationship between the mind's faculties that is dialogic rather than hierarchic but this is a proposition too advanced for Milton's day.

In an important passage, Bhabha points to 'the "*ambivalence*" of the stereotype' as a concept whose consequences 'remain[] to be charted' and which invites attention from postcolonial scholars.[12] Seventeenth-century England surrounded itself with stereotypes which partook of each other and which were opened to ambivalence by the transactions between them. Bhabha regards ambivalent others as increasing the room for manoeuvre and the operational flexibility of the dominant self. But multiple others also complicate the space of the self, reaching into and compounding the self's nascent uncertainty. An uncertain self is capable of operational flexibility but inconsistency might be its more characteristic deportment. As it endeavours (or is obliged) to make itself explicit the uncertain self can find itself dismantled by its dissensions.

Within these observations the failed second Israel can be tentatively cartographed as a divided self in contention with an imperial Catholic-Spanish other, that maintains a fifth column in the self. The first Israel fell victim repeatedly to its fifth column. It should have been the type to England's truth. Unfortunately, instead of retreating as a type, it advances intimidatingly as a metaphor. The second Israel should have rewritten the first. Instead, the first writes the second with a repetitive force which only enlightened understanding can frustrate.

Enlightened understanding must resist the temptation to see its future as epic and to use the instruments of empire to achieve the epic statement. *Paradise Regained* displays the epic temptation more and more extensively as Satanic. The victor's feast (offered by Satan in the initial round), the pursuit of glory (empire as character building), the liberating mission which retrieves Israel / Ithaca, and the strategic alliance with Parthia (an alliance was necessary to found Rome) are all constituents of the epic-imperial undertaking. The Son does not totally dismiss them. It would be more accurate to say that he recontextualizes them, placing them around the primacy of the interior kingdom. The inner kingdom can be described as a kingdom not of this world. It is better described as a site of loyalty to the divine imperium which makes possible creative action in this world.

World power is the maximum objective of the imperial epic, and world power exercised in the interests of justice elevates the imperial claim into nobility. The Son before he was twelve (*PR* 1.209–10) had dreamed of a world-wide subduing of 'Brute violence' and 'proud Tyrannic pow'r' (*PR* 1.219). He is sharply conscious of the systematic ravaging to which the name of 'glory' can be attached:

> They err who count it glorious to subdue
> By Conquest far and wide, to overrun
> Large Countries, and in field great Battles win,
> Great Cities by assault: what do these Worthies,
> But rob and spoil, burn, slaughter, and enslave
> Peaceable Nations, neighboring, or remote,
> Made Captive, yet deserving freedom more
> Than those thir Conquerors.   (*PR* 3.71–8)

This is not the best poetry Milton ever wrote but it remains an emphatic condemnation of the havoc wrought by empire builders. The last two lines are particularly notable, given the compulsion of every imperialism to devalue and despise subjected peoples. The condemnation however carries a responsibility with it. Christ's own kingdom has to be defined by contrast. It is imaged in two striking and traditional similes:

Know therefore when my season comes to sit
On *David's* Throne, it shall be like a tree
Spreading and overshadowing all the Earth,
Or as a stone that shall to pieces dash
All Monarchies besides throughout the world,
And of my Kingdom there shall be no end.   (*PR* 4.146–51)

The tree and the stone are based on Nebuchadnezzar's vision (Daniel
4:2; 2:35). Commentary treats both texts as typological anticipations of
the Son's kingdom. In a god-centred universe, the tree (as in more than
one major mythology) can be regarded as having its roots in heaven. Its
spreading canopy offers the world protection. The stone fits in less easily
with characterizations of the new heroism. It is Samson's way of doing
things rather than the Son's. One can argue that neither way can wholly
rule out the other and 1.226 comes to our rescue as a gloss. But there is a
relish in the lines on the stone which reminds us that Milton even at his
most pacific, is not slow to rejoice in the evidence of God's wrath.[13]

In *Paradise Regained*, the Son's imaging of his kingship follows his
response to Satan's Roman temptation. Rome is offered as a worldwide
empire. If Parthia is an exemplum of military strength, Rome is an
exemplum of geopolitical expansiveness. Thanks to Satan's 'Optic skill'
(*PR* 4.40), the Son is able to take in the full scope of this expansiveness
which, in Satan's presentation, may extend as far as Sumatra.

An expert merchandizer of empires such as Satan would not have
expected the shrewd bargainer he imagines the Son to be to settle for
the paltry offer of Parthia. Rome is the real prize and is cried up
accordingly. Its connections to seventeenth-century England are evident. Catholic Rome is the enemy and classical Rome is both a precedent and a warning. More immediately, Cromwell's 'global imperial
designs,' as Christopher Hill calls them, and the 'fantastic scope' of
Cromwell's foreign policy are reflected in Satan's panoramic display.[14]

The Roman imperium however is not merely territorial and legal.
Satan himself draws attention to its 'Civility of Manners, Arts, and Arms'
(*PR* 4.83), qualities which Parthia evidently lacks.[15] We have to take
civility of arms not as oxymoronic, but as implying magnanimity to the
conquered. Rome's epic, *The Aeneid*, goes further and Anchises's outlining of the Roman mission to Aeneas deserves more than a cursory
reading. Dryden's translation quoted below is not untouched by seventeenth-century views of empire:

Let others better mold the running Mass
Of Mettals, and inform the breathing Brass;
And soften into Flesh a Marble Face:
Plead better at the Bar; describe the Skies,
And when the Stars descend, and when they rise.
But *Rome,* 'tis thine alone, with awful sway,
To rule Mankind: and make the World obey;
Disposing Peace, and War, thy own Majestick Way.
To tame the Proud, the fetter'd Slave to free;
These are Imperial Arts, and worthy thee.[16]

Other translators are more generous to Greece than Dryden, who trivializes that country's achievement. Rome, on the other hand, is the destined ruler of mankind, with the ethics of imperialism justifying her 'Majestick Way.' Imperialism is not only an art but an art informed by godlike responsibilities. In fact taming the proud and freeing the fettered are objectives remarkably close to the Son's boyhood ambitions.

Secularizing the sacred is an old inevitability. The Son's insistence on the divine imperium is meant to remove empire from the world of terrestrial politics. Unfortunately, its long-term result can be the recrudescence of terrestrial empires armed with sacred empowerments and self-justifyingly claiming Providence as their guide. The transcendentalizing move reconciles dissent with obedience and can even make dissent the sign of a higher obedience. It grounds sectarianism in a celestial totalizing which will bring together all committed seekers in the collective harvesting of the truth. These strategies respond to the day's religious imperatives as well as to its political pitfalls. But they also make a poet who is fundamentally antiimperial sadly vulnerable to appropriation by imperial thought.

An empire ostensibly dedicated to noble causes can claim to be serving rather than subverting the divine imperium. Imperialism armed with a conscience is all the more formidable and Satan understands that all too well. Milton's fragile safeguard is that an inner kingdom must control exterior actions and that the divine imperium will control that inner kingdom through the mediating presence of the image of God in man.[17] These connections rest on a vigilant and incessant answerability that is psychologically impossible to sustain. They seem almost destined to be swept aside by events.

Despite his safeguarding manoeuvres, Milton contributes considerably to the mainstream of imperial discourse. In *Milton and the Imperial*

Vision, Paul Stevens and Willy Maley examine his devaluations of the Amerindians and of the Irish. The rhetoric of these devaluations becomes routine in its application to subjected peoples. Nicholas von Maltzahn in the same compilation shows how in the reception of Milton's work, a republican statement mutates into an imperial one. The hierarchic principle can become an instrument of empire. The Adam-Eve relationship can be reactivated (as in Sydney Owenson's novel, *The Missionary*) in the relationship between dominant and subjected cultures, as Rajan has argued.[18]

We can register the manner in which Milton's work was read by imperial events; but in a postcolonial era, another trend needs to be registered. We have to ask how Milton's work contributed to the resistance statement and how it may still speak to us within the language of that statement. *Paradise Regained* in particular seems a text concerned not merely with the futility of empires but with the relationship of that futility to the domestication of the other in the fallen self and even of its inherence in that self.

The Rome Satan offers to the Son is under Tiberian tyranny. Israel was to be freed from the Roman yoke, and Rome is now to be freed from the yoke it has imposed on itself. An imperial other that has generated its own servitude is a mirror held before a second Israel. It warns us that the subjugation of others cannot protect a nation from its downfall and may indeed contribute to its inner decay. A people appointed to reform reformation has failed signally in its service to the divine imperium. It has to return with contrition to that service. Mirrored in Rome and Israel's bondages, the bondage of the second Israel reminds us of the pervasiveness of bondage, the strength and stubbornness of the enemy within. External tyrannies project an internal usurpation. The home of the other is the self.

Only an internal reconstitution, a deeply felt return to the divine image within us can successfully confront not merely the tyrannies of the moment, but the permanence of tyranny until the self is freed. This is the resistance statement, the firm ground of the Son's retreating refusals. Satan can offer the empires (not the kingdoms) of the world. Only the divine can offer the kingdom (not the empire) of the self.

The Son is not John Milton, but his rejection of the classical world cannot be without an echo of Milton. It is as if Rome betrayed a promise to which Milton was too enthusiastic in subscribing. To say that the Romans 'conquer'd well, / But govern ill' (*PR* 4.134–5) is to concede more to imperialism than is permissible today. Conquest is not compatible with justice and Milton says as much in other places, including book 3, lines 71–8 of *Paradise Regained* (already quoted). But Milton can also lean the other way, finding the Roman conquest of Britain (as Linda Gregerson reminds us) civilizing in its effects.[19] His views on this matter are divided and perhaps stubbornly divided. Sallust fortified by original sin, makes for a potent antiimperial mixture but even Milton may have been reluctant to drain it to the last drop.[20] He might not have been hostile to a Roman precedent that kept alive the possibility of a Protestant empire. Others in seventeenth-century England interested in combining the republican with the imperial would have found such a demonstration helpful. One can be irate with the self-indulgence that ruled it out.[21]

The image of the spreading tree, which follows immediately upon Rome's dismissal and which defines the universality of the Son's kingship, is thus not wholly dissociated from what Rome might have become. It may be Milton's exasperation at the waste of an unprecedented potential for greatness that leaks into the Son's rejection, giving it a special intensity of contempt. Castigation extends even to the Roman wine list (*PR* 4.116–19). The climactic 'These thus degenerate, by themselves enslav'd' (*PR* 4.144) is stingingly disdainful with the sibilants curling in the air of the speaker's scorn. There is nothing for Satan to do but to try another temptation. It has to be 'non-canonical' since as Satan himself points out, he has run out of kingdoms (*PR* 4.88–9).

Athens is a poor second to Rome in Dryden's estimation, but as Satan might say, there is no accounting for the Son's tastes. Moreover the Son's obstinate insistence on the primacy of the inner kingdom makes the offer of an inner kingdom inevitable. Significantly, learning is offered not as a kingdom but as the basis of an empire (*PR* 4.284). In testing Christ as king, Satan is consistent in offering only empires.

Michael had seen learning as an empire in *Paradise Lost* (12.576–81), but it was an empire to be superseded by quietly cultivating the paradise within. The young Milton had viewed learning imperially in the Seventh Prolusion (*CPW* 1:296). There is no question that on the hill from which the Son looks down at the world's kingdoms and which Adam's hill anticipates (*PL* 11.381–4), Milton is saying farewell to part of himself. In the course of proceeding to that farewell he wrote an encyclopaedic poem with all knowledge as its provinces. He is not necessarily saying farewell to that poem. The elation of knowing and of organizing knowledge into a preparation for wisdom is real. It has to be elation and not hubris.

The Son's dismissal of Athens is more temperate than his rejection of Rome and even includes an 'Alas' (*PR* 4.309). It remains characterized by that stern logic which has marked his accumulating refusals. Stripped of its loyalty to the divine imperium, the kingdom of the mind opens itself to subversion by the incipient arrogance of knowledge. This is a conclusion which may be in the making from the time we first see Adam and Eve in paradise:

> in thir looks Divine
> The image of thir glorious Maker shone,
> Truth, Wisdom, Sanctitude severe and pure,
> Severe, but in true filial freedom plac't;
> Whence true autority. (*PL* 4.291–5)

The repeated 'true' couples authority to filial freedom, insisting doubly on the authenticity of both. 'Whence' is a decisive statement of primacy. The outer claim without the inner allegiance amounts to no more than 'Tyrannic pow'r.' And even the inner allegiance can be located in a filial freedom that is less than true. It must be subjected to an unceasing scrutiny indicated by the repeated 'severe.' The passage bristles with cautions against the appropriation of the image – an appropriation to which imperial thought inevitably proceeds.

The mind no less than material empires, can be the territory of a desecrated image, dedicated to its external attributes rather than to its inner life. It cannot be its own place as Satan once insisted. The place is always inhabited by God, by Satan, and in our own time's thinking, by the cultural persuasions of the moment. Set apart and at the same time fundamentally involved, the mind's ideological kingdoms can be doubly dangerous because of the actions they promote under the semblance of true intellectual authority. Before lamenting the Son's dismissal of learning – it is a placing rather than a dismissal – we should remember that the world of thought is not deficient in the number of its victims. Too much of recent history is the result of the collusion between Rome and Athens.[22]

When the last empire is renounced the epic possibility dwindles. Containment and closure, the triumphant advance towards a manifest destiny, are no longer appropriate to the human project. That project must be humble before providence, resistant to the kingdoms of the world, vigilant in fending off the tyranny within. Milton's own epic falls arrestingly short of closure, leaving the human future perilously open to a free will which Christ can address but to which he does not dictate.

The rules of the meditative combat are remarkably simple. Satan has to make Christ an offer he cannot refuse. The Son, through his retreating refusals, has to demand from Satan an offer he is unable to make. The only offer Satan cannot make is that of a kingdom constituted by creative dependence on a divine will to which Satan has been made alien. Since Satan cannot offer this connection, his only remaining possibility is to test its sustaining strength. He falls and the Son stands on the result of that testing.

As a resistance statement *Paradise Regained* proceeds on the assumption that the power of the world is predominantly Satanic and that human nature must struggle unceasingly with the destructive propensity implanted in itself. Epic heroism is too much of a bludgeon for so complex a combat, as dangerous to the self as to the enemy. A different poem is written on the pinnacle. The road runs from that poem to Shelley's Promethean heroism and from there to the strategies of resistance that in our own time have brought about the undoing of empires. Milton's thought tends itself to imperial appropriation; it lends itself equally to imperialism's dismantling.

II

Milton's writing takes two very different routes across the terrain of imperial history. The routes come together in the peripeteia of the colonial classroom, with the teachers imparting one lesson and the students learning another. A particular incident comes to mind. The windows of the classroom look out on a beach. A political demonstration is beginning to form itself on the yellow, mud-flecked sands in front of the catamarans and fishing boats. The lecturer armed with Verity's influential notes, instructs the students on the classical strain in Milton. If he has one eye on the demonstration he may point to the limitations of 'immortal hate' and the 'study of revenge' (*PL* 1.105–9). The students find these limitations effaced by the crowd's nonviolent behaviour as it faces a lathi charge by the police. The 'unconquerable Will' and 'courage never to submit or yield' are what Milton carries into the political moment.

Students can read more adventurously than their instructors, and some students are aware of subversive English critics who argue that Satan is the real hero of the poem. They wonder if even a divine imperialism can be altogether free of the self-justifying compulsions by which the imperialism they know is characterized. The lecturer inaptly quotes Walter Raleigh's conclusion in his 1900 study of Milton that *Paradise Lost* is a monument to dead ideas,[23] and the students wonder what ideas the demonstration may be burying. The great organizing imperatives which will override these problematics and which will dominate Milton scholarship for the next two decades have not yet come into being. Lovejoy has not yet published *The Great Chain of Being*, and C.S. Lewis has yet to popularize the hierarchic principle. For minds unsettled by the distraction of reality outside those windows, *Paradise Lost* stands out as a text of Promethean resistance.

The colonial classroom reminds us that poems are read by events as well as by readers but not every poem opens itself as strongly as *Paradise Lost* to readings so dramatic in their differences. We have yet to ask ourselves about the character of a work that is able not only to allow, but also to sustain responses as vigorous as these in their undoing of each other. Ambivalence is a feeble characterization even if we add, perhaps insultingly, that Milton was representative in his ambivalence. A writer responds to his world and does not merely register it. He intervenes in a debate; and if the word means anything, it means that the debate will not be quite the same after the intervention.

Milton's intervention takes in the Puritan dilemma as well as the complications of English imperialism in its early modern phase. The combination is fluid enough to befuddle any thinker. It cannot be said that Milton navigates its treacherous waters with the masterful self-confidence that was once the sign of his talent. But at least we are conscious throughout of a navigator and not of someone helplessly compliant to whatever wind happens to seize his sails. Janel Mueller's study of the dismantling logic in Milton's engagement with his time's imperialism shows a mind concerned not only with responding to the cultural pressures around it but also with achieving a structure in that response.[24]

Overdetermination tends to substitute the conflicted site for the uncertain author. Milton's case suggests that far from being in hiding, he is at work obstinately on the site. He may even be the owner of some of his ambivalences. He earns his title to them by struggling through them, making a statement which is thoughtful because it is not conclusive, because it must live with difficulties in the grain of Milton's work as well as in the persuasions of the moment. The difficulties which harass the movement of that work are not necessarily ideological. More profoundly, they concern the imperial manner of his antiimperialism and the imperial scope of the very design within which imperialism is exposed to questioning.

The problems of Milton's commitment become evident when Comus argues for a brave new world of conspicuous consumption and when the Lady replies that youth and joy are the children of moderation. The reply is respectable doctrinally and should be impeccable in our own time. It does not succeed poetically and that may not be because Milton's imagination is not on the side of the Lady. It may be because imagination cannot be on the Lady's side, because poetry itself is a form of conspicuous consumption.

The split between imagination and doctrine is the oldest issue in Milton criticism, allowing us to meditate on where the poem lies or on how to read it against its argumentative grain. But the epic voice in *Paradise Lost* is also the voice of the imperial imagination, of sumptuous orchestration, of metaphorical opulence, the encyclopaedic, outreaching, all-encompassing voice, the voice of the unifying imperative. No one articulates this voice more resplendently than Milton; and no one struggles against it more insistently.

The struggle unravels much that seems in the nature of poetry. To write the imperial other eloquently into the language of the self and then to confront it as an other which one can only disavow, not vanquish, is Milton's ironic act of courage. Christian heroism, the paradise within, creative dependence on the divine connection within us, the uncertain steps towards dialogue between Adam and Eve that replace their stately and settled hierarchic exchanges, the perilous openness of a history offered to the interplay between agency and providence rather than withheld from chaos by imperial closure, all argue for a new poetry, but one that cannot come into being until an older poetry is completely renounced.

Paradise Regained moves in this direction, reducing Satan to a salesman of empires and characterizing the Son's voice by obliquities and ironies which conceal the real power that 'Virtue, Wisdom and Endurance'[25] can exert. Milton exposes the gaudiness of empire. He does not quite succeed in exposing its emptiness. The day of the epic is over. The nostalgia for epic remains. We can feel this nostalgia in the curtness of the Son's dismissals as he confronts and chastises an adversary embodying some of the interregnum's hopes.

As Christian heroism supersedes classical heroism, we might expect a Milton purged of the classical strain to be purged also of the imperial disposition.[26] The quiet voice of resistance could then come forward on the unadorned stage of the new verse. But Milton would not be Milton without the classical strain that connected him to Roman republicanism once and connected him to Roman imperialism later. The imperial persuasion outlives the powerful ideological shift which the last books of *Paradise Lost* project but are not quite able to bring into being. The current of that persuasion runs so deep that Blake, even in cleansing Milton, cannot emancipate his own poetry from the proclamatory force of Milton's language. Milton's collusion with imperialism is not with an ideology he criticizes or with a discourse he more than once demystifies. It is in the stride and accent of his poetry. In waging war against his own splendid excess, he problematizes at the deepest level a necessity which continues to perplex us: to achieve the extinction of empire not simply in our ideological commitments, but in the language we write and which writes us as we write it.

NOTES

1 Martz, '*Paradise Regained*: The Meditative Combat,' 223–47.
2 Lewalski, *Milton's Brief Epic: The Genre, Meaning and Art of 'Paradise Regained.'*
3 Quint, *Epic and Empire: Politics and Generic Form from Virgil to Milton*, 340.
4 Elizabeth Pope was the first to point out that Christ was in no serious danger on the pinnacle (*'Paradise Regained': The Tradition and the Poem*, 84–7). See further Rajan, *The Lofty Rhyme: A Study of Milton's Major Poetry*, 125–6.
5 *Poems*, edited by Carey and Fowler (1968), 1109n.
6 *The Lusiads of Luis de Camões*, 349–50.
7 *The Lusiads*, 368 ff.
8 Sims, 'A Greater Than Rome. The Inversion of a Virgilian Symbol from Camões to Milton'; 'Camões' *Lusiads* and Milton's *Paradise Lost*: Satan's Voyage to Eden'; and 'Christened Classicism in *Paradise Lost* and *The Lusiads.*' See also chapter 8, note 15 of this volume and Quint, *Epic and Empire*, 253–67 and esp. 264–6.
9 Sauer, 'The Politics of Performance in the Inner Theater: *Samson Agonistes* as Closet Drama,' 204.
10 Said, *Culture and Imperialism*, 131–62.
11 Radigund in book 5 of Edmund Spenser's *The Faerie Queene* exemplifies the Celtic Amazonian. Characterization of Ireland can be studied initially in *Representing Ireland: Literature and the Origins of Conflict, 1534–1660*, A proliferation of studies has followed this book.
12 Bhabha, *The Location of Culture*, 66.
13 Commentators do ingenious things with the stone in adapting it to the new dispensation. See Lewalski, *Milton's Brief Epic*, 278–80.

14 Hill, *God's Englishman: Oliver Cromwell and the English Revolution*, 167, 165. Hill points out that the 'Western Design' included designs on India (160). The aim was to protect the sea route to India round the Cape of Good Hope by occupying Assada, an island near Madagascar. It was not until 1810 with the capture of Mauritius from the French that the aim was fully realized.

15 Civility is a term much used in establishing Ireland's otherness. Bhabha's 'Sly Civility,' a reverentially subversive response to dominance (*The Location of Culture*, 93–101) is filled in by being joined to these seventeenth-century discussions.

16 Dryden, *The Works of Virgil ... Translated into English Verse* (1697), vol. 5: 566, book 6. 1168–77.

17 See Quint, *Epic and Empire*, 368: 'Perhaps only Milton among epic poets could reject both kingship and territorial empire, displacing this concentrated power from human politics onto his God, and onto the will of the individual believer.'

18 Stevens, 'Milton and the New World,' Maley, 'Milton "and the complication of interests,"' von Maltzahn, 'Acts of Kind Service,' and Rajan, 'Feminizing the Feminine: Early Women Writers on India.'

19 Gregerson, 'Colonials Write the Nation: Spenser, Milton, and England on the Margins,' 169–90.

20 'From the daily Scene effeminate' (*PR* 4.142) may echo Sallust's remark that the end of an empire is in sight when men begin to dress like women. Feminizing the other is a standard move in imperial rhetoric, including Rome's (Quint, *Epic and Empire*, 24–9). Sallust's comment underlines the deterioration of the self into the other. It was known well enough to be quoted by an important member of the Spanish opposition. See Elliott, *Spain and Its World 1500–1700*, 251.

21 On the other hand, one can be uncomfortably aware that self-indulgence may be in the nature of imperial practice, that the inner kingdom is placed under stress when it reaches too far into the kingdom without. It is safer to live within manageable frontiers. The Roman failure and its demonization in Spanish imperial behaviour are admonitions to an English Israel. Setbacks to the 'Western Design' strengthen the proposition that the elect nation should concentrate on improving itself rather than on diluting its identity in imperial adventures.

In 'John Milton: Poet Against Empire,' 223–4, Armitage discerns a shift in the 'later 1660s' from 'territorial expansion and empire-building' to 'an espousal of the calmer policy of self-containment' and 'rejection of conquest in favour of commerce.' If Milton contributes to this shift, he is also critical of it. His sustained questioning of the dissociation between commerce and empire suggests that the shift does not go far enough.

22 Edward Said's *Orientalism* and Ronald Inden's *Imagining India* demonstrate the lamentable extent of this collusion.

23 Walter Raleigh, *Milton*, 85.

24 Mueller, 'Dominion as Domesticity: Milton's Imperial God and the Experience of History.'

25 Shelley, *Prometheus Unbound*, 4.562.

26 The cleansing appropriates Milton to a Romantic cultural nationalism which seeks to replace Rome rather than to excel it, as Julia M. Wright shows in '"Greek & Latin Slaves of the Sword": Rejecting the Imperial Nation in Blake's *Milton*.' Excelling Rome was the basis of the eighteenth-century elevation of Milton, Nicholas von Maltzahn argues in 'Acts of Kind Service: Milton and the Patriot Literature of Empire,' 233–54.

7 The Two Creations: *Paradise Lost* and the *Treatise on Christian Doctrine*

Headnote

An early version of this essay was presented at the Seventh International Milton Symposium at Beaufort, South Carolina, in 2002. 'The Poetics of Heresy' (chapter 2) was written before the authorship of the *Treatise on Christian Doctrine* emerged as an important issue in Milton scholarship. Like the date of *Samson Agonistes*, the authorship question carries an agenda with it. As with *Samson Agonistes*, Rajan in the present essay chooses to bypass the controversy and the view of Milton that it seeks to reshape, concentrating instead on the way in which the two texts illuminate each other. The essay examines the considerable divergence between the account of the creation in the seventh book of *Paradise Lost* and that offered by the *Treatise*. It also examines a *sotto voce* account of the creation in the book that is more compatible with the *Treatise*.

The *sotto voce* account offers us a cosmology that is democratic rather than imperial. It provides an alternative platform within the poem to a statement which might otherwise be overwhelmingly hierarchic. The world of today is not without its connections to Milton's double view of the politics of first matter.

The two accounts of the creation in *Paradise Lost* form an enigma and the enigma deepens as we realize how little attention has been paid to its teasings. Students, including graduate students, are surprised to learn that two accounts exist. Their surprise is justified since scholars commenting on the creation in *Paradise Lost* often write as if there were only one account. Even those who, like Regina Schwartz and John Rumrich,[1] are aware of two accounts pay only passing attention to the third book version. Annotators who by the nature of their calling must recognize both accounts, are reluctant to dwell on the divergences between them. John Rogers, who could have quoted the third book version as supporting his refreshingly new view of seventeenth-century science, does not choose to cite it in this context.[2] In a recent collection of essays, John Leonard and W.B. Hunter also treat the two accounts as if there were no problem in their conflation.[3] This essay attempts to argue that the two versions differ and that the differences align themselves with differing directions in Milton's thought. The complication of commitments becomes more basic as we carry it back to two versions of the creation fable. The choice is then no choice but a vacillation.

Surprise at the neglect of the third book account increases when we look at the strongest growth industry in the economy of Milton diversified – namely the status of the *Treatise on Christian Doctrine* and its relationship to *Paradise Lost*. For those addicted to Maurice Kelley's table of equivalences,[4] the seventh book account presents formidable difficulties. First matter is presented as implacably threatening, 'Outrageous as a Sea, dark wasteful, wild,' with mountainous waves seeking to assault 'Heav'n's highth, and with the Centre mix the pole' (*PL* 7.212, 215). In contrast, the Columbia translation of the *Treatise* advises us almost resoundingly, that first matter is 'intrinsically good, and the chief productive stock of every subsequent good.'[5] Carey's translation in the Yale edition of Milton's prose is more cautious: 'This original matter was not an evil thing, nor to be thought of as worthless: it was good, and it contained the seeds of all subsequent good.'[6]

It is difficult for translators of the *Treatise* to keep *Paradise Lost* completely out of mind. Carey's language certainly engages the seventh book account more effectively by conceding the appearance of evil to first matter. It then reassuringly tells us that the appearance is not the reality. One might almost conclude that Raphael's pedagogical purpose is to frighten Adam rather than to enlighten us.

Such a conclusion of course would be shockingly unwarranted but it draws attention to a deep divergence at this point between the *Treatise* and the epic, a divergence which A.S.P. Woodhouse attempted to underline in a hitherto neglected article written over fifty years ago.[7] No one can read the seventh book account without being intensely aware of the dangerously thin line that is Milton's 'just Circumference' (*PL* 7.231) and that separates an exquisitely diversified creation from a chaos that rages outrageously against it. The golden compasses seem to have been a printer's ornament. We can regard them figuratively as circumscribing the creation that is the book against the assault of the wild sea of language. The *Treatise* simply does not convey this persuasion that order can only be wrought within containment and that notwithstanding the containment, the outside remains ineradicably inside, eager to resume its precreation loyalties.

Throughout this discussion chaos has been identified with first matter. The *Treatise* does not seem to have anything to say about chaos, separating it strikingly from a poem which the threat of chaos dominates. In the absence of a prechaos narrative, the most plausible inference would be that chaos is first matter prior to processing. *Paradise Lost*, in yet another of its divergences from the *Treatise*, refers to first matter only once. When Raphael expounds the scale of nature to Adam, he tells him that all things proceed from and return to God and that all things are formed from 'one first matter' (*PL* 5.470–2). Since he is conversing in Paradise with an Adam innocent of the idea of chaos it seems evident that he is referring to first matter after processing. The extensive activities described in 7.225–40 indicate that much has to be gone through before chaos can be prepared for the possibility of order. In this preparation, the crucial steps are infusing vital virtue and warmth into chaos and purging away the 'dark, tartareous, cold, Infernal dregs / Adverse to life' (*PL* 7.238–9). Despite the *Treatise*'s reassurances, the line's four epithets are insistent in asserting the embedded presence of destructiveness in first matter,[8] its deep opposition to the prospect of order. It is only after these carefully directed ministrations that first matter is brought to a point where its creative possibilities can be discerned. Kelley puts Raphael's words into his table of equivalences[9] but the seventh book account gives no indication that any capability for creativeness resides in first matter. Indeed it gives every indication that chaos is the rampant denial of a capability that must be injected into it by the creative will of God.

The truth is that the seventh book account gives little imaginative support to the idea of a creation *ex deo* – a conclusion which the *Treatise* advocates as the less difficult of two vexing choices (*CPW* 6:307–8).[10] It can be less difficult only in a context that allows us some awareness of the goodness of first matter. That awareness urged on us by Raphael's laying out of the scale of nature, is something the seventh book seems determined to place in debate. It is not an exercise in monism. Indeed philosophical monism is difficult to embody in a poem that relies so heavily on binaries. We should not be surprised at finding the main account of the creation dramatically dualistic and resistant to the intimations of continuity, the reduction of the difference between the human and the divine, that are persistent elsewhere in the poem. *Paradise Lost* is deeply self-contesting. That is the nature of the educated imagination. It is not the nature of a systematic theology.

Such support as there is in *Paradise Lost* for a creation *ex deo* has to be found in a much disputed preamble to the creation in the seventh book that has been subjected to diametrically opposite readings. There is no real counterpart to this passage in the *Treatise*. Indeed the creation is of minor importance in the *Treatise* which devotes only 27 pages to it out of 807 in the Yale format.

In the preamble, an 'uncircumscrib'd' God brings about creation either by withdrawing his presence from boundlessness, or by reasserting his presence in a boundlessness from which he had previously withdrawn. The language helpfully lends itself to both interpretations, since 'retire' can be read either as referring to an action already taken or to one that is pending. The initial confrontation was between Denis Saurat who proposed the first reading and Maurice Kelley who advocated the second.[11] I have not sedulously followed the box-score since then but my impression is that it stands at about 65–35 in favour of Kelley. I accept Kelley's view not out of deference to the will of the majority, but because it seems to me to make superior sense.

If God reasserts his presence in the boundless deep, creation and the scale of nature are brought about by differentiating and diversifying that presence. Chaos is simply maximum absence. The condition of maximum absence is that it should be unable to find any trace of presence in itself. Presence must therefore be 'infus'd' into it (*PL* 7.236). The infusion sculpts the thin line and the enormous distance that separates chaos from creation and that can be obliterated either by the divine will, or by the dangerous autonomy conferred upon human agency. This precariousness is evident in Raphael's educational mandate where the poetry lives out the instability through wavering repetitions that come to rest warningly on the strong internal pause that follows 'mutable' (*PL* 5.233–7). It is also expressed in one of the most glorious lines that even Milton ever wrote – 'And Earth self balanc't on her Centre hung' – where the sheer beauty of the perilous equilibrium seems to justify the potentially tragic cost of its existence.[12]

If we read *PL* 7.167–73 as Kelley does, and construe its implication as I have attempted to do, we can bring the book 7 account into concordance with the *Treatise*. But some strenuousness of scholarship is needed to achieve this agreement, largely because the imaginative effect of the poem is so deeply different from the *Treatise*'s view of first matter. Of course, systematic theologies are not interested in imaginative effects, or in the troubled engagement of divine doctrine by human history. Poems happened to be concerned about such matters and this should make the importance of the *Treatise* in reading the epic less than central even if both were written by the same hand at about the same time.

The hand is disputed now and the table of equivalences has been complicated to the point where we can consider dispensing with its assistance. The poem could then hang self-balanced on its centre which is the way in which I would prefer to approach it. If the seventh book account were the only one, we could reinstate Woodhouse's misgivings and ask that the creation be considered, both against the continuing menace of its disengagement from chaos and in the compensatory plenitude of its unfolding.

There are, as we know by now, two accounts. Raphael's compelling narrative has all but erased the earlier version, not simply because it is given an entire book, strategically located in the twelve book version, but because it is so profoundly representative of the poem's idea of itself. Uriel's account takes less than twenty lines. It is staged as information given to a traveller who missed the creation but has heard reports of it and wishes to observe it at first-hand. Uriel is conveniently taken in by a depth of hypocrisy which according to the authorial voice, only God can penetrate. Eve solicited by the same voice is expected to do better. The deluded cherub congratulates Satan on his scientific passion for on-the-site inspection which some less Baconian angels do not share. He ends by disastrously pointing out the precise location of '*Adam's* abode' (3.733–5).

Uriel's 'excited reminiscence,' as Fowler calls it,[13] is hurried as well as excited. Two travellers whose paths diverge, have time only for a passing exchange. The brevity of the account encourages us to fold it into the book 7 narration and the connections seem sufficient to allow the folding. But there are also differences that resist incorporation and that taken together, encourage us to see Uriel's remembrance as another rendering of the greatest of all events. It would be surprising if only one rendering were possible.

The circumstances of staging justify Uriel's brevity but also invite us to read what he says with more than passing attention. His account comes first and first impressions take root. It takes place on the sun where illumination is to be expected. Uriel's 'I saw' (*PL* 3.708) makes it apparent that his is the statement of an eyewitness, despite the length of the Son's journey 'Far into *Chaos* and the World unborn' (*PL* 7.220). Moreover, the first account is given by the first among archangels. The order of precedence is Uriel, Raphael, Gabriel, and Michael. Milton follows this sequence scrupulously when it comes to dispensing information or guidance. Gabriel is taken out of it when it comes to homeland security. Finally, Uriel speaks to Satan as one angel to another. What he says is free of an educational mandate.

First matter is described by Uriel as a 'formless Mass / This world's material mould' (*PL* 3.708–9). The language is diligent in avoiding the high solemnity which the seventh book courts at every turn in its eloquence. Genesis tells us that the earth was 'without form,' but it was also 'void.' A void is not a mass though Milton in negotiating the prevarication between the empty and the formless, does refer to chaos as a 'fluid Mass' (*PL* 7.237). The 'vast Abyss' of 1.21, the abyss covered by 'Darkness profound' of 7.233–4, the 'dark, unbottom'd, infinite Abyss' of 2.405, and 'the void profound / Of unessential Night' of 2.438–9 inch closer to an ultimate nothingness to which form is not only alien but inconceivable. Scholastic thought sees evil as the total voiding of goodness and this understanding subtends Raphael's exposition of the scale of nature. But the confrontational structure of *Paradise Lost* requires evil to be more of an active principle, the negative manifestation that erupts from the total voiding. If we imagine night as an ontological zero we can imagine the chaos of book 7 as penetrated by the negativity on the far side of this zero. The chaos in book 3 is penetrated from the other direction. 'Unessential Night' is particularly powerful in evoking the zero state, a darkness no longer 'visible' (*PL* 1.34), stripped even of its own attributes as darkness.[14] In contrast, 'Mass' intimates not only substance but also the dormancy of form and 'material mould' strengthens the intimation. Moreover the material mould comes 'to a heap' (*PL* 3.709) at God's command. The ungainly phrase is oddly appropriate in suggesting the awkwardness of the primal coming together, the unfamiliarity rather than the alienness of order to first matter in its unbidden state. The confusion which hears God's voice and the 'wild uproar' (*PL* 3.710) which consents to be ruled by that voice are concordant with book 7 but their comparative matter of factness is quietly different from the grand style of Raphael's presentation.

Chaos cannot attain form without the divine intervention but the divine intervention here seems to urge into creativity an all but erased capability through which chaos can discover the seeds of form in itself.

Chaos in book 7, on the other hand, is hostile to creation, not unable to achieve it. Order has to be imposed on it rather than brought out of it. In Uriel's narration, wild uproar 'stood rul'd' and 'vast infinitude' stood 'confin'd' (*PL* 3.711). 'Stood' is a highly charged word with Milton and its repetition underlines the awakening of first matter to a force within itself that the divine bidding summons. Golden compasses are not needed to prescribe the circle of confinement. Uriel's subsequent language confirms this trend. Darkness *flees*, order *springs* from disorder, the 'cumbrous Elements' (*PL* 3.715) *hasten* to their 'several Quarters' (*PL* 3.714) and the 'Ethereal quintessence' (*PL* 3.716) no longer impeded by the weight of these elements, *flies* upward. Light does 'spring from the deep' in the seventh book, but the cumulative effect, the repeated positive responses to God's bidding, are stronger and far more persistent in book 3. 'Order from disorder sprung' (*PL* 3.713) gains its force from a carefully tailored context of which it can become the crystallization. Connecting with 'confusion' three lines earlier, 'disorder' suggests the frustration of order rather than its negation.[15] The words point with persuasiveness to a capacity for form that exists within first matter but that remains imprisoned until the divine creativeness reclaims it. We can deem this relationship analogous to the liberation of the fallen will by grace. If we do so we can contrast it with a sentence by Peter Du Moulin which must be considered crushing in its clarity: 'The degree of Predestination is that whereby God hath appointed what he will do with us and not what he will have us do.'[16] The seventh book leans in this direction with its utter alienation of first matter from the divine. The third book leans the other way. So too does much of *Paradise Lost*. Yet it would be wildly erroneous to conclude that the seventh book's imagining of origins is in discord with the poem. It is in fact, profoundly authentic in voicing it. But it is not the only authenticity. There are other voices which must be heard as principal voices in a poem whose orchestration is persistently contrapuntal. The voice which describes chaos to an Adam, who until now has been unaware of its existence, speaks for a present and persistent danger from a condition both utterly alien and potentially intimate. Creation, as the old anarch tells Satan, is only a brief walk from chaos (2.1007). The self-balanced earth can regress into it with the slightest tremor in its perilous equilibrium.

Danger is more distant in the third book version. The emphasis shifts to what first matter can do with itself when the impossibility of doing anything is removed. When the self-suffocating ordinance is lifted, first matter's possibilities can be nurtured, rather than held in being by monarchic absolutism from above. The third book opens the way to a political order that allows its *materia prima* some voice and to scientific understandings that are found in things rather than read into them. It is not unimportant that these authorizations should be anchored in the nature of the creation fable.

The complication is that there are two versions of the fable, one gesturing to the republican and the other anchored in the imperial,[17] one allowing first matter some share in the writing of order and the other insisting that order can be written only by the divine hand. We could argue that the first account is inserted to allow *sotto voce* compliance with the *Treatise*'s view of first matter from which the seventh book dramatically diverges. Muted acknowledgments may have been all that could be ventured, given the *Treatise*'s theologically inflammatory nature. Milton himself had narrowly escaped being on the 'most wanted' list of the Restoration police. This argument disallows Milton the heroic recklessness or the stubborn honesty that some among us would be happier to find in him. It further assumes not merely that the *Treatise* and the epic were written by the same hand, but also that doctrinal identity between the two had to be maintained, though in a language of maximum tact about the dangerous *liaison*.

One would prefer an explanation that did not give the *Treatise* this kind of automatic dominance and that treated the two works as two creations, each with its own rights. The present controversy and its dissociation of the epic from the *Treatise* reflects an uneasiness about this insistent identification, about what might be called the tyranny of the table. Yet, piling up differences rather than equivalences acknowledges the table in the endeavour to dispense with it. It is possible that the *Treatise* was not written by Milton or that not all of it was fully rewritten by Milton. Conjectures about the *Treatise*'s authorship (and scholarship on this matter can only be conjectural) can lead to various degrees of disengagement between it and the epic. Skills worthy of Miltonists are displayed in this exercise but the display helps us to avoid examining the extent of an author's entitlement to differ from himself. In essay 2 in this collection I have argued that the heresies in the *Treatise*, taken together rather than individually, form a structure that may be crucial in imagining *Paradise Lost*. If this argument is found persuasive, it implies an engagement between the poem and the *Treatise* that runs far deeper than mere doctrinal coincidence. Yet in my first book on Milton, written thirty years before the essay on his heresies, I had argued that a poem doctrinal and exemplary to a nation could not be written if its purpose was to foreground sectarian beliefs, however fervently those beliefs were held by their author. I was pleading then for disengagement and continue to do so. The poem's intimate associations with the *Treatise* and its sometimes dramatic differences from it are part of the weave of its fabric. It should not be necessary to raise questions of authorship in order to admit these differences. Instead, we should discard the limiting assumption that differences between two works by the same author can be differences only of genre or of mode. We should recognize more readily how the eloquence of difference lies in the way two works of the mind are conceived, rather than in the way they are presented. One speaks to history and the other to permanence. One speaks to experience and the other to those structures that must unassailably inform the reading of experience. We are still far from recognizing the force of these distinctions, not to mention the poem's imaginative autonomy, the extent to which it can debate the power of authorship, rewriting itself in the process of being written. The recognition is more complex because *Paradise Lost* more than many other poems, is balanced and contended for by differences within itself.

As I have already suggested, at least two translations are necessary and should be engaged in our understanding of the greatest of all events.[18] One is hospitable to democratic thought and scientific inquiry. The other asks us to imagine the maximum otherness against which the circumference of human selfhood can be drawn. The poem walks between these versions as it does with other differences and bridgings that inhabit its landscape, notwithstanding the distancing force of its antithetical statements. Because of its location in history, its rending awareness of the revolution betrayed, *Paradise Lost* has to see the human condition as fraught with danger but not stripped of opportunity. Another view less stark, is not foregrounded. But it is also not eradicated. Its presence in the poem remains part of the intimations of continuity and connectedness that counterpoint the poem's binary severances. It is creative rather than clandestine.

NOTES

1 Schwartz, *Remembering and Repeating: Biblical Creation in 'Paradise Lost'*;
   Rumrich, 'Milton's God and the Matter of Chaos.'
2 Rogers, *Matter of Revolution: Science, Poetry, and Politics in the Age of Milton.*
3 See Leonard, 'Milton, Lucretius, and "the void profound of unessential
   Night"'; Hunter, 'The Confounded Confusion of Chaos.'

4 Kelley, *This Great Argument: A Study of Milton's 'De Doctrina Christiana' as a Gloss upon 'Paradise Lost.'* See pp. 73–7, 82–3, 85–1, 101–6, 108–9, 123–8, 132–4, 135–9, 140–3, 143–7, 151–3, 154–5, 157–60, 164–7, 168–70, 171–2, 174–8, 179–81, 182–3, 186–9.

5 *De Doctrina Christiana*, ed. Hanford and Dunn, trans. Sumner, 15:21–3.

6 *Christian Doctrine*, trans. Carey, *CPW*, 6:308.

7 Woodhouse, 'Notes on Milton's Views on the Creation: The Initial Phase.' Like others, Woodhouse does not take the book 3 version into account. His article and the differences from the *Treatise* to which it draws attention have come into their own with the present controversy regarding the authorship of the *Treatise*. See chapter 4, note 9 of this book.

8 This excess of language has not escaped attention. Rogers (*Matter of Revolution*, 137) refers to it as an 'intractable theological aporia' and Schwartz (*Remembering and Reporting*, 11) finds 'the inference of an evil chaos so difficult to escape that it is not worth trying.' Hunter, who finds chaos neutral rather than evil, points out reassuringly that 'the problem vanishes' if 'Milton did not author the chapter on creation in the treatise' ('The Confounded Confusion of Chaos,' 229). Even so, one can still argue for an aporia caused by the divergence between the third and seventh book accounts, an aporia all the more significant because it is resident in a single text and not the result of a collision between two texts. Perhaps it is naive to continue assuming that authors strive to avoid aporias at all costs, but are driven by the nature of language to a threshold from which they cannot retreat. Not all aporias are language-induced, and perhaps the most interesting among them arise from divergent alignments in a poem neither of which the poem is prepared to renounce.

> Spenser appears to associate evil with chaos:
> > For in the wide wombe of the world there lyes,
> > In hatefull darkenesse and in deepe horrore
> > An huge eternall *Chaos*, which supplyes
> > The substances of natures fruitfull progenyes.   (*FQ,* 3.6.36.6–9)

The purpose here is replenishment not creation (3.6.36.2). Everything fetches its being from first matter. Forms come into existence and perish but 'The substance is not chaunged, nor altered' (3.6.38.1). Though the 'darkenesse' and the 'horrore' of chaos are acknowledged, they are backgrounded by nature's unceasing plenitude.

9 Kelley, *This Great Argument: A Study of Milton's 'De Doctrina Christiana,'* 125.

10 For a succinct exposition of these choices see Kelley, *Complete Prose Works*, vol. 6, introduction, 89.

11 Saurat, *Milton: Man and Thinker*, 236–8. Kelley, *This Great Argument: A Study of Milton's 'De Doctrina Christiana,'* 80–2, 209–12. There is an unexpected convergence between Milton's language and Marlowe's in *Tamburlaine Part Two*

> ... he that sits on high and never sleeps
> Nor in one place is circumscriptible
> But everywhere fils every Continent
> With strange infusion of his sacred vigor.   (2.2.2906–9)

The 'infusion' of 'sacred vigor' (csf. *PL* 7.136) points to a putting forth rather than a retraction of presence.

12 In 'On the Morning of Christ's Nativity,' the 'well-balanc't world' is 'on hinges hung' (122). In *PL* the world is hung from heaven by a golden chain (2.1051–3) with the 'self-balanc't' earth at its centre (7.242). The hinges are transferred to the gates of heaven (7.205–7) implementing the creation itself of 3.99: 'Sufficient to have stood, though free to fall.'

13 *Poems*, edited by Carey and Fowler (1968), 605n.

14 Milton's capacity to imagine nothingness could encourage those who do not know better to read *Paradise Lost* as supporting a creation *ex nihilo*.

15 The view of Milton's chaos offered by Catherine Gimelli Martin fits well with the book 3 account. In fact her quotation from John Ray (165) helps us to read Uriel's remembrances of 'confusion' and 'disorder' as a disarray which the divine bidding rectifies; see *The Ruins of Allegory: 'Paradise Lost' and the Metamorphosis of Epic Convention*.

16 Du Moulin, *The Anatomy of Arminianism*, 85. Du Moulin's statement is relentlessly imperial. Milton's steadfast upholding of free will (the theological ancestor of agency), and of the cosmic price paid in order to keep it in being, need to be read in this context.

17 In the 1805 text of *The Prelude*, Wordsworth's account of the vista from the summit of Mount Snowdon attaches itself to Uriel's version of the creation. In the 1850 text, the seventh book creation is evoked. In the *Form of the Unfinished*, 136–9, I examined Wordsworth's imperializing of the Snowdon experience but did not note how the imperializing tracks the movement from book 3 to book 7.

18 Multiple fables of the creation in Hindu mythology should persuade us that the creation needs to be continuously remythologized if it is to be actively understood.

8 Milton and Camões: Reinventing the Old Man

Headnote

An earlier version of this essay was printed in 'Post-Imperial Camões,' a special issue of *Portuguese Literary and Cultural Studies* 9 (fall 2002): 177–87. The original version was read at the conference, 'Post-Imperial Camões, a Colloquium' at the University of Massachusetts, Amherst, MA, in 2002. The background for the current essay is provided in Rajan's chapter, '*The Lusiads* and the Asian Reader,' in *Under Western Eyes: India from Milton to Macauley* (1999), 31–49. Pages 31–41 of the chapter in *Under Western Eyes* examine the circumstances of da Gama's voyage and pp. 45–9 explore current interpretations of *The Lusiads*, showing how almost all of them seek to reconsider its centre-margin relationship.

Readings of *The Lusiads* are predominantly the work of Western scholars. Rajan in *Under Western Eyes* insists that the reading community must be regarded hereafter as global, and that erstwhile subjected peoples must be given their proper place in it. Subjected peoples will be resistant to triumphalist rhetoric and to having their civilizational heritages reduced to commercial opportunities. The reading offered embraces these resistances. It suggests that the best way to confront them is not to rebuild the poem around its uneasinesses but to see it more straightforwardly as a seminal statement, peremptory in its nature, of the early modern moment. Its commercial emphases are brought to fruition in the commercially dominated globalism of today. A critique of that globalism is called for in relation to the poem of the moment that launched it. The Old Man whose protest was left behind on the receding shoreline of an obsolete world view must be placed on an approaching horizon. He has to be reinvented to speak with authority in a world that is strange to him. Rajan discusses *Paradise Lost* in this essay as offering a path towards that reinvention.

This essay forms part of Rajan's larger argument that imperialism has always been a companion of commerce (see *Under Western Eyes*), and that today's globalism reduces itself to a highly sophisticated form of imperialism (see Rajan's 'Imperialism and the Other End of History' [2004]).

If we are to study the status of Camões in a postimperial world one overwhelming question needs to be asked. How does the poem now look to a citizen of those territories which *The Lusiads* made into the emblems of Portuguese glory? The banners of Camões's vision (seen from a hilltop similar to the one on which Christ in *Paradise Regained* refused the kingdoms of the world)[1] are no longer to be seen on Asian soil. But more than the banners have vanished. Independence also means the independence of the Asian reader to assess the poem against his own history. If Camões is a world poet what are the terms of a global understanding about him or more tentatively, the terms of that conversation within which such an understanding might be sought?

It is twenty-five years since Edward Said's *Orientalism* reconfigured our perception of intercultural relationships. Postcolonialism at its outset lacked historical depth, assuming disarmingly that the world began with Kipling. In the years that followed it has reached back to the time of Columbus and Vasco da Gama, demonstrating that its patterns of perception can indeed engage historically distant periods with the present and can give to the term 'early modern' a significance which is penetrating rather than polemical. In the process the canon which might be taken to be imperialism's steadfast stronghold has been shown to be heavily conflicted and to be built around fault lines that oblige it to struggle with itself. Voices of protest are prominent in *The Lusiads* and might be taken to be evidence of these fault lines, but paradoxically they are prominent because the poem seems determined to deny them entry. Moreover they are dismissive rather than disarticulating. It is not easy to make them the revisionary centre of a work that stubbornly remains the most triumphalist of Western epics.

Not all differences in poems lead to openings around which the poem can be rearticulated. Richard Helgerson for example treats *The Lusiads* as a heroic poem of Portuguese nationhood[2] whereas William Mickle, its eighteenth-century translator, describes it as 'the epic poem of the birth of commerce, and, in a particular manner, the epic poem of whatever country has the control and possession of the commerce of India.'[3] In finding Mickle's reading 'bizarre,' Helgerson accounts for it by assigning it to a different reading climate, a different position on the 'hermeneutic spiral.'[4] We in our time occupy yet another location on that spiral from which another view of The Lusiads needs to be launched. I leave aside this principal item on our agenda for the moment in order to point out that Mickle's allegedly 'bizarre' view is not without roots in the text. Epic catalogues in the later books of The Lusiads are catalogues of spices not of heroes. One might argue that the commercial and the heroic run convergent courses which meet in today's global economy where the bottom line has been elevated to transcendence and where CEO's are either deified or satanized. To say this is only to remind the Asian reader that commerce and the pursuit of imperial glory have colluded persistently and with deplorable results. The aristocratic/middle class distinction that separated the two in the sixteenth century seems less a debate about the imperial mission than a division of labour in its implementation. It does not offer the solace of a fault line around which the poem can be rebuilt.

A postimperial era is not simply an era of vanishing empires. It is also a time in which others hitherto ventriloquized can speak as themselves and not be heard simply in allotted voices which they can do no more than modulate by their own voices of protest. When the constraints of a dominant discourse are removed the line of the unacceptable will be drawn more firmly and deeply. Occasions for the willing suspension of disbelief will become less profuse. We can no longer leave our ideologies in the cloakroom as we enter the literary seminar. Some things that have been said cannot be lived with even in the name of literature. Perhaps we can live with them in the name of history. We then reduce them to documentary status. Another possibility is to estrange them and to ask ourselves what we learn from the estrangement. There can be both dissociation and connectedness as we negotiate the line of cleavage and joining. Historicizing the unfamiliar can become a crude, polemical tactic when civilizations of today are dismissed as medieval. It is a different matter when Milton pushes historicization to its limits by making the principles of ideal order Edenic. The Fall is the maximum estrangement. We are the total other of our origins. The fissure is the poem and we read the poem along changing approaches because so much can be poured into the fissure.

The Lusiads is not a poem into which the human condition can be emptied. I would say this of the Mahabharata but in the Western world there may be only one such poem. *The Lusiads* is less capacious than *Paradise Lost* and perhaps for that reason less riven within itself. Like the *Aeneid* to which it alludes eighty times and claims to surpass, it is the story of a dangerous voyage, but a voyage in the bronze world of reality rather than the golden one of poetic feigning.[5] Unlike the *Aeneid*, *The Lusiads* is not the narrative of a dispossessed people, journeying across strange seas to establish a new homeland. That story should be familiar in New England and I am sometimes surprised that the *Aeneid* is not the American epic. The waste of war, the weariness of wandering, and the tragic cost of destiny suffuse the Virgilian hexameter, the 'stateliest measure,' according to Tennyson, 'ever moulded by the lips of man.'[6] There is enough in the poem to turn it against its *telos* for those wishing to doubt the imperial enterprise.

The Lusiads is more self-confident than the *Aeneid*. It has to be confident because it is more than the epic of Portugal. It is the poem of the early modern moment.[7] It offers us a beginning and beginnings can be peremptorily clear. They can also be tentative, wrapped in ambivalences and offering multiple routes out of their nuclei whose consequences can diverge and entwine. *The Lusiads* is in the former category. Bold beginnings often leave something behind, such as an old man on the seashore. He speaks with wisdom as the narrator notes but wisdom falters as the paradigm shifts. It is a shift that in its nature has to be peremptory, that must ignore rather than take in the Old Man, that must refrain from engaging itself with the world-view it abandons. Misgivings can only come later, as the shift opens itself to the consequences which its initial clarity elides.

Early modernism is marked by competing nascent empires. Commerce with Cathay and curiosity about the Far East's fabled civilizations were the motives for Columbus's westward voyage. When the New World came in the way, conquest, plunder, and settlement became agreeable options. In the East, the military balance of power made regime change impractical. Since Portugal was given the East by papal dispensation,[8] commerce had to be the prize, along with glory, establishing links with distant Christian communities, including the elusive Prester John, and converting infidels in whom the East abounded. Vasco da Gama's voyage was an audacious move, typical of an exuberant nationhood, eager to assume a world destiny. Commerce with the East had been in existence for centuries but it had been largely Arab-controlled, moving along the Silk Road and through ports on the Arabian Sea to Venice. Da Gama's mission was to open a sea route to the Indies that would undermine the

Venetian dominance and break open the Arab grip on commerce between Asia and Europe. The Old Man had said that if glory was important, Portugal should seek it in battle with the traditional enemies of
Christendom. He was not thinking of economic victories which were to
count as much in the future as military triumphs. Da Gama's voyage was
not simply from Lisbon to Calicut but from a premodern to an early
modern world-view.

The cost of the voyage was high and its tactics were daring. They
involved plunging west where the shoreline of Africa turns east and
journeying deep into the Atlantic before making the turn that would
enable trade winds to carry the three ships to the Cape.[9] Da Gama's men
were out of sight of land for ninety-six days. Though the epic does not
suggest this, the passage from the Cape to India was less of an advance
into the unknown. Commerce between India and the Eastern African
and Arabian coasts had been intensely active for centuries. Another
Braudel is needed to write the history of the world of the Indian Ocean.[10]
Da Gama's difficulties were further eased by the services of an experi-
enced pilot who may have been the legendary Ibn Majid.[11]

Nevertheless one third to one half of da Gama's men did not return to
Portugal. When Camões set sail for Goa fifty-five years later in a flotilla of
four ships, three were lost on the way out and the one remaining did not
survive the return journey. The cost was higher than in the Second
World War when German submarines operating from Dakar preyed
upon Allied shipping obliged to take the Cape route.

A cost-benefit analysis may seem beside the point in circumstances
where international standing among empires was more important than
the return on venture capital. It can be observed, nevertheless, that the
Portuguese bid for eminence, both commercially and in world imperial
rankings, was at the outset, spectacularly successful. Albuquerque had
prophesied that if a sea route to the Indies was opened, 'Cairo and
Mecca will be entirely ruined, and to Venice will no spices be conveyed,
except what her merchants go and buy in Portugal.'[12] By the early
sixteenth century 75 per cent of spices from the East were arriving in
Portuguese vessels and profits of 90 per cent were being reaped.

The moment passed almost as soon as it materialized. Portugal lacked
the money and the ships to maintain the dizzying reach of its imperial
design. The blockade of Arab ports could not be maintained and the loss
of skilled manpower on dangerous voyages took a toll that became
increasingly hard to sustain. By the end of the century Portugal's share in
the pepper trade fell to a mere 20 per cent. Aden could not be captured

and Ormuz, the emporium of the Orient, was taken from the Portuguese in 1622. Even more devastating was an ill-fated military expedition to Moorish Africa launched in June 1578 with considerable pomp and circumstance. In five hours of battle under a searing sun the flower of Portugal's manhood was destroyed. Eight thousand men were killed and fifteen thousand taken prisoner. No more than a hundred found their way back to Portugal. Camões, with the deathbed wit that was part of his time's tragic gaiety, remarked that he was glad to perish not only in but also with his country.

Camões must have been aware of Portugal's decline at the time he wrote *The Lusiads*. We have to ask ourselves to what extent that awareness is taken into his poem. We could have had a poem that was elegiac rather than triumphalist. We could even have had a poem that foresaw in Portugal's decline, the eventual dubiousness of the imperial enterprise. It is obvious that we do not have either. Doubts about the imperial mission are expressed in *The Lusiads* but they are marginalized in relation to a triumphalist core. They circulate at the fringes of an undertaking which seems determined not to allow them into its space. Attempts have been made to move them closer to the centre and indeed revisionary readings of *The Lusiads* are heavily dedicated to such attempts. They seem to me to skew the poem immoderately.

Skewed interpretations are the order of the day. When literary texts make statements we find difficult to accept, we search for and foreground the text's anxieties so that the statements are undermined or at least contested. We do so with the justification that this is how the text reaches out to its future. We want to think of a poem that endures as resisting its own indoctrination, as not being able to avoid its honesty. Literature could not be heard with involvement outside the auditory in which it was first performed if we did not listen to its contrapuntal music. Skewed readings are needed but skewing beyond a certain point is wilful rather than accommodative. Disputes can and do occur about the permissible degree of reorientation but I remain persuaded that efforts to reconstitute the poem around the Old Man's harangue pull it too far away from its anchorage.

Among reflections on *The Lusiads*'s self-dismissals, an article by Jack Tomlins is particularly interesting. He argues that Camões after his return from India 'saw the Oriental conquest – with India as the brightest diamond in the crown – as mere vanity and total ruin.' The opening dedication, the Old Man's rebuke, and the disillusioned envoi of the epic were all composed after the poet's return and reflect this deep change in understanding. The poem thus 'flies apart at three junctures' undoing 'the very business of the epic.'[13] Tomlin's recuperation via chronology can only be conjectural and is not supported by any evidence except the desirability of the recuperative arrangement. Nevertheless it concedes the marginality of the poem's misgivings about itself. His argument is that the marginality is the result of the recantations coming too late to enter a central space already occupied by a previous poem. If so, the two poems are simply not sufficiently engaged for them to fly apart. What we have is a collision rather than a critique.

Our difficulty is that the countervoice in the poem must be more than merely dismissive. It has to provide the basis for a revisionary turn within the poem itself. The Old Man is not saying that a different version of *The Lusiads* ought to be written. He is arguing that the epic should not be written at all.[14] If, as I have already argued, da Gama's voyage is to be seen not just as a voyage from Lisbon to Calicut but as an opening up of the early modern world, the Old Man's speech may have to be deposited in what Hegel derisively called the lumber room of history. In fact the Old Man is advocating almost that abandonment of history which the last books of *Paradise Lost* were once chided for embodying.

A protesting voice is needed but its location has to be different. It has to come out of the world the poem sails into rather than from the world it leaves behind. Milton more than any other poet, seems to me to initiate this voice. Milton does not mention Camões but books have been written about Milton's relationship with authors he did not mention. J.H. Sims's many articles on the subject show that the connection of *The Lusiads* with *Paradise Lost* is more substantial than the two alliterative reminiscences that can be heard in Milton's poem.[15] *Paradise Lost* actually lies in close chronological proximity not to *The Lusiads*, but to its first English translation by Richard Fanshawe, which was not published until 1655. A blind poet growing older, who had given his best years to a faltering revolution, might well have remembered a marginal voice on a receding shoreline. Milton does indeed step into the Old Man's shoes but the man in the shoes is imperiously Milton.

Commerce and empire are blended in the beginnings of early modernism from which they flow into their consummation of today's globalism and the imperial power of the consumer ethos. Columbus's voyage and da Gama's embrace the world between them. The world we live in is the result of that dubious embrace. The Old Man can say nothing about the synergy between commerce and empire because he does not speak out of the early modern moment. Milton begins his detection of that synergy with a famous speech by Comus which can be read as a prospectus for da Gama's voyage.[16] The lady replies by counselling temperance, and talk about temperance can be tedious, particularly for those who wish to find commendations of temperance sustained paradoxically by the plenitude of language. This is a difficulty Milton often confronts. Temperance becomes more acceptable when it is metamorphosed into the collective self-restraint that is necessary to safeguard our planet.

In *Paradise Lost* the argument against the early modern synergy is more clearly focused and driven with greater sternness. Satan is the original imperialist and his journey from Hell to Paradise, laden with evocations of the spice trade,[17] is the infernal matrix of the heroic-commercial quest. The argumentative thrust is even clearer in the quite different accounts of forbidden fruit consumption provided in *Areopagitica* and in *Paradise Lost*. The prose tract tells us that the knowledge of good and evil leaped into the world 'from out the rinde of one apple tasted.'[18] *Paradise Lost* has none of this delicate nibbling. Eve does not tentatively puncture the rind of an apple. She eats it rind and all. In fact, she seems to eat several apples. Having done so, she tears off a branch from the tree and carries it to Adam who after some hesitation shares with her the delights of unrestricted apple eating. None of this staging is to be found in Genesis or in any commentary that I know of on Genesis. Pleasing and sating the 'curious taste' is in Comus's perverse ecological reasoning, not merely a right but a responsibility bestowed upon us by earth's abundance.[19] In *Paradise Lost* the justification for unrestricted consumption is embedded in our origins and carried to its lethal extreme.

The Old Man does suggest that original sin lies at the root of da Gama's enterprise but he suggests this as part of the vaguely inclusive proposition that all mistaken undertakings are the result of original sin. He can say no more because he is on the wrong side of an historical divide. His is a discourse no longer relevant. The poem, to form itself, must move away from that discourse. Milton can say more because he is speaking from within the discourse that *The Lusiads* authenticates. One hundred and seventy-five years of early modernism generate a critique that can be planted with precision not merely in the cultural stipulations of the moment but more fundamentally in the deep-rooted propensity to destructiveness which is so stubbornly part of the nature of our beginnings.

The Old Man's remarks on the vanity of human endeavour are more difficult to sharpen and direct. Augustine touches a responsive chord in Milton. Yet despite the almost overwhelming presence of the weight of

woe within it, *Paradise Lost* is pledged to history as the Old Man's declamation is not. Even that classical heroism which is denounced as the
poet tunes his note to 'tragic,' is embodied in a splendour of language
that reinstates what it rejects and that Milton cannot quite bring to the
'better fortitude.'[20] The poet against empire writes a poem that is resplendently imperial, commanding and directing the history of Western literature into a work seeking to contain a history that rages against
the borders of poetic form, as chaos did until it was compelled into
order. *Paradise Lost* does not turn its back on history. History is its theme
and its obsession. As a poem containing history (the phrase is Ezra
Pound's)[21] it has to proceed on the premise that history can be compre-
hended through containment, that it can be written and not merely
endured, that its creative promise will prevail over its tragic momentum.
But the conditions for that writing, the sweeping aside of all collective
action until the rebellious self is fully aligned with the divine, will constitute a deferral as destructive as the premature action it bleakly anato-
mizes. The powerful foregrounding of fallenness does not sufficiently
address a spectrum of religious and moral understandings which are
with us today and in which fallenness does not play a crucial part. In a
postimperial world the time has come for the critique to be critiqued.

To conclude, I regard *The Lusiads* as a quintessential poem of the early
modern moment. Its self-confidence is part of the moment's character.
Protests against that self-confidence are driven to the poem's margins
and essentialized to a point where they no longer seem pertinent. In
recording a historical event *The Lusiads* is itself an event in cultural
history, an intervention that shifts the parameters of debate. That debate
remains in progress today.

Asian readers resent the commercial emphasis of *The Lusiads* and the
trivial commodifications which resolutely bypass all that Asian civilizations have offered to world understanding. Yet that very reductiveness
leads into and underlines the impoverishments of the economic universalism now being put forward as our final paradigm. It also advises us
that commerce is the ally of imperialism, not its replacement. The
synergy between the two, which *The Lusiads* is so prophetic in making
evident, will not be dismantled simply by being globalized. It will be
dismantled only by commitment to a universalism adequately in accor-
dance with human dignity, worth, and aspirations. Previous universalisms
have built themselves on concerns more elevated than the profit principle. The enlightenment offered us a world governed by universal
reason free from the selectiveness imposed by a right reason which had

to be reconstructed from the debris of fallenness and which therefore had to be theologically certified.[22] We need to proceed further into a world which is governed by conscience as well as by reason, a world in which to modulate Shelley's description of the poetic imagination 'the pains and pleasures of [the] species must become [man's] own.'[23] Today we are threatened by citizenship of a world order in which what cannot be commodified does not exist. We are at the end of da Gama's journey. Once again the Old Man needs to be reinvented but in a manner which speaks specifically to our time as well as more amply to eternity.

NOTES

1 *The Lusiads*, 10.77. All references to *The Lusiads* are to the translation by Leonard Bacon. The mountain which Christ ascends (*PR* 3.251–66) is specifically compared to the highest hill in Paradise (*PL* 11.377–82) from which Adam views the havoc wrought by his fall. Characteristically the approach to the hill of vision in *The Lusiads* is strewn with emeralds and rubies.

2 Helgerson, *Forms of Nationhood: The Elizabethan Writing of England*, 155–76, 189–90.

3 Mickle, *The Lusiads or The Discovery of India: An Epic Poem*, cxlvii.

4 Helgerson, *Forms of Nationhood*, 190.

5 Camões does argue that the bronze world of his poem is as exemplary as the golden and has the added advantage of being actual rather and fictive.

6 Tennyson, 'To Virgil," in *The Poems of Tennyson*, 1313, l. 20.

7 Recognized characteristics of early modernism include the ending of feudalism, the rise of the nation-state, the emergence of a middle class, and the expansion of commerce. The emergence of competing empires and the collusion between imperial and commercial interests have been insufficiently acknowledged. Before the term 'early modern' came into use, the era was seen as a dystopic beginning in which things fell apart, unity of being and culture became fragmented, sensibility was dissociated, and the mind became disinherited. Technology undermined the individual self-consciousness which Burckhardt saw as the heart of the Renaissance. Eliot and Yeats are prominently associated with this view.

8 Under the Treaty of Tardesillas, signed in 1494. The absence of a reliable computation of longitude led to complications. See J.R. Hall, *Renaissance Exploration*, 45.

9 See e.g., Hall, *Renaissance Exploration*, 29–45. Developing the 'wind route' was

important because shorter and more predictable travel times would lead to higher profits. Da Gama's ships (unlike Columbus's) were specifically built to provide the maximum carrying capacity consistent with seaworthiness.

10 Braudel, *The Mediterranean and the Mediterranean World in the Age of Phillip II*. An important beginning in this direction has been made in Chaudhari's *Asia before Europe: Economy and Civilization of the Indian Ocean from the Rise of Islam to 1750*. It is carried further in Richard Hall's superb *Empires of the Monsoon*.

11 Geoffrey Vaughan Scammell confidently identifies the pilot as Ibn Majid, 'the most distinguished navigator of the time' (*The World Encompassed: The First European Maritime Empire c. 800–1650*, 235). See also J.R. Hall, *Renaissance Exploration*, 40. Portuguese sources describe him as the 'Moor of Gujarat' and as Maleme, Cana, or Canaqua (Captain Astrologer). It is hard to think of a Muslim pilot helping the Portuguese to destroy the very monopoly from which he himself was profiting. These difficulties are taken into account by Richard Hall, *Empires of the Monsoon*, 179–83, who nevertheless concludes that the Majid was the pilot.

12 As quoted in Mukherjee, *The Rise and Fall of the East India Company*, 100–1.

13 Tomlins, 'Gil Vicente's Vision of India and Its Ironic Echo in Camões "Velho de Rosselo."'

14 The Old Man could be read as voicing the conservative opposition to the king, particularly in his view that reformation at home was more important than adventures abroad. This is a stereotypical caution against expansionist enterprises which must be made specific to be effective. Instead it becomes lost by being distanced into fundamentalist statements about original sin and the vanity of human endeavour. The declamation takes in prevailing misgivings but it takes them in through a rhetoric designed to be dismissed.

15 Sims, 'Camoëns' *Lusiads* and Milton's *Paradise Lost*: Satan's Voyage to Eden'; 'Echoes of Camoens' *Lusiads* in Milton's *Paradise Lost* (1–4)'; 'Camoës, Milton, and Myth in the Christian Epic'; 'Christened Classicism in *Paradise Lost* and *The Lusiads*'; 'Delicious Paradise' in *Os Lusiadas* and in *Paradise Lost*'; 'The Epic Narrator's Mortal Voice in Camões and Milton'; 'A Greater than Rome: The Conversion of a Virgilian Symbol from Camoës to Milton'; 'Milton as a Camoist'; and '*Os Lusiadas*: A Structural Prototype of *Paradise Lost*.' The alliterative reminiscences are in *PL* 2.639 and *PL* 11.399.

16 *A Masque Presented at Ludlow Castle, Poems*, 11. 705–54. J. Martin Evans shows how 'Comus's great hymn to Nature's fecundity' reflects encounters with the New World (*Milton's Imperial Epic: 'Paradise Lost' and the Discourse of Colonialism*, 47–50).

17 See in particular, *PL* 2.636–43.

18 *Areopagitica, CPW* 2: 514. Comus's 'curious taste' is taken up in the tasting of the apple but uninhibited consumption is here shrunk to a tentativeness that underlines the drama of the sentence as the twins leap explosively into the world. Syntactic deferrals add to the suspense of the drama.

19 It is remarkable how the sheer perversity of the argument is ignored by admirers of Comus's eloquence. If the firmament displays the glory of its maker it is so that we can treat it with a sense of reverence.

20 *PL* 9.31; 1–41.

21 Pound, *Make it New*, 86. See also Rajan, *The Form of the Unfinished*, 288.

22 The influential book by Theodor W. Adorno and Max Horkheimer, *The Dialectic of Enlightenment*, has been read as arguing that the Enlightenment is the source of most of our woes. The real objection of the authors seems to be to the totalizing trend implicit in all universalisms and of the degree to which totalizing forces in alliance with the momentum of technology have deprived us of the human dimension. There is another side to this dystopic view of the Enlightenment, which is that human rights as we now know them are the Enlightenment's consequence.

23 Shelley, *A Defence of Poetry*, in *Shelley's Poetry and Prose*, 488.

9 Warfaring and Wayfaring: Milton and the Globalization of Tolerance

Headnote

This hitherto unpublished essay, composed in 2004, marks a further stage in Rajan's continuing attempt to bring Milton's work into engagement with the contemporary world. 'Banyan Trees and Fig Leaves' (chapter 5), 'The Imperial Temptation' (chapter 6), and 'Reinventing the Old Man' (chapter 8) are other illustrations of this effort. 'Early modern' is a term designed to invoke this connection. Nevertheless much seventeenth-century scholarship tends to estrange the seventeenth-century world from our time rather than to make the connection that 'early modern' invites.

Estrangement does draw attention to the distinctiveness of seventeenth-century discourse, both in its terminology and its idiom, in dealing with matters such as toleration which are crucial in constituting both today's world and Milton's. Estrangement resists the easy assimilation of one world into another. It calls for translation rather than transference. On the other hand, 'early modern' implies that the two worlds are far from opaque to each other and that translation is not only possible but natural if we are to understand the beginnings of the world in which we live. The constitution of the subject has been presented as a defining characteristic of early modern thought. It establishes an epistemic continuity between 'early modern' and 'today' which subtends economic and cultural continuities. Attention to difference should not blur these continuities. This chapter endeavours to show how the overflowing images of *Areopagitica* connect themselves to contemporary problems of tolerance, despite the specialized language and restricted horizons of seventeenth-century Protestant discourse.

Toleration in Milton's time was a restricted problem. Its dimensions were religious and confined to a single religion. There were boundaries to toleration even within that religion. Papists and Turks lay outside the pale and were habitually conjoined in the language of abhorrence. Jews could be lived with only because their conversion was the prelude to a Second Coming which many regarded as imminent.

Toleration today is not simply between religions. It is between different cultural formations, different mindsets and the different ways in which history has embedded them. Globalizing tolerance and multiplying its dimensions cannot be posed as a problem even on the horizons of Milton's thought. Can the imagery which sustains that thought be taken out of the moment of its kindling and into situations which Milton never foresaw? It is a large demand to make of the poet's claim to timelessness.

Milton remains a poet even in his prose. At times the poetry seems almost incongruous. The wars of truth are barren in their language. Deep issues are involved but they are imprisoned within the swirl of controversy and the narrowings of a discourse that reduces truth to doctrine. Sword-play in these militancies needs to be precise, to be 'suttle and sinewy,' as in Milton's description of the talents of his countrymen.[1] The prose of the pamphlet explosion does not meet this characterization and Milton's own prose is made even more distant from it by the estranged voice of the imprisoned poet. The overburdened sentences of the prayer in *Of Reformation* (*CPW* 1:614–17) seem self-defeating in their compensatory excess. Even the wonderful closing sentence of Section IV of *Animadversions* (*CPW* 1:707): 'The voice of thy Bride calls thee, and all creatures sigh to bee renew'd,' is not to the point though it comes as a welcome relief from the heavy-handed thrust and parry of the exchanges that have preceded it.

A powerful successor to Milton is needed to tell us that the road of excess can lead to the palace of wisdom and that the future can be fertilized by language that overflows its channels. Milton's imaginings often pivot on this overflow, on the almost symbiotic relationship between discipline and excess. That pivoting is embodied as language performance both in the heavenly dance in *Paradise Lost* (5.618–27) and in the eulogy on discipline in *The Reason of Church Government* (*CPW*

1:751–3) where the self-supplementing energy of the sentences takes us beyond the principles of church organization into a cosmic realm of order discovered in plenitude. *Areopagitica* translates this mutual dependence into the relationship between its argument and its imagery. For the first and perhaps the only time in Milton's prose, the liberated right hand achieves parity with the left (*CPW* 1:808).

The overflow of language and the supplementation the future finds in that spillage are the basis on which a work of the mind endures and is born of the moment without being the moment's prisoner. There is nothing original, we are assured, in *Areopagitica*. Roger Williams, Henry Robinson, William Walwyn, and the author of M.S. to A.S. were saying the same things as Milton in the months before he said them. The only thing original about *Areopagitica* is its eloquence.[2]

Eloquence is nearly all in *Areopagitica*. It is the reason why a text little recognized in its own time has now assumed classic status, not simply as a plea for the 'liberty of unlicens'd printing' but as a plea for the mind's right to seek itself and for identity made real in community.

In the rhetoric of persuasion, the imagery is expected to apprentice itself to the argument. This is not so in *Areopagitica*. Milton's figural language has a generative power that overruns the train of the argument, sometimes sweeping that argument to the sidelines with its momentum. The images do not simply follow each other as waves do. They reinvent each other so that the space they collectively animate is alive with possibilities remarkably beyond the immediate interests they support.

Excess invigorating discipline, the surplus in which a work opens itself to its future, becomes apparent early in *Areopagitica*. A good book, Milton tells us, is 'the pretious life-blood of a master spirit' (*CPW* 2:493). The phrase passes into everyone's familiar quotations, with the term 'master spirit' curiously unscrutinized. Also unscrutinized is Milton's pursuit and enlargement of his metaphor. Suppressing a book is an act of homicide. Enduring the suppression is martyrdom. In the end we become witnesses to a massacre, to a program of genocide directed against intelligence (*CPW* 2:502–3). The momentum carries us into a different era where the right drably described as freedom of information subtends the very possibility of thought.

As we turn to the legend of Cupid and Psyche, we find Milton overwriting the myth so as to engage it with his own time and then suggesting through the overflow of his language, how the myth reaches forward to a point where we can engage it:

> Good and evill we know in the field of this World grow up together almost
> inseparably; and the knowledge of good is so involv'd and interwoven with
> the knowledge of evill, and in so many cunning resemblances hardly to be
> discern'd, that those confused seeds which were impos'd on *Psyche* as an
> incessant labour to cull out, and sort asunder, were not more intermix't.
> (*CPW* 2:514)

It is important to remember that in the original narrative of the story by
Apuleuis, Psyche's task was onerous but not difficult. The six different
kinds of seeds in the heap set before her by Venus could be distinguished without trouble. Psyche's real difficulties lay in the size of the
heap and in the impossibility of meeting the deadline imposed by Venus.
She was enabled to do so by a helpful army of ants.[3]

Milton does not mention the ants but he expects us to remember
them. As they come to Psyche's rescue in her lonely task, they advise us
that no one is alone. They anticipate the figures of collective effort that
abound in *Areopagitica* and that come to be its signature. As Milton
overwrites the story, making the work of disentanglement immensely
more difficult, he looks forward to future images in which the work of
understanding is possible only because it is shared. *Areopagitica* is in fact
the most community minded of Milton's works, a work in which toleration is not just the protective right to which it was later reduced, but a
necessary component of consensus building.

Intelligence, aroused and watchful, is needed in our predicament
rather than the diligence of the ants. Milton insists on cunning resem-
blances (in which Spenser's Archimago was a specialist),[4] on the interweaving of the knowledge of good and of evil, and on labour which is
incessant not because a deadline has to be met, but because eternal
vigilance is the price of Christian liberty. The enemy is within. The
confusion among the seeds is embedded in the act of perceiving them.
In wrestling with the treacheries of understanding, the imagery propels
the thought into depths it may not have anticipated: 'It was from out the
rinde of one apple tasted, that the knowledge of good and evill as two
twins cleaving together leapt forth into the World' (*CPW* 2:514). 'Involv'd'
and 'interwoven,' despite their sombre weight, now seem no more than
euphemisms as we contemplate an inseparability that has become bio-
logical, an elemental part of the birth and nature of knowledge.

As Milton melts down the antitheses that enable us to talk of evil
empires he is, of course, opening a door into the modern world. Much
passes through that door but much that passes moves around a textual

crux that now needs to be examined in some detail: 'He that can apprehend and consider vice with all her baits and seeming pleasures, and yet abstain, and yet distinguish, and yet prefer that which is truly better, he is the true warfaring Christian' (*CPW* 2:514–15). The Yale text prints 'warfaring' as do most of *Areopagitica*'s later editors.[5] The 1644 text of *Areopagitica* (and the only one published in that century) prints 'wayfaring.' Wayfaring has been changed by hand into 'warfaring' in at least eight copies of 1644, including four presentation copies. The hand may or may not be Milton's (Helen Darbishire questions the claim that it is) but the assiduity with which the alteration was pursued, makes it likely that the intention was Milton's. Nevertheless it does not follow that the 1644 wording was a printer's mistake. It may have been a wording which Milton first sponsored and then chose to overwrite.[6]

England in 1644 was in a state of war which it was helpful to elevate into a state of Christian warfare. *Areopagitica* is a work enlisted in the wars of truth and is therefore full of images evoking combat. It is also full of images of seeking, finding, and building, of a collective effort which potentially engages the search for understanding everywhere and is not held within the constraints of a Christian society. That search involves cooperation rather than contentiousness. In the passage just quoted, considering, abstaining, distinguishing, and preferring are not activities one would normally place in a combat zone. They do not even belong to a state of Christian warfare, internalized, as *Jihad* is supposed to be. Some grimness in the struggle against the enemy within is needed to justify the use of 'warfare' as a metaphor. 'Prefer' is a curiously gentle word suggesting a scale of values instead of an implacable opposition. The Lady does not say, 'I'd rather not' to Comus.[7]

A few lines later, Milton cites Spenser as a better teacher than Scotus or Aquinas (*CPW* 2:516). *The Faerie Queene* relies felicitously on the slippage from warfaring into wayfaring. Milton's tract vacillates between the two and the vacillation must be deemed crucial for its overflow into our world. The globalizing of toleration calls for wayfaring as the proper figure of a necessarily intermittent and evasive progress. Warfaring can have its place, if it has to have one, but it must be in the theatre of the self and not the world's arena.

The Faerie Queene begins with an overconclusive encounter in which both error and the entire brood of error are destroyed (1.1.13–26). Thereafter, Elizabeth's knights discover through six books and many wanderings, that the birth rate among dragons may be greater than any death rate they are able to inflict. Reformation can be accomplished with encouraging swiftness, but the reforming of reformation is an 'endlesse worke.' Spenser could see on the horizon of his poem and embody in its unfinished nature the relinquishment of the unifying design which his 'Letter to Raleigh' had announced.[8] He passes on this legacy to a successor confronted with even more formidable difficulties in the long-delayed building of the true church.

Spenser is a more cosmopolitan poet than Milton. The fifth book of *The Faerie Queene* displays a considerable interest in Egyptology.[9] Milton could be impatient with such allegorical dalliances. In *Paradise Lost*, the likes of Isis and Osiris are dismissed with one thunderous word – 'abominations' (*PL* 1.389). Milton's 'On the Morning of Christ's Nativity' is slightly more charitable, with the false gods trooping to the 'infernal jail' instead of being plunged into the torments of hell (ll. 232–3). *Areopagitica* stands apart from these compulsive repudiations. In its solitary reference to Egypt, the quiet voice of a better teacher than Aquinas is reborn and strengthened by Milton's propulsive eloquence:

> Truth indeed came once into the world with her divine Master, and was a perfect shape most glorious to look on: but when he ascended, and his Apostles after him were laid asleep, then strait rose a wicked race of deceivers, who as that story goes of the *AEgyptian Typhon* with his conspirators, how they dealt with the good *Osiris*, took the virgin Truth, hewd her lovely form into a thousand peeces and scatter'd them to the four winds. From that time ever since, the sad friends of Truth, such as durst appear, imitating the carefull search that *Isis* made for the mangl'd body of *Osiris*, went up and down gathering up limb by limb still as they could find them. We have not yet found them all, Lords and Commons, nor ever shall doe, till her Masters second comming; he shall bring together every joynt and member, and shall mould them into an immortall feature of loveliness and perfection. (*CPW* 2:549)

Plutarch, in narrating the Osiris legend, calls on us to treat it as an allegory of the pursuit of truth.[10] Transported into the seventeenth century that treatment seeks to provide the essential middle way between the Scylla of the Westminster Assembly and the Charybdis of proliferating sects.

The Assembly saw itself as a theological legislature with parliament as its executive. Parliament was not altogether happy with the role the Mullahs assigned to it. On the other hand, it was not eager to open the door to the 'miscellaneous rabble' (*PR* 3.50) of the sects. The complication of interests was to be compounded by the army, which, having done

God's work on the field of battle, thought it deserved its share in nation building. In the midst of these cross-currents, Milton was closer to the whirlpool than the rock. His steady conviction that doctrine was meaningless unless it was made real by an inner commitment controls his withering remarks about Church Fathers (*CPW* 1:626), his derision about tickets from Cranmer, Latimer, and Ridley (*CPW* 1:535), and his conclusion that even truth can become a heresy if it is believed in only because the Assembly says so (*CPW* 2:543). His will to order was passionate but his inner self had to authorize that order. Perhaps he might have steered differently, with more apprehensions about the dissidence of dissent and with a stronger sense of the need for accommodation in building any consensus, if he had not believed with others, that the existing turbulence was God's work and not that work's undoing (*CPW* 1:795). The end of history was imminent and a final dispensation would set all things in order.

It is hard to enter the mood of an era in which the Second Coming was at hand, not in the dystopian falling apart of which Yeats's rough beast remains the slouching sign,[11] but in the gathering coherence of a dedicated effort to build the true church in the image of its impending consummation. We underrate the urgency of 'thou the Eternall and shortly-expected King' (*CPW* 1:616), or the intense longing of 'thy Kingdome is now at hand, and thou standing at the dore' (*CPW* 1:707). 'We reck'n more then five months yet to harvest,' Milton writes in *Areopagitica.* 'There need not be five weeks, had we but eyes to lift up, the fields are white already' (*CPW* 2:554). When God 'shakes a kingdome with strong and helpful commotions,' he is about to offer a special dispensation of light to an elect nation, tardy in reformation (*CPW* 1:525) but chosen despite that tardiness, to be in the vanguard of an approaching fulfilment (*CPW* 1:799; 2:566).

The end of time is no longer in sight or threateningly around the corner as it is in Marvell's appeals to his coy mistress. The emphasis must now fall on a collective search, incremental in its recognitions of what we share and ready to share differences without reducing difference to disagreements. The space of deferral in Milton's figure has widened enormously so that a far more protracted quest can be undertaken. The thousand fragments of the body of truth (fourteen in the original) have been not only scattered, but scattered to the four winds. The task of retrieval is global. And the retrieval will not result and may not even move towards the '*homogeneal,* and proportionall' form which Milton prophesies (*CPW* 2:551).

Truth, substantiated in the world's religions, has many forms, not one.

A global exchange of understandings among these religions should seek enrichment rather than finality. Progress should be measured by that enrichment and not by a reduction in the number of forms. Milton does not move boldly into this range of possibilities. On the other hand, he does not entirely preclude it. In the Osiris allegory, a space of deferral, strikingly compressed in Milton's time, separates unity from what will later be called contiguity. As the space expands, it offers room for errancy and Milton's circumventions of his own imagery make possible an extension into that space. If the image of the search which *Areopagitica* enshrines is read back into the tract, the tract itself can be seen as a searching among images which ends in the persuasion that more than one image is needed and that the interplay between images choreographs a space of understanding which all images address but which no single image takes over. Vacillation is an important element in this choreography. If Milton vacillates between warfaring and wayfaring and between discipline and excess, he also comes to vacillate more cautiously between homogeneal truth and truth diversified. An early reference to the 'teeming womb of Truth,' aborted by the alliance of custom and error (*CPW* 2:223–4), seems to recognize the multiform possibility. More probing is a passage in *Areopagitica* which contrasts the binding of Proteus who will otherwise assume form after form, with the unbinding of Truth who can assume her true form only when she is liberated. Having come this far, the thinking suddenly turns across itself:

> Yet is it not impossible that she [Truth] may have more shapes then one. What else is all that rank of things indifferent, wherein Truth may be on this side, or the other, without being unlike her self. (*CPW* 2:563)

Indifferency is an important concept in seventeenth-century religious discourse. Ideally, it should have safeguarded all those areas in which discretionary thought was permissible because the Bible was silent. Unfortunately, the long history of biblical interpretation had occupied much of this territory. Augustine was prominent in these annexations. Independency in the seventeenth century tended to consist of exemptions (granted by institutions whose very status was being interrogated) instead of being claimed as a right to free thought in any terrain not inhabited by a scriptural text.

A book could be written on *Paradise Lost* as an exercise of the imagination in the *ideal* area of indifference, an envelopment of the Bible sufficiently comprehensive to renegotiate our understanding of that text. The actual area of indifferency was much more restricted and vulnerable to erosion. Preserving and enlarging that area was one way of enlarging the scope of religious toleration. The other and far more important way was to separate civil from religious power.

The separation of the two powers from each other is fundamental in today's political thinking. It marks not the dividing line but the un-bridgeable gulf between democracies and theocracies. Civil power, more-over, is now seen as economic and not merely legal. It even extends to the language of civil institutions which is expected to be free of inflec-tions that favour one religious community over another. In renouncing any incursion into the religious realm, civil power in secular nation-states has, in fact, become defensive, asserting itself only when religious zeal overflows into the realm of public order.

Milton's reflections on the relationship between church and state begin with two entries in the Commonplace Book contrasting Camden, who says bluntly that 'separation between religion and the state cannot be,' with the 'very wise chancellor of France,' who is 'of the opposite opinion' (*CPW* 1:421). Later entries from Dante and Machiavelli lean in the direction of the wise chancellor (*CPW* 1:475–7). *The Reason of Church Government* con-tains a passage (highlighted by Gardiner) arguing for separation (*CPW* 1:831–2).[12] Milton does not seem to return to the subject until 1649 with a paragraph in *Observations Upon the Articles of Peace* similar in tenor to the one in *Church Government* (*CPW* 3:310–11). The *Second Defence* (*CPW* 4:678) and Sonnet 17, 'To Sir Henry Vane the Younger' (*Poems*, ed. Hughes, 161) once again argue for separation. *The Treatise of Civil Power* (1659), Milton's first *in extenso* consideration of the subject, is uncompromisingly against the use of civil power in ecclesiastical causes.

Milton's view of the relationship between the two powers is strikingly consistent but before 1659 his attention to the subject seems sporadic. *Areopagitica*, unlike *The Bloudy Tenent*, is conspicuously silent on this matter in a context where its sustained consideration seems not merely appropriate but demanded. The silence comes perilously close to open-ing a black hole in the argument. The Yale editor suggests that Milton adopted this silence to avoid alienating the Erastian wing of parliament. He is supported in this view by Nigel Smith.[13] Milton, despite his con-frontational nature, is not incapable of tactical avoidances but his scanty reflections on the subject in his early tracts suggest that it was not really in the foreground of his mind. It was brought to the foreground by the growing scope and complexity of the problem of toleration and by his own accumulating heterodoxies.

To compensate for his silence, the Yale editor continues, Milton 'enormously enlarges' the scope of things indifferent (*CPW* 2:170). If so, one would expect an argument for enlargement more diligent and sustained than in the passage quoted earlier. The only other reference to things indifferent in *Areopagitica* (*CPW* 2:565) does not advance a compensatory strategy which must be more insistent to have its proper impact. Milton's references to indifferency are important but not because of the advice they offer regarding its scope. They are important because they offer the dance of truth as an alternative to the wars of truth.

The shapes of truth in Milton's figure lie on both sides of an imaginary line drawn by the movements of truth across it. Truth, unlike Proteus, is recognizably herself in the many forms she assumes. The seeker after truth can find it in more than one shape and can presumably move from one shape to another in the pursuit of a more generous understanding. The consequences of this view in a world searching for toleration that must in its nature be multicivilizational do not require underlining.

Toleration today must be interactive not permissive. It must learn from difference and not simply put up with it until difference thinks better of itself. Accepting the permanence of differences and agreeing that they contribute to a multifaceted wisdom rather than challenging a wisdom that is unique are moves beyond the constraints of seventeenth-century Puritanism with its root and branch mentality and its demonization of otherness. Milton writes within the discourse of his time and even within that discourse is less progressive than Roger Williams, who is prepared to live in peace with Turks and papists. 'Extirpate' is the word Milton uses in relation to the papist principle as he perceived it. *Areopagitica*'s solitary reference to the Koran five years before its translation into English suggests that it only survives by extirpating alternatives (*CPW* 2:548, 565).

This essay is concerned less with Milton's argument than with the figures of understanding which in sustaining that argument carry themselves beyond the argument's boundaries. The Siamese twinning of good and evil makes it less easy to treat them as forming the ultimate antithesis. Milton compounds the difficulties of those addicted to antithetical formations (in which *Paradise Lost* shows him to be no novice) by arguing that the substance of good and evil is the same (*CPW* 2:527). Good and evil then elide into truth and error, and error can be treated as a wandering from the truth or more philosophically, as truth's insufficient presence. Warfaring slips into wayfaring. The collective search for the torn body of Osiris points to a commitment in which all civilizations can participate. The homogeneal and proportional form of truth is contested by the recognition that truth can have many forms before the one form of a deferred finality.[14]

If different civilizations are to come together in shared recognitions substantiated by their differences, a figure of understanding is needed which, like the search for the fragments of the torn body of Osiris, will emphasize discovery through collective efforts. Unlike the Osiris figure, it must focus not on unification, but on the embedding of diversity. Milton responds to these requests of the future with a figure of understanding which must be deemed visionary in its forward reach:

> Yet these are the men cry'd out against for schismaticks and sectaries; as if, while the Temple of the Lord was building, some cutting, some squaring the marble, others hewing the cedars, there should be a sort of irrationall men who could not consider there must be many schisms and many dissections made in the quarry and in the timber, ere the house of God can be built. And when every stone is laid artfully together, it cannot be united into a continuity, it can but be contiguous in this world; neither can every peece of the building be of one form; nay rather the perfection consists in this, that out of many moderat varieties and brotherly dissimilitudes that are not vastly disproportionall arises the goodly and gracefull symmetry that commends the whole pile and structure. Let us therefore be more considerat builders, more wise in spirituall architecture, when great reformation is expected. (*CPW* 2:555)

As Ernest Sirluck notes, the 'squaring' and 'hewing' of the marble and the cedars for Solomon's temple were done away from the site so that the quiet of the holy place might not be disturbed.[15] This fact became an argument for conformity, or for a consensus achieved before the work of building began. Milton on the contrary is arguing that the consensus does not lie in the preliminary blueprint but has to be achieved in the act of building itself. The artful play on schisms and dissection is lost to us but would have reverberated in seventeenth-century minds. It converts dismal forebodings into creative necessities. Even more important is the way in which Milton rewrites the allegory of the torn body of truth which a few pages earlier had seemed a defining event in his imagination's seizure of the moment. What takes place is not an act of retrieval; it is an act of making and shaping and of laying the constituents 'artfully together.' A distinction between contiguity and continuity follows which has escaped comment because it eludes annotation. There is a meaning in what is built which cannot be fully known by the builders, that lies in the commitment to 'spirituall architecture' rather than in the architecture itself.

The continuity/contiguity distinction significantly rewrites the relationship between approximate and final form in the Osiris legend. Not all the pieces of Truth's torn body will be found by the community of seekers. Some will remain to be found at 'her Masters second comming.' The work of bringing 'every joynt and member' together and of moulding them 'into an immortall feature of loveliness and perfection' will not be accomplished in the realm of time.

The house of God on the contrary is not an unfinishable edifice. It is put together by choosing rather than finding pieces, and by the human effort of 'moulding' them so that they fit with 'gracefull symmetry' into a 'pile and structure.' Every stone will be 'laid artfully together' in the commitment to building the temple. But those who build it will see only the contiguity of the edifice, its togetherness rather than its animating principle. The implicit form will not be known in time. But it is brought into existence by the earnestness of its builders. The shift from the insufficiency of human effort to the enduring validity (as yet not discernible) of that effort is important. It takes a cleavage (and linkage) between time and the timeless, which Milton's imagination persistently problematizes, and negotiates a juxtaposition which the play on words both distinguishes and joins. As an accomplishment in the art of ambivalence it is, as it should be, both absorbing and evasive.

'Neither can every peece of the building be of one form,' Milton continues. The 'homogeneall' form of truth is being relinquished not as a compromise, but in pursuit of a better aesthetic: 'Nay rather the perfection consists in this.' The subsequent references to 'moderat varieties' and 'brotherly dissimilitudes' can be read as attempts to contain the eruptive energy of the manifold; they can also be read as not simply 'tolerating' but welcoming difference to the maximum extent compatible with the existence of structure. That the dissimilitudes not be 'vastly disproportionall' is indeed a remarkable rewriting of a previous insistence on the 'proportionall' body of truth.

The architecture of understanding is not diversified in order to be inclusive. It is diversified because inclusiveness is its strength. A symmetry arises from its accommodations and multi-foliate tolerances that is both 'goodly and gracefull.' That symmetry 'commends the whole pile and structure' not only for what it is, but for what has gone into making it. 'Pile,' as Laura Lockwood points out,[16] is a word used in describing Herod's temple (*PR* 4.547). Nevertheless pile contests structure as accumulation contests containment. The 'contiguity' between the two concepts is best seen in non-European forms of sacred architecture such as the *gopuram* and the *Ziggurat*.[17] It is a contiguity that the future needs to embody.

Milton tells us that in his prose he knows himself inferior to himself, having the use only of his left hand. *Areopagitica* is an exercise in the politics of the right hand and of the right hand's imaginative extensions. The poet comes into his strength beginning late, when the left hand has written profusely and written in vain. In meditating on the failed revolution, his overarching theme is the profound relationship between responsibility and freedom. The theme connects itself passionately with the Puritan dilemma but does not directly engage the problem of toleration which articulated itself between that dilemma's horns. Yet the creation itself can be construed as a deep act of toleration. God could have constructed a universe which was failure proof. Instead he constructed one which was failure prone. He did so in order that the earth could hang precariously and exquisitely 'self-balanc't' on its centre (*PL* 7.242), symbolizing and ennobling the right to self-determination regardless of the tragic cost of that right. Free will, the theological ancestor to agency, is the fulcrum on which the fate of the cosmos rests. Foreseeing what will happen makes even more momentous the decision to allow it to happen. Compared with the toleration of disobedience, the toleration of dissent seems minor.

'Necessity and Chance / Approach not mee' is God's declaration as the creation begins (*PL* 7.172–3). With the death of the author, God is left as the only author. Others are written as they write. God alone writes with an immunity which no taint of contingency can approach. Given this absolute freedom, how is God imaged? What representation of the divine is chosen amid an infinity of choices? Surely some of the unconstrained must be reflected in the form of limitation it chooses as its metaphor. The universe must walk the precarious tightrope between necessity and chance, between determinism and randomness, between the rock and the whirlpool, between emergent form with its gathering articulations and the preemptive clarity of the 'great Idea' (*PL* 7.557). The politics of the city of God translate the perils of this tightrope. Toleration is needed for the tightrope to even exist.

Areopagitica offers us the cunning resemblance, the bewildering twinning of good and evil in every moral choice that we confront. In *Paradise*

Lost, Michael tells Adam that 'true Liberty' is twinned with 'right Reason' and has no 'dividual being' apart from her (*PL* 12.83–5). Twinning here points to the right relationship, the relationship between Urania and Eternal Wisdom which the deformed birth in *Areopagitica* parodies. Our task is to find our way from the destructive alliance to the creative sisterhood. That way can only be pursued by seeking, respecting, and bringing to the work of retrieval every available fragment of the world's wisdom.

After the fall Adam and Eve, having spent 'fruitless hours' in mutual accusation' (*PL* 9.1187–8), save themselves by listening to each other. Dialogue is surprisingly one of the gifts of fallenness. The changeless, even when subject to 'grateful vicissitude,' needs only to enunciate and not to debate itself. Dialogue arises when choices have to be made in a world offering its plethora of parodies. The web of conversation which we should strive to bring about must be spun from the intersections of that dialogue.

The globalization of tolerance has so far been treated as inherently desirable.[18] We have to recognize that this idealist projection is not on globalism's agenda and is only peripherally on its radar screen. Globalism is a homogenizing movement in which the human image has been shrivelled into the will for material betterment. If global toleration can be commodified, that image can be enriched. Commodification is most likely at the local level. It is unlikely at the civilizational level of the nation-state which can interrogate or even threaten the Mammon-given rights of global citizens. 'Spirituall architecture' is alien to globalism though it can remain a thing indifferent as long as it does not intrude into the realm of global civil power. These relationships will prevail until the human race finds itself sufficiently disenchanted with the image it sees in globalism's looking-glass.

NOTES

1 Milton, *Areopagitica*, *CPW* 2:551.
2 Williams, *The Bloudy Tenent, of Persecution, for Cause of Conscience Discussed*; Robinson, *Liberty of Conscience: Or the Sole Means to Obtaine Peace and Truth*; Walwyn, *The Compassionate Samaritane*; *M.S. to A.S. with a Plea for Libertie of Conscience*. Thomason dates *Areopagitica* 24 November 1644. *CPW* 2:73–92 provides a background against which Milton's 'originality' can be assessed.

Four pamphlets in the eight months before Milton's stately statement (including three in the single month of July) make evident the celerity with which the scholarly journalism of the day could assemble itself around a current topic. The response time looks forward to the internet.

3 Apuleius, *The Golden Ass or Metamorphoses*, 101–2 (book 6).

4 Spenser, *The Faerie Queene*, 1.2.9–11. Cited as *FQ*. The false Florimell (3.7.1–10) is an even more cunning resemblance in which Archimago plays no part.

5 The textual crux and the correction by hand in eight copies are discussed fully by the editor of *Complete Prose Works*, volume 2, Ernest Sirluck (515n102). The possibility that the hand making the alterations may be Milton's is advanced by G.A. Bonnard in 'Two Remarks on the Text of Milton's *Areopagitica.*' It is doubted by Helen Darbishire, 'Pen-and-Ink Corrections in Books of the Seventeenth Century.' Darbishire concludes that Milton intended the alteration even if the hand was not his.

In 'The Ways and Wars of Truth,' Ruth M. Kivette finds the textual case for 'warfaring' persuasive, but not overwhelming. Unlike Hughes and Sirluck, she argues that 'wayfaring' fits better into the frames of evocation provided by Milton's work. Unless 'his [Milton's] responsibility for the correction can be proved beyond a reasonable doubt, we might allow ourselves the liberty of preferring "that which is truly better"' (85). My own view is that the two terms elide into each other and that the slippage between them is encouraged by the elision. Internal Christian warfare is 'exercised' by life's pilgrimage.

6 The following editions of *Areopagitica* print 'warfaring': *CPW* 2:515; Hughes, ed., *John Milton, Complete Poetry and Major Prose*, 728; Flannagan, ed., *Areopagitica, The Riverside Milton*, 1006. Flannagan (n156) observes that the 'general consensus of editorial opinion' is that the 'wayfaring' of the printed text 'is wrong.' Hughes (n102) allows more circumspectly that 'wayfaring' has 'the weight of priority' but prefers 'warfaring' on both textual and contextual grounds.

7 Milton, *A Mask Presented at Ludlow Castle, Poems*, 659–813. The Lady's journey through the 'hideous wood' (520) to the Castle connects her to wayfaring. On the other hand, her derisive rejection of Comus and her threat in 791–8 associate her with warfaring, as does the Elder Brother's description of her as 'clad in complete steel' (421).

8 Spenser, 'Letter to Raleigh,' in *FQ* 15–18. See also the editorial note on the Letter, 1068–70.

9 Spenser, *FQ* 5.7.2–22.

10 Plutarch, *Moralia*, 351–2. See *CPW* 2:549, n222.

11 Yeats, 'The Second Coming,' in *The Variorum Edition of the Poems of W. B. Yeats*, p. 402, l. 22.

12 Gardiner, *The Fall of the Monarchy of Charles I 1637–1649*, 2:442. Merritt Hughes cites the same passage from Milton in characterizing the separation of church and state as 'one of his [Milton's] most passionately and clearly entertained beliefs' (Milton, *Observations Upon the Articles of Peace*, edited by Hughes, *CPW* 3:310–11n29).

13 *CPW* 2:169–70, 176; Nigel Smith, '*Areopagitica*: Voicing Contexts, 1643–5,' 104.

14 These slippages pave the way for the far more drastic slippage in *Of True Religion* whose truth and error (with truth self-evidently the preferred term) are replaced by error and heresy (with error the preferred term). Error here partakes of errancy, the wanderings in the labyrinth of those committed to the attainment of truth. See Steadman, *The Hill and the Labyrinth*. Heresy, in Milton's dealings with the term, is consistently weighted in favour of its etymological association with choice at the expense of its historical association with deviation from the orthodox. Milton's final manoeuvre is to argue that the deepest heresy is the forbidding of choice. The aim which is to defend freedom of conscience against religious absolutism is undoubtedly to be commended, but the argument is less than logically respectable. For a judicious reading of Milton's views on heresy, see Mueller, 'Milton on Heresy.'

15 Sirluck, editor, *Areopagitica*, in *CPW* 2:555n244.

16 Lockwood, ed., *John Milton, Selected Essays: Of Education, Areopagitica, The Commonwealth; with Early Biographies of Milton*, 122n8.

17 The trapezoidal forms of the *gopuram* and the *Ziggurat* allow accretions by the eye of the mind. A spire does not permit accretion. Its symbolic shape is that of a pointer to eternity.

18 A huge amount of scholarship on globalism now exists. I am not aware of any scholarly essay on globalism's relationship to worldwide toleration. The omission speaks volumes, but the volumes have yet to be written.

Afterword: His More Attentive Mind

JOSEPH A. WITTREICH

'After Blake,' C.S. Lewis avers, 'Milton criticism is lost in misunderstanding,' not finding its way again until Lewis's own time when, according to Douglas Bush, the Second World War helps in 'the righting' of our perception of Milton, especially of his *Paradise Lost.*[1] In the century and a half between Blake's offending document, *The Marriage of Heaven and Hell,* and Lewis's redeeming *Preface to 'Paradise Lost'* are a series of critical skirmishes culminating in Walter Raleigh's turn-of-the-century battle-cry – '*Paradise Lost* ... is a monument to dead ideas.'[2] In its aftermath come the battle wounds inflicted by T.S. Eliot's abrupt dismissal of Milton as a poetic influence no longer relevant, then deepened by F.R. Leavis's rude dislodgment of this poet whose epic he read and underscored, almost line-by-line, in the trenches during the Second World War. Some critics would now turn the story of man's fall into Milton's fall. If Milton had become an 'historical problem, a literary enigma,'[3] it was because, increasingly, his epic poem seemed like a field of contending forces, which, acknowledged by all, were reconcilable – or irreconcilable – depending upon the critical camp with which a reader was allied or to which she or he was listening.

Through his erasure of the Blakean moment from Milton criticism, as well as its nineteenth- and early twentieth-century phases, Lewis hides a politicized Milton, sometimes divided against himself, and already claimed by the nineteenth century 'as a figure of world importance.'[4] He cloaks what, in the words of Denis Saurat, was the then 'new conception of Milton' as both an international poet and a cultural icon.[5] By the 1940s, various critics were reading *Paradise Lost,* the fixation of the moment, and, if usually finding the same elements in the poem, were also valuing them differently. Contradictory views of Milton had already been ex-

plained – if not explained away – as contradictions *within* Milton: uncon-
scious meanings at war with conscious intent and spilling over into the
poetry, early and late – into *Lycidas* as readily as *Paradise Lost.* Or just as
unsettling to some, what once had been viewed as the conflicting agendas of a rebellious theologian (in *De Doctrina Christiana*) and a poet of
Christian orthodoxy (in *Paradise Lost*) were coming to look, rather insistently, like complementary, not competing, roles with Milton, in poetry
and prose alike, casting off custom, tradition, and the tyranny of error;
simultaneously, defecting from Christian orthodoxies; and, in the words
of Maurice Kelley, 'den[ying] the most sacred and central of Christian
doctrines,' even as he defied any easy mythologizing of himself as heretical in youth and orthodox in maturity.[6]

The congruity between the radical theologian and revolutionary poet
was affirmed by Blake when he reported to Henry Crabb Robinson that
'Milton ... in his old age ... returned back to God whom he had had in his
childhood'[7] and, subsequently, was attested to by both William Ellery
Channing and Joanna Baillie in the immediate aftermath of the publication of *De Doctrina.* Yet what came under review during the Victorian
period, the conviction that the authors of *De Doctrina* and *Paradise Lost*
were the same, has come under challenge since – repeatedly. What Lewis
wanted most to silence, not unlike Eliot, was the audacity of Milton's
speculations, his transgressive politics and poetics, equally marks of
Milton's modernity. The recourses available to criticism were obvious:
either discredit, dislodge, and denounce the poet; or recuperate him by
renouncing his supposedly heretical tendencies, by recovering this poet
for orthodoxy by making him look like a thoroughly consistent thinker,
a compendium of stock beliefs, and an epitome of the common glosses
of theologians. If criticism, both historical and new, was about to fetishize
ambiguity and tension in poetry, brakes would be applied; and in the
process, the critic's job would be redefined with him, or her, now setting
out to dispel the mists of ambiguity and attendant clouds of misunderstanding to which tensions in poetry, and perceived conflicts, had been
giving rise.

Milton's apologists of the 1940s pave the way for the repudiations and
eventual mediations of the same decade. If the 'chance of war' brought
people together, often in a peculiar mix, if it sought to forge a community within a world divided, as Lewis reports, it also produced changes in,
as well as enforced an ideology on, reading inflections. Thus, Lewis finds
in Milton no struggles, no resistances between classical and Christian
mythologies: 'There is *fusion*, or integration' in *Paradise Lost*, in this 'very

map of poetry,'[8] in every way conforming to the idealisms of unity, consistency, and coherence. Any hint of conflicting ideologies or competing voices needed silencing within a criticism which worried over being blindsided by questions and whose repeated tactic was evasion. Hierarchical thinking, deriving from 'the ancient orthodox tradition of European ethics' and 'the indwelling life of the whole' of *Paradise Lost*, is supposedly at the very core of Milton's epic of enforced orthodoxies wherein heresies, even if occasional intrusions, are notable only because they are ultimately 'uninfluential,'[9] hence plainly irrelevant. What mattered, according to the subtitle of G. Wilson Knight's book, is that this epic is 'The Message of John Milton to Democracy at War.'[10]

If Milton's fame was now of special moment, that was because, as Bush explains, Milton's poetry, having 'outlived many wars,' is part of the heritage for which those wars have been fought. Especially *Paradise Lost*, rather as *Samson Agonistes* has become today, was a bible for waging war and for winning, in Bush's words, a 'lasting peace.' Milton is a poet who understands a world in which 'good and evil are distinct realities'; he is a 'thoroughly orthodox' poet with 'very little of the specifically Puritan in ... the whole body of ... [his] poetry' and in all 'essential respects' conforming to 'the theology of the seventeenth-century Anglican divines.' Above all, there is 'no antinomy ... between Milton's intention and the result'; and while we may discern in *Paradise Lost* 'incidental antinomies,' we discover 'no central antinomy' inasmuch as conflicts evident in Milton are anchored in a mythology that, bound by, Milton could not therefore resolve.[11] In a moment of disarming sincerity, Bush owns up to things being 'in literary criticism, as [they are] in other forms of propaganda,' with John S. Diekhoff thus given licence to break ranks by distinguishing between Milton's 'heterodox and eclectic ... theology' and the 'narrative and ... ethic' of *Paradise Lost*, both completely 'conventional.'[12] Fissures, long ago detected in *Paradise Lost*, were now becoming a feature of Milton criticism itself. Themselves reacting against reactionaries, Lewis, Bush, and Diekhoff, through their denials and evasions, effect what will become an unwelcome counterstatement to their own observations.

What quickly becomes apparent in the 1940s is that, ever since Blake, 'attempts to refit *Paradise Lost* for the modern mind' have involved acknowledging, as does A.J.A. Waldock, 'the presence of unresolved conflicts in Milton's mind,' with questions concerning those conflicts usually shelved instead of settled. For Waldock, however, problems in a poem are as germane to criticism as meaning, especially when a poet like

Milton transfers from his source stories, themselves 'lined with difficulties of the gravest order,' rifts of which the poet is unaware and which then become, in the 'tremendous enlargement' of *Paradise Lost*, a huge gulf: '... deep underlying ambiguities ... begin to make themselves really felt ... subterranean weaknesses ... start the earth cracking at the surface. Rifts begin to open, hair lines at first; then they become wider, and presently there is a chasm.'[13] In this poetry of paradoxes and problems with its clashing narrations and commentaries, in this poetry of risk taking with its eventual suppression of intentions, 'coherencies' devolve into uncertainty as Milton, unaware according to Waldock, thinks he has created 'an unassailable imaginative whole' even if, because of such menacing moments, he has created a poetry, notwithstanding its originality and daring, its 'bold and startling speculations,' with 'embedded ambiguity at the heart of it.'[14] Criticism was now begging for mediation, soon forthcoming in the diplomacy of Balachandra Rajan and signalled by the rejoinder that Milton, not writing unknowingly, knew full well what he was doing, both in prose works and poems, where he was registering shifts of mind as well as modifications of value.

As a mediating voice, Rajan ushered in a new phase – what would eventually modulate into the postmodern phase – of Milton criticism. It would emerge from the understanding that, as Rajan puts it, 'We can no longer leave our ideologies in the cloakroom as we enter the literary seminar' (125). Rajan's first injunctions are multiple. Let's historicize. Let's contextualize. Let's mark Milton's traditions, orthodox and dissenting, those to which he submits and those he will spurn. Let's understand that the topic of Milton and tradition has hidden within it the questions: Milton and which traditions? In which of their manifestations? Let's attend to the reader, the typical and at times harassed reader, both of Milton's time and of posterity; and doing so, let's understand that critics should match their efforts to Milton's when it comes to the attention given to readers and the exercise expected of them. One thread in this line of criticism leads to Stanley Fish and affective stylistics; another, to Hans Robert Jauss and Wolfgang Iser, to the former's horizons of expectation and to their shared aesthetics of reception. The history of Milton's reception, in his own time and in ours, is a reminder that over the centuries Milton criticism mimics itself, repeating the same gestures, so many of them aiming at containment of Milton's subversions, even erasure of them.

Paradoxically, to situate Milton in his own times may eventuate in radicalizing, not conventionalizing, his thinking; may showcase his intel-

lectual 'daring and independence,' his sensitivity to 'the speculative issues of his time' by attending to his affiliations with 'heterodox ... minority traditions.'[15] Again paradoxically, locating Milton's poetry in his own
age is an unexpected way of bringing it into dialogue with our own time,
attesting anew to Milton's relevance. This line of criticism stretches from
Rajan, to Christopher Hill and John Carey, to the revisionist historians
and critics, and carries with it the reminder that conventions, continually
checked by Milton's unconventionality, force us to scuttle the idea that
Milton is 'a hanger on to platitudes, a man who says nothing unless seventeen people have said it.'[16] Moreover, this same line of criticism
branches towards both the contextualists and intertexualists – towards
those like Mary Ann Radzinowicz, and those like Rajan and Elizabeth
Sauer, who states in her introduction to this volume that 'the whole
body of Milton's work ... [is] a reading context for each of its constituents' and that its still proliferating contexts allow for Milton's writings, in
Sauer's words, 'to be differently assessed from diverse reading locations'
(7, 14). At the same time, Rajan never allows us to forget that if there
were two Wordsworths there was but one Milton, with shifting opinions
perhaps, but also with settled principles: a prose writer and poet, himself
a true poem, whose poetry and prose in tandem are mutually reflective
and illuminating, each of them a song of the poet's own self.

Contexts matter. Yet, as with tradition, the pressing questions are:
which are the right contexts? Or, what happens when works are read in –
and out of – context? For example, as Rajan argues, when read by itself
as an epic poem, *Paradise Lost* 'reverberate[s] orthodoxy'; but when read
within the context of the *Treatise on Christian Doctrine* it is an 'Arian'
poem.[17] What, then, are we to conclude: that Milton's poetry is orthodox
or merely looks that way; is slyly submitting to orthodoxy, or subverting
it, or being hopelessly bridled by it; is summoning competing truths into
concord or holding them in animated suspension? Is Milton's an encyclopedic or, more exactly, a kaleidoscopic mind? With his compendious
intervention, Rajan displaces the certainties of Lewis, Bush, and Waldock
with a hermeneutic of suspicion, one of whose initial objectives is to
contradict Milton and his critics out of their contradictions.

What Peter C. Herman calls 'the masterplot of Milton criticism'[18] is
evident in Rajan's early writings and their representation of *Paradise Lost*
as an epic that coheres, as well as their description of the critic's task to
make the poem cohere, to make the unconventional conventional. But
Rajan also writes at a crossroads in Milton criticism and, himself moving
in new directions, pushes later critics to follow after him. First, he puts to

rest the idea that *Paradise Lost* is 'a monument to dead ideas' (Raleigh 85). Eventually, he embraces alternative propositions: that as it interrogates itself from within, *Paradise Lost* comes increasingly to 'walk a tightrope between dissent and obedience, frayed slowly by its own internal stresses'; that not so much a poem of fissures as a fissure, Milton's epic, 'riven within itself,' is to be read 'along changing approaches because so much can be poured into the fissure (67, 126, 125). What is remarkable in such moments is the way in which Rajan's speculations simultaneously resonate with, and upend, criticism of sixty years ago. They have had the power of an oracle. When we are told that 'Milton clearly recognizes the possibility of alternative perspectives, even as he proceeds with his own,' without always clarifying just what his own position actually is,[19] we are apt to think of Rajan just because he set forth such propositions first.

The best recent criticism continues to be an exfoliation of, and supplement to, Rajan's critical writings. Rajan's now contestatory Milton is a poet of contraries, whose poems, admitting to more than one interpretation, present 'two ways of seeing on two sides of a crisis,' not choosing between propositions but, instead, 'celebrat[ing] the world that is brought into being between them, the push and the pull of contrary understandings in the systole and diastole of the imagination' (24). Rajan's Milton is a poet often contemptuous of traditions except when its voices are intelligent enough to agree with him. When Rajan's Milton embraces traditions, moreover, their representatives are typically exemplars of revolutionary thinking; and when those traditions are also inclusive of heresies, the heresies themselves, rife with complexities, are an aspect of, as well as further testimony to, Milton's humanism and often find their counterparts in his aesthetics.

Circumspection on Milton's part is not to be confused with conformity, nor does it rule out unorthodox interpretations. Under Rajan's tutelage, we learn that the stilling of controversy is Satan's way, not God's, and that if Milton's anti-Trinitarianism brings God closer to man, his Arminianism (with its insistence that we participate in our own redemption) brings man closer to God. Before William B. Hunter ever mounted his challenge to Milton's authorship of *De Doctrina Christiana* on the grounds that its heretical theology was at odds with the conformist thinking of Milton's last poems,[20] we were reminded by Rajan that Byron, Keats, and Shelley, all dead when *De Doctrina* was published, had already tuned into the heretical depths of Milton's poetry. Before Hunter's challenge, Rajan saw what would be at stake in the segregation of

Milton's theological treatise from his last poems: very simply, the loss of 'an identity sign' (68). Indeed, Rajan cuts to the quick in his insistence that the poet may write the poem 'but major poems sometimes rewrite their authors (43).

As quickly as Hunter, Rajan acknowledges 'deep divergence' (113). between the *Treatise on Christian Doctrine* and *Paradise Lost* but also invokes generic difference, not different authorship, to account for such divergence. Rajan is also a step ahead of others in the studied attention he gives to Milton's bridgings of difference. Despite its 'theologically inflammatory nature,' the Treatise evinces a consistency, which sometimes puts the tract at odds with Milton's contestatory poem, the latter acting as a signature not for 'a systematic theology' but for an 'educated imagination' (119, 115). Three different accounts of Creation in *Paradise Lost* figure alternating directions of Milton's thinking or, as Rajan explains, 'the extent of an author's entitlement to differ from himself,' even if sometimes contrary opinions on a graduated scale are articulated within a huge range of interpretative voices, differently calibrated, thus giving to *Paradise Lost* 'its investigative sweep' (61). Ironically, it was an attempt to dislodge Milton from a hierarchy of poetic voices, and thus diminish the authority of his voice, that led to a catapulting of Milton from a poetic universe of which he had been the creator. Milton himself, long before T.S. Eliot, fashioned an aesthetics of the unfinished and a complementary poetics of indeterminacy for a poetic universe in which the poet is an elusive, yet still powerful presence, as in book 3 of *Paradise Lost*, where Milton's God quotes Milton, thus carrying the poet's message, championing his thinking and even his theology. It is no coincidence that an age which declares God to be dead will, correspondingly, announce Milton's dislodgment – and the death of his ideas as well. Nor should it come as any surprise that Milton is much more powerfully the poet of our cultural moment than of early modernism.

To say that the poet is fully implicated in his poems may rub against the grain of a criticism prizing authorial erasure but no more so than it is an irritation to a criticism obsessed with the poet's omnipresence in, and even tyranny over, his writings. Frontispiece portraits often tease us into searching surfaces for what is hidden in the interstices of a poem and into expecting fully delineated portraits where there are merely sketches or fragments thereof. The poet may be now a strong and now a muted presence, or hidden inscription, but in his very elusiveness is also a reminder that, often at odds with himself, he speaks in contradictions and is in troubled dialogue with his own writings. As Rajan goes on to explain (as if in concert with Louis Martz),[21] a poem like *Paradise Lost*, written against its times, by a poet on the margins, in exile, 'cannot be wholly one with its claims' (56) and often will be an active complication of them. To be in exile, however, is not synonymous with being in hiding: Milton always is there, 'obstinately active on the site' (67).

In such a poetic universe, we are as apt to observe truths fragmenting as coalescing; for as Rajan never tires of acknowledging, *Paradise Lost* 'is a central statement of the seventeenth-century mind, the window through which we look at Protestant Christendom':

> It is not simply a poem of the mainstream but a poem which prescribes the nature of the mainstream. In writing itself it writes the history and even some of the future of literature. As the best-known commentary on Genesis it overlays Genesis to such an extent that the sacred text must be read in the secular shadow. We need to remind ourselves that this decisively central document was written on the margin of a paradigm shift, on the brink of an epistemic fissure. Milton's poem responds to these possibilities by resolutely looking backwards, by claiming the future out of its own obsolescence. It is natural to think of *Paradise Lost* as a supremely representative poem of its time. We need to think of it as also a poem against its time ... A lifelong nonconformist writes a poem of estrangement, of implacable otherness, defiant even in its versification. His function is to tell the tale of the tribe to a tribe that refuses to listen. (48–9)

A contribution to the art of exile, *Paradise Lost* is also a reminder, says Rajan, 'that there is no art but in exile' (49).

No one has been more sensitive than Rajan to the 'powerful ideological shift which the last books of *Paradise Lost* project' (109), but which is not brought into full being until the 1671 poetic volume. 'A different poem is written on the pinnacle,' says Rajan, with roads running into the future – to Shelley's *Prometheus Unbound* and 'from there to the strategies of resistance that in our own time have brought about the undoing of empires' (106), their dismantling and collapse. In the early 1970s, Rajan nudged us into consideration of the copresence of *Paradise Regained* and *Samson Agonistes* in a single poetic volume, arguing that Milton put the two poems together because he meant to say something through their juxtaposition. Rajan thus ensured that the relationship between these two poems would be 'much discussed' (97) – so much so that thirty years later Sharon Achinstein allows that '[t]here is still room to think about the ways in which Milton's two works are interconnected.'[22] Rajan might easily have predicted that *Samson Agonistes* would eventually become the poem of the moment, quintessentially so of these early years of the twenty-first century, which, as he would likely allow, is 'the world the poem sails into rather than ... the world it leaves behind' (129).

To read through the essays compacted into this volume is to watch Rajan gradually awakening to the avant-garde possibilities of his own criticism, which, without ever surrendering its mediatorial role, becomes steadily more methodologically adventurous and intellectually bracing. In the process, the boundaries of Milton criticism have been extended and its circumference redrawn. Instead of reorienting Milton criticism, Rajan has resituated it. It is tempting to say that Rajan writes within the Empsonian tradition,[23] but that temptation is a trap; for Rajan was there first and is still furthering the defence of Milton's artistic value against his detractors, while resisting those who would make Milton's poetry the preserve of Christian orthodoxy. Rajan's critical writings dwell in their own possibilities. They reach for ever higher strains of ethical insight and new expanses of vision. Rajan knows, as Blake once said, that the man who never alters his opinions is like standing water and breeds reptiles of the mind; and he is the best exemplar of his own words: 'A writer responds to his world and does not merely register it. He intervenes in a debate; and if the word means anything, it means that the debate will not be quite the same after the intervention' (107). Rajan's changing yet unfailingly attentive mind, his altering eyes and reinflected voice, have blazed the way for a new Milton criticism alert to fault lines, bracing for controversy, and, re-fitting Milton to the twenty-first-century mind, less taken with certainties than with new opportunities.

NOTES

1 Lewis, *A Preface to 'Paradise Lost,'* 129; and Douglas Bush, *'Paradise Lost' in Our Time: Some Comments*, 5.
2 Raleigh, *Milton*, 85.
3 Logan Pearsall Smith, *Milton and His Modern Critics*, 82.
4 Ibid., 6–7.
5 Saurat, *Milton: Man and Thinker*, 344, 345. Saurat credits this new conception of Milton to Edwin Greenlaw and James Holly Hanford.

6 Kelley, *This Great Argument: A Study of Milton's 'De Doctrina Christiana' as a Gloss upon 'Paradise Lost,'* 4.

7 William Blake, quoted from *The Romantics on Milton: Formal Essays and Critical Asides,* 96.

8 Lewis, *A Preface to 'Paradise* Lost,' v, 5, 7.

9 Ibid., 73, 79, 129.

10 See Knight, *Chariot of Wrath.*

11 Bush, *'Paradise Lost' in Our Time,* 2, 3, 57, 45, 60, 44, 71, 101.

12 Ibid., 2; Diekhoff, *Milton's 'Paradise Lost': A Commentary on the Argument,* 10.

13 Waldock, *'Paradise Lost' and Its Critics,* 8, 2, 18, 19, 42.

14 Ibid., 143, 21, 19, 145.

15 Rajan, *'Paradise Lost' and the Seventeenth Century Reader,* 9–10.

16 Ibid., 13.

17 Ibid., 25.

18 Herman, *Destabilizing Milton: 'Paradise Lost' and the Poetics of Incertitude,* 95.

19 Gay, *The Endless Kingdom: Milton's Spiritual Society,* 139.

20 For a consolidation of his argument, see Hunter, *'Visitation Unimplor'd: Milton and the Authorship of 'De Doctrina Christiana.'*

21 See Martz, *Poet of Exile: A Study of Milton's Poetry.*

22 Achinstein, *'Samson Agonistes,'* 419.

23 The best assessment of William Empson's place in Milton criticism is afforded by Gregory, *'In Defense of Empson: A Reassessment of Milton's God,'* 73–87.

Publications by Balachandra Rajan

'The Motivation of Shelley's *Prometheus Unbound*.' *The Review of English Studies* 19.75 (July 1943): 297–301.

Focus One: Frank Kafka and Rex Warner, edited by Balachandra Rajan and Andrew Pearse. London: Dennis Dobson, 1944.

'"Simple, Sensuous and Passionate."' *The Review of English Studies* 21.84 (Oct. 1945): 289–301.

Focus Two: The Realist Novel in the Thirties, edited by Balachandra Rajan and Andrew Pearse. London: Dennis Dobson, 1946.

'Georgian Poetry: A Retrospect.' *The Critic* 1.2 (1947): 7–14.

'Yeats and Indian Philosophy.' *The Listener* 4 September, 1947, 392–3.

'India and the English Mystics.' *The Listener* 20 November, 1947, 901–2.

T.S. Eliot: A Study of His Writings by Several Hands, edited by Balachandra Rajan. London: D. Dobson, 1947; New York: Funk and Wagnalls, 1948.

'Paradise Lost' and the Seventeenth Century Reader. London: Chatto and Windus, 1947; reprinted 1962, 1966; Ann Arbor: University of Michigan Press, 1967.

The Novelist as Thinker, edited by Balachandra Rajan. London: Dennis Dobson, 1948.

'W.B. Yeats and the Unity of Being.' *The Nineteenth Century and After* 146 (Sept. 1949): 150–61.

'Bloomsbury and the Academies.' *The Hudson Review* 11.3 (autumn, 1949): 451–57.

'Arjuna's Education.' *The Nineteenth Century and After* 176 (Feb. 1950): 119–25.

'Imagism: A Reconsideration.' In *Modern American Poetry*, edited by Balachandria Rajan, 81–94. London: Dennis Dobson, 1950.

Modern American Poetry, edited by Balachandra Rajan. Poetry selected by Vivienne Koch. London: Dennis Dobson, 1950.

The Dark Dancer (novel). New York: Simon and Schuster, 1957; London: Heinemann, 1958.

Too Long in the West (novel). London: Heinemann, 1961; New York: Athenaeum, 1962.

'Now Days are Dragon-ridden.' *The American Scholar: A Quarterly for the Independent Thinker* 32.3 (summer 1963): 407–14.

John Milton, 1608–1674. Paradise Lost, Books 1 & 2, edited and intro. by Balachandra Rajan. New York: Asia Publishing House, 1964.

'*Paradise Lost:* The Critic and the Historian.' *University of Windsor Review* 1 (spring 1965): 42–50.

W.B. Yeats, a Critical Introduction. London: Hutchinson University Library, 1965. Enlarged and reprinted, 1969.

'The Indian Virtue.' *The Journal of Commonwealth Literature* 1 (Sept., 1965): 79–85.

'English as a Highway or as Barrier.' *Times Literary Supplement* no. 3, 316 (16 Sept. 1965): 796.

'Yeats and the Absurd.' W.B. Yeats Centenary Issue. *Tri-Quarterly* (1965): 130–7.

'Identity and Nationality.' In *Commonwealth Literature: Unity and Diversity in a Common Culture,* edited by John Press, 106–9. London: Heinemann Educational Books, 1965.

Makers of Literary Criticism, compiled and edited with A.G. George. New York: Asia Publishing House, 1965.

'Conflict, More Conflict.' *University of Toronto Quarterly,* 35.3 (1966): 315–20.

'The Overwhelming Question.' *The Sewanee Review* 74 (1966). Reprinted in *T.S. Eliot: The Man and His Work,* edited by Allen Tate, 363–81. London: Chatto and Windus, 1967. Also reprinted in *The Overwhelming Question: A Study of the Poetry of T.S. Eliot.* (1976).

'The Higher Heroism.' *Times Literary Supplement* no. 3, 441 (8 Feb. 1968): 134.

'In Order Serviceable.' *Modern Language Review 63.1 (1968): 13–22. Reprinted in The Lofty Rhyme.*

Sophocles' 'King Oedipus,' in the Translation by W.B. Yeats; with Selections from 'The Poetics of Aristotle,' translated by G.M.A. Grube, edited and intro. by Balachandra Rajan. Toronto: Macmillan of Canada, 1969.

'*Paradise Lost:* The Web of Responsibility.' *Paradise Lost: A Tercentenary Tribute,* edited by Rajan, [106–40.] Toronto, 1969. Reprinted in *The Lofty Rhyme.*

Paradise Lost: A Tercentenary Tribute: Papers given at the Conference on the Tercentenary of Paradise Lost, University of Western Ontario, October 1967, edited by Balachandra Rajan. Toronto: University of Toronto Press in association with University of Western Ontario, 1969.

The Lofty Rhyme: A Study of Milton's Major Poetry. London: Routlege and Kegan Paul, 1970.[1]

'*Paradise Lost* and the Balance of Structures.' *University of Toronto Quarterly* 41 (1972): 219–26.

'Yeats and the Renaissance.' In *Literature and Ideas*, edited by R.G. Collins and Kenneth McRobbie, 110–18. *Mosaic* 5.4. Winnipeg: University of Manitoba Press, 1972.

'Yeats, Synge and the Tragic Understanding.' In *Yeats Studies*, 2: 66–79. Shannon: Irish University Press, 1972.

'To Which Is Added *Samson Agonistes*.' In *The Prison and Pinnacle*, edited by Rajan, 82–110. Toronto, 1973.

The Prison and the Pinnacle: Papers to Commemorate the Tercentenary of 'Paradise Regained' and 'Samson Agonistes' 1671–1971, edited by Balachandra Rajan. Toronto: University of Toronto Press in association with University of Western Ontario, 1973.

'The Dialect of the Tribe.' In *'The Wasteland' in Different Voices*, edited by A.D. Moody, 1–14. London: Edwin Arnold, 1974. Reprinted in *The Overwhelming Question*.

'India.' In *Literature of the World in English*, edited by Bruce King, 79–97. London and Boston: Routlege and Kegan Paul, 1974.

'The Cunning Resemblance.' *Milton Studies* 7 (1975): 29–48.

The Overwhelming Question: A Study of the Poetry of T.S. Eliot. Toronto: University of Toronto Press, 1976.

'A Note on the Coriolan Poems.' In *A Political Art: Essays and Images in Honour of George Woodcock*, edited by William H. New, 95–104. Vancouver: University of British Columbia Press, 1978.

'Andrew Marvell: The Aesthetics of Inconclusiveness.' In *Approaches to Marvell: The York Tercentenary Lectures*, edited by C.A. Patrides, 155–73. London: Routledge and Kegan Paul, 1978. Reprinted in *The Form of the Unfinished*.

'Milton and Eliot: A Twentieth-Century Acknowledgment.' In *The Presence of Milton*, edited by Balachandra Rajan, 115–29. *Milton Studies* 11 Pittsburgh: University Pittsburgh Press, 1978.

'The Presence of Milton,' edited by Balachandra Rajan. Special issue of *Milton Studies* 11. Pittsburgh: University of Pittsburgh Press, 1978.

'The Poetry of Confrontation: Yeats and the Dialogue Poem.' In *Myth and Reality in Irish Literature*, edited by Joseph Ronsley, 119–28. Waterloo: Wilfrid Laurier University Press, 1977.

'*Lycidas*.' In *A Milton Encyclopedia*, general editor William B. Hunter; edited by John T. Shawcross, John M. Steadman, Purvis E. Boyette, and Leonard Nathanson, 40–57. Lewisburg: Bucknell University Press, 1978–83.

'Osiris and Urania.' *Milton Studies* 13 (1979): 221–35.

'Milton, Humanism, and the Concept of Piety.' In *Poetic Traditions of the English Renaissance*, edited by Mack Maynard and George deForest Lord, 251–69. New Haven: Yale University Press, 1982.

'Browne and Milton: The Divided and the Distinguished.' In *Approaches to Sir Thomas Browne: The Ann Arbor Tercentenary Essays*, edited by C.A. Patrides, 1–11. Columbia: University of Missouri Press, 1982.

'*Paradise Lost*: The Uncertain Epic.' 'Composite Orders: The Genres of Milton's Last Poems,' edited by Richard S. Ide and Joseph Wittreich, 105–119. Special issue of *Milton Studies* 17. Pittsburgh: University of Pittsburgh Press, 1983. Reprinted with additions in *The Form of the Unfinished*.

The Form of the Unfinished: English Poetics from Spenser to Pound. Princeton: Princeton University Press, 1985.

'Its Own Executioner: Yeats and the Fragment.' *Yeats: An Annual of Critical and Textual Studies* 3 (1985): 72–87.

'Closure.' In *The Spenser Encyclopedia*, edited by A.C. Hamilton, 169–70. Toronto: University of Toronto Press, 1990.

'Scholarship and Criticism.' In *Literary History of Canada: Canadian Literature in English*, edited by W.H. New, 133–58. 2nd ed. Vol. 4. Toronto: University of Toronto Press, 1990.

'Milton, Eliot, and the Language of Representation.' In *The Fire and the Rose: New Essays on T.S. Eliot*, edited by Vinod Sena and Rajiva Verma, 117–29. Delhi, India: Oxford University Press, 1992.

'T.S. Eliot.' In *The Johns Hopkins Guide to Literary Theory & Criticism*, edited by Michael Groden and Martin Kreiswirth. Baltimore: Johns Hopkins University Press, 1994. www.press.jhu.edu/books/ Hopkins_guide_to_literary_theory/ entries./t._s._eliot.html. Revised for 2nd edition, 2004.

'Banyan Trees and Fig Leaves: Some Thoughts on Milton's India.' In *Of Poetry and Politics: New Essays on Milton and His World*, edited by P.G. Stanwood, 213–28. Binghamton, NY: Medieval & Renaissance Texts & Studies, 1995. Revised and enlarged in *Under Western Eyes*.

'Feminizing the Feminine: Early Women Writers on India.' In *Romanticism: Race and Imperial Culture, 1780–1834*, edited by Alan Richardson and Sonia Hofkosh, 160–72. Bloomington: Indiana University Press, 1996. Revised in *Under Western Eyes*.

'*The Lusiads* and the Asian Reader.' *English Studies in Canada* 23.1 (March 1997): 1–19. Revised and enlarged in *Under Western Eyes*.

'Monstrous Mythologies: Southey and The Curse of Kehama.' *European Romantic Review* 9.2 (spring 1998): 201–16. Revised in *Under Western Eyes*.

'Milton Encompassed.' *Milton Quarterly* 32 (1998): 86–9.

'Excess of India.' *Modern Philology* 95.4 (May 1998): 490–500.

'The Imperial Temptation.' In *Milton and the Imperial Vision*, edited by Balachandra Rajan and Elizabeth Sauer, 294–314. Pittsburgh, 1999.

Milton and the Imperial Vision, edited by Balachandra Rajan and Elizabeth Sauer.
Pittsburgh: Duquesne University Press, 1999.
Under Western Eyes: India from Milton to Macaulay. Durham, NC: Duke University
Press, 1999.
'Milton and Camões: Reinventing the Old Man.' 'Post-Imperial Camões.'
Special Issue of *Portuguese Literary and Cultural Studies* 9 (fall 2002): 177–87.
'Imperialism and the Other End of History.' *University of Toronto Quarterly* 73.2
(2004): 707–24.
'A Note on "Further India."' In *Imperialisms: Historical and Literary Investigations,*
1500–1900, edited by Balachandra Rajan and Elizabeth Sauer, 177–84. New
York: Palgrave Macmillan, 2004.
Imperialisms: Historical and Literary Investigations, 1500–1900, edited by
Balachandra Rajan and Elizabeth Sauer. New York: Palgrave Macmillan, 2004.

NOTES

1 Several chapters of *The Lofty Rhyme* have been reprinted. Some are noted in
the list of publications. However, since this list records only first appearances
in print, information on the other reprintings is provided below.
'*Paradise Lost*: The Hill of History.' *Huntington Library Quarterly* 31.1 (1967):
43–63.
'*Comus*: The Inglorious Likeness.' *University of Toronto Quarterly* 37.2 (1968):
113–35.
'Jerusalem and Athens: The Temptation of Learning in *Paradise Regained.*'
In *Th'Upright Heart and Pure; Essays on John Milton Commemorating the
Tercentenary of the Publication of 'Paradise Lost,'* edited by Amadeus P. Fiore,
61–74. Pittsburgh: Duquesne University Press, 1967. Reprinted and
enlarged in *The Lofty Rhyme.*
'*Lycidas*: The Shattering of the Leaves.' *Studies in Philology* 64.1 (1967): 51–64.
'*Paradise Lost*: The Providence of Style.' *Milton Studies* 1, edited by James
Simmonds, 1–14. Pittsburgh: University of Pittsburgh Press, 1969.

Works Cited

Abrams, M.H. *Natural Supernaturalism: Tradition and Revolution in Romantic Literature.* New York: Norton, 1971.

Achinstein, Sharon. *Milton and the Revolutionary Reader.* Princeton: Princeton University Press, 1994.

– '*Samson Agonistes.*' In *A Companion to Milton,* edited by Thomas N. Corns, 411–28. Oxford: Blackwell, 2001.

Adorno, Theodor W., and Max Horkheimer *The Dialectic of Enlightenment.* 1944. Translated by John Cummings. London: Verso, 1997.

Apuleius, *The Golden Ass or Metamorphoses.* Translated by E.J. Kenney. London: Penguin, 1998.

Armitage, David. 'John Milton: Poet Against Empire.' In *Milton and Republicanism,* edited by David Armitage, Armand Himy, and Quentin Skinner, 206–25. Cambridge: Cambridge University Press, 1995.

Bakhtin, M.M. *The Dialogic Imagination.* 1965. Edited by Michael Holquist. Austin: University of Texas Press, 1981.

Belsey, Catherine *John Milton: Language, Gender and Power.* New York: Blackwell, 1988.

Bennett, Joan. 'Milton's Antinomanism and the Separation Scene in *Paradise Lost.*' In *Reviving Liberty: Radical Christian Humanism in Milton's Great Poems,* 94–118. Cambridge, MA: Harvard University Press, 1989.

Bhabha, Homi K. *The Location of Culture.* London: Routledge, 1994.

– 'Afterword: An Ironic Act of Courage.' In *Milton and the Imperial Vision,* edited by Balachandra Rajan and Elizabeth Sauer, 315–22. Pittsburgh: Duquesne University Press, 1999.

Bonnard, G.A. 'Two Remarks on the Text of Milton's *Areopagitica.*' *The Review of English Studies* 4.16 (Oct. 1928): 434–8.

Books and Readers in Early Modern England: Material Studies, edited by Jennifer

Andersen and Elizabeth Sauer. Philadelphia: University of Pennsylvania Press, 2002.

Bowra, C.M. *From Virgil to Milton.* London: Macmillan, 1963.

Braudel, Fernand. *The Mediterranean and the Mediterranean World in the Age of Phillip II.* Translated by Sean Reynolds, illustrated ed. New York: Harper & Row, 1972.

Broadbent, J.B. *Some Graver Subject.* London: Chatto and Windus, 1960.

Browne, Thomas. *Religio Medici: A New Edition with Biographical and Critical Introduction* by Jean-Jacques Denonian. Cambridge: Cambridge University Press, 1955.

Burden, Dennis H. *The Logical Epic: A Study of the Argument of 'Paradise Lost.'* London: Routledge & Kegan Paul, 1967.

Bush, Douglas. *'Paradise Lost' in Our Time: Some Comments.* 1945. Gloucester, MA: Peter Smith, 1957.

Camões, Luís de. *The Lusiads of Luis de Camões.* Translation and introduction by Leonard Bacon. New York: Hispanic Society of America, 1950.

Campbell, Gordon. *'De Doctrina Christiana*: Its Structural Principles and Its Unfinished State.' *Milton Studies* 9 (1976): 243–60.

Campbell, Gordon, et al. 'Final Report on the Provenance of *De Doctrina Christiana.' Milton Quarterly* 31 (1997): 67–121.

Carey, John. *Milton.* London: Evans Brothers, 1969.

Cawley, R.R. *Milton and the Literature of Travel.* Princeton: Princeton University Press, 1951.

Chaplin, Gregory. '"One Flesh, One Heart, One Soul": Renaissance Friendship and Miltonic Marriage.' *Modern Philology* 99.2 (2001): 266–92.

Chaudhari, K.N. *Asia before Europe: Economy and Civilization of the Indian Ocean from the Rise of Islam to 1750.* Cambridge: Cambridge University Press, 1990.

Colie, Rosalie. *Light and Enlightenment.* Cambridge: Cambridge University Press, 1937.

Darbishire, Helen. 'Pen-and-Ink Corrections in Books of the Seventeenth Century.' *The Review of English Studies* 7.25 (Jan. 1931): 72–3.

Darian, Stephen G. *The Ganges in Myth and History.* Honolulu: University of Hawaii Press, 1978.

Davies, Godfrey. 'Arminianism versus Puritanism in England c. 1620–50.' *Huntington Library Bulletin* 5 (1934): 157–79.

de Man, Paul. *Blindness and Insight.* New York: Oxford University Press, 1971.

Diekhoff, John S. *Milton's 'Paradise Lost': A Commentary on the Argument.* New York: Columbia University Press, 1946.

Dobranksi, Stephen B. 'Samson and the Omissa.' *Studies in English Literature* 36 (1996): 149–69.

– *Milton, Authorship, and the Book Trade*. Cambridge: Cambridge University Press, 1999.

Donnelly, Phillip J. 'The Telos of Genres: *Paradise Lost* and *De Doctrina Christiana*.' *Milton Studies* 38 (2000): 74–100.

Drew, John. *India and the Romantic Imagination*. Delhi: Oxford University Press, 1987.

Dryden, John. *The Works of Virgil … Translated into English Verse*. 1697. Edited by William Frost. In *The Works of John Dryden*. Gen. ed. Alan Roper. Vol. 5. Berkeley and Los Angeles: University of California Press, 1987.

Du Moulin, Peter. *The Anatomy of Arminianism*. London, 1626.

Duncan, Joseph E. *Milton's Earthly Paradise: A Historical Study of Eden*. Minneapolis: University of Minnesota Press, 1972.

Early Travels in India, 1583–1619, edited by William Foster. London: Humphrey Milford; Oxford: Oxford University Press, 1921.

Elliott, J.H. *Spain and Its World 1500–1700*. New Haven: Yale University Press, 1989.

Evans, J. Martin. *Milton's Imperial Epic: 'Paradise Lost' and the Discourse of Colonialism*. Ithaca: Cornell University Press, 1996.

Fallon, Stephen M. '"Elect Above the Rest": Theology as Self-representation in Milton.' In *Milton and Heresy*, edited by Stephen B. Dobranski and John P. Rumrich, 93–116. Cambridge: Cambridge University Press, 1998.

– 'Milton's Arminianism and the Authorship of *De doctrina Christiana*.' *Texas Studies in Literature and Language* 41 (1999): 103–27.

Ferry, David. *The Limits of Mortality: An Essay on Wordsworth's Major Poems*. Middletown, CT.: Wesleyan University Press, 1959.

Fish, Stanley. *How Milton Works*. Cambridge, MA: Harvard University Press, 2001.

– 'Why Milton Matters; or Against Historicism.' *Milton Studies* 44 (2005): 1–12.

Fisher, Michael H. *The First Indian Author in English: Dean Mahomed (1769–1851) in India, Ireland, and England*. Delhi: Oxford University Press, 1996.

Flannagan, Roy, editor. *Areopagitica* by John Milton. In *The Riverside Milton*, 987–1024. Boston and New York: Houghton Mifflin, 1998.

Fletcher, Harris F. *Milton's Rabbinical Readings*. Urbana: University of Illinois Press, 1931.

Froula, Christine. 'When Eve Reads Milton: Undoing the Canonical Economy.' *Critical Inquiry* 10 (1983): 321–47.

Frye, Northrop. 'A Tribute to Balachandra Rajan.' In *Northrop Frye on Milton and Blake* (2005), edited by Angela Esterhammer, 178–81. *The Collected Works of Northrop Frye*, gen. ed. Alvin Lee. Toronto: University of Toronto Press, 1996–.

Gardiner, Samuel Rawson. *The Fall of the Monarchy of Charles I 1637–1649*. London: Longmans Green, 1882.

Gascoigne, Bamber. *The Great Moghuls.* New York: Harper & Row, 1971.

Gay, David. *The Endless Kingdom: Milton's Spiritual Society.* Newark: University of Delaware Press, and London: Associated University Presses, 2002.

Godley, A.D., ed., *The Poetical Works of Thomas Moore.* London: Humphrey Milford, Oxford University Press, 1915.

Goldberg, Jonathan. 'Dating Milton.' In *Soliciting Interpretation: Literary Theory and Seventeenth-Century English Poetry*, edited by Elizabeth D. Harvey and Katharine Eisaman Maus, 199–220. Chicago: University of Chicago Press, 1990.

Graves, Robert. *Wife to Mr. Milton: The Story of Mary Powell.* 1944. New York: Noonday Press, 1962.

Gregerson, Linda. 'Colonials Write the Nation: Spenser, Milton, and England on the Margins.' In *Milton and the Imperial Vision*, edited by Balachandra Rajan and Elizabeth Sauer, 169–90. Pittsburgh: Duquesne University Press, 1999.

Gregory, Tobias. 'In Defense of Empson: A Reassessment of *Milton's God.*' In *Fault Lines and Controversies in the Study of Seventeenth-Century English Literature*, edited by Claude J. Summers and Ted-Larry Pebworth, 73–87. Columbia: University of Missouri Press, 2002.

Grossman, Marshall. 'The Rhetoric of Feminine Priority in *Paradise Lost.*' *English Literary Renaissance* 33 (2003): 424–43.

Guillory, John. *Poetic Authority: Spenser, Milton and Literary History.* New York: Columbia University Press, 1983.

Hall, J.R. *Renaissance Exploration.* New York: W.W. Norton, 1968.

Hall, Richard. *Empires of the Monsoon.* London: Harper Collins, 1996.

Hanford, James Holly. *John Milton, Englishman.* New York: Crown Publishers, 1949.

Hansen, Waldemar. *The Peacock Throne: The Drama of Mogul India.* New York: Holt, Rinehart and Winston, 1972.

Hartman, Geoffrey. *Wordsworth's Poetry, 1787–1814.* New Haven: Yale University Press, 1964.

Helgerson, Richard. *Forms of Nationhood: The Elizabethan Writing of England.* Chicago: University of Chicago Press, 1992.

Herman, Peter C. *Destabilizing Milton: 'Paradise Lost' and the Poetics of Incertitude.* New York: Palgrave Macmillan, 2005.

Hill, Christopher. *God's Englishman: Oliver Cromwell and the English Revolution.* New York: Harper and Row, 1970.

– *Milton and the English Revolution.* New York: Viking Press, 1978.

– 'Professor William B. Hunter, Bishop Burgess, and John Milton.' *Studies in English Literature* 34 (1994): 165–93.

Hughes, Merritt Y., ed. *John Milton, Complete Poems and Major Prose.* New York: Macmillan, 1957.

Hunter, William B. 'The Center of *Paradise Lost.' English Language Notes* 7 (1969): 32–4.

– 'Milton on the Exaltation of the Son: The War in Heaven in *Paradise Lost.' English Literary History* 36 (1969): 215–31.

– 'The Provenance of the *Christian Doctrine.' Studies in English Literature* 32 (1992): 129–42.

– 'The Provenance of the *Christian Doctrine:* Addenda from the Bishop of Salisbury.' *Studies in English Literature* 33 (1993): 191–207.

– '*Visitation Unimplor'd: Milton and the Authorship of 'De Doctrina Christiana.'* Pittsburgh: Duquesne University Press, 1998.

– 'Responses.' *Milton Quarterly* 33 (1999): 31–7.

– 'The Confounded Confusion of Chaos.' In *Living Texts: Interpreting Milton,* edited by Kristin A. Pruitt and Charles V. Durham, 228–36. Selinsgrove: Susquehanna University Press, 2000.

Hunter, William B., C.A. Patrides, and J.H. Adamson. *Bright Essence: Studies in Milton's Theology.* Salt Lake City: University of Utah Press, 1971.

Hutchinson, F.E. *Milton and the English Mind.* London: Hodder & Stoughton, 1946.

Inden, Ronald. *Imagining India.* Oxford: Basil Blackwell, 1990.

Johnson, Samuel. *Life of Milton.* In *Milton 1732–1801: The Critical Heritage,* edited by John T. Shawcross, 290–310. London and Boston: Routledge & Kegan Paul, 1972.

Kelley, Maurice. 'Milton's Arianism Again Reconsidered.' *Harvard Theological Review* 45 (1961): 195–205.

– *This Great Argument: A Study of Milton's 'De Doctrina Christiana' as a Gloss upon 'Paradise Lost'* [1941]. Princeton Studies in England. Vol. 22. Gloucester, MA: Peter Smith, 1962.

– 'Milton and the Trinity.' *Huntington Library Quarterly* 33 (1970): 315–20.

– 'On the State of Milton's *De Doctrina Christiana.' English Language Notes* 27 (1989): 43–8.

– 'The Provenance of John Milton's *Christian Doctrine:* A Reply to William B. Hunter.' *Studies in English Literature* 34 (1994): 153–63.

Kerrigan, William. *The Sacred Complex: On the Psychogenesis of 'Paradise Lost.'* Cambridge, MA: Harvard University Press, 1983.

Kivette, Ruth M. 'The Ways and Wars of Truth.' *Milton Quarterly* 6 (1973): 81–5.

Knight, G. Wilson. *Chariot of Wrath.* London: Faber and Faber, 1942.

Kolbrener, William. *Milton's Warring Angels: A Study of Critical Engagements.* Cambridge: Cambridge University Press, 1997.

Kristeva, Julia. *Desire in Language: A Semiotic Approach to Literature and Art.* Edited by Leon S. Roudiez and translated by Thomas Gora, Alice Jardine, Leon S. Roudiez. New York: Columbia University Press, 1980.

Latham, R.E., trans., *Marco Polo: The Travels*. London: Penguin, 1958.

Lawry, Jon S. *The Shadow of Heaven: Matter and Stance in Milton's Poetry*. Ithaca: Cornell University Press, 1969.

Leonard, John. 'Milton, Lucretius, and "the void profound of unessential Night."' In *Living Texts: Interpreting Milton*, edited by Kristin A. Pruitt and Charles V. Durham, 198–217. Selinsgrove: Susquehanna University Press, 2000.

Lewalski, Barbara K. *Milton's Brief Epic: The Genre, Meaning and Art of 'Paradise Regained.'* London: Methuen, 1966.

– *Protestant Poetics and the Seventeenth Century Religious Lyric*. Princeton: Princeton University Press, 1979.

– 'The Genres of *Paradise Lost*: Literary Genre as a Means of Accommodation.' *Composite Orders: The Genres of Milton's Last Poems*, edited by Richard S. Ide and Joseph Wittreich, 75–103. Special issue of *Milton Studies* 17. Pittsburgh: University of Pittsburgh Press, 1983.

– *'Paradise Lost' and the Rhetoric of Literary Forms*. Princeton: Princeton University Press, 1985.

– 'Milton and *De Doctrina Christiana*: Evidences of Authorship.' *Milton Studies* 36 (1998): 203–28.

Lewalski, Barbara K., and John T. Shawcross. 'Forum: Milton's *Christian Doctrine*.' *Studies in English Literature* 32 (1992): 142–62.

Lewis, C.S. *A Preface to 'Paradise Lost.'* 1942. London, New York, and Toronto: Oxford University Press, 1956.

Lieb, Michael. '*De Doctrina Christiana* and the Question of Authorship.' *Milton Studies* 41 (2002): 172–230.

Lockwood Laura E., editor. *John Milton, Selected Essays: Of Education, Areopagitica, The Commonwealth; With Early Biographies of Milton*. The Riverside Literature Series. London: George G. Harrap, n.d.

Low, Anthony. 'The Parting in the Garden in *Paradise Lost*.' *Philological Quarterly* 47 (1968): 30–5.

Major, R.H. (Richard Henry), editor. *India in the Fifteenth Century: Being a Collection of Narratives of Voyages to India*. London: Hakluyt Society, 1857.

Maley, Willy. 'Milton and "the complication of interests" in Early Modern Ireland.' In *Milton and the Imperial Vision*, edited by Balachandra Rajan and Elizabeth Sauer, 155–68. Pittsburgh: Duquesne University Press, 1999.

M.S. to A.S. with a Plea for Libertie of Conscience. Rev. ed. July 1644.

Marcus, Leah. *Unediting the Renaissance: Shakespeare, Marlowe, Milton*. New York: Routledge, 1996.

Martin, Catherine Gimelli. *The Ruins of Allegory: 'Paradise Lost' and the Metamorphosis of Epic Convention*. Durham: Duke University Press, 1998.

Martz, Louis L. '*Paradise Regained*: The Meditative Combat.' *English Literary History* 27 (1960): 223–47.

– *The Paradise Within.* New Haven: Yale University Press, 1964.
– *Poet of Exile: A Study of Milton's Poetry.* New Haven: Yale University Press, 1980.
McColley, Diane K. 'Free Will and Obedience in the Separation Scene of *Paradise Lost.*' *Studies in English Literature* 12 (1972): 103–20.
– *Milton's Eve.* Urbana: University of Illinois Press, 1983.
McHenry, James Patrick. 'A Milton Herbal.' *Milton Quarterly* 30 (1996): 45–115.
Mickle, William Julius. *The Lusiads or The Discovery of India: An Epic Poem.* Oxford: Jackman and Lister, 1776.
Milton and the Imperial Vision, edited by Balachandra Rajan and Elizabeth Sauer. 255–72. Pittsburgh: Duquesne University Press, 1999.
Milton and Gender, edited by Catherine Gimelli Martin. Cambridge: Cambridge University Press, 2004.
Milton and Republicanism, edited by David Armitage, Armand Himy, and Quentin Skinner. Cambridge: Cambridge University Press, 1995.
Milton, John. *The Works of John Milton,* edited by Frank Allen Patterson et al. 18 vols. New York: Columbia University Press, 1931–8.
– *De Doctrina Christiana.* In *The Works of John Milton,* vols 14–17, edited by James Holly Hanford and Waldo Hilary Dunn, and translated by Charles R. Sumner. New York: Columbia University Press, 1933–4.
– *Complete Prose Works of John Milton.* Edited by Don Wolfe et al. 8 vols. New Haven: Yale University Press, 1953–82.
– *Complete Poems and Major Prose.* Edited by Merritt Y. Hughes. New York: Macmillan, 1957.
– *Areopagitica.* In *Complete Prose Works of John Milton.* Vol. 2. Edited by Ernest Sirluck, 480–570. New Haven: Yale University Press, 1959.
– *The Poems of John Milton.* Edited by John Carey and Alastair Fowler. London: Longmans, 1968.
– *On Christian Doctrine.* In *Complete Prose Works of John Milton.* Vol. 6. Edited by Maurice Kelley, and translated by John Carey. New Haven: Yale University Press, 1973.
– *Areopagitica.* In *The Riverside Milton,* edited by Roy Flannagan, 997–1024. Boston and New York: Houghton Mifflin, 1998.
Mueller, Janel. 'Contextualizing Milton's Nascent Republicanism.' In *Of Poetry and Politics: New Essays on Milton and His World,* edited by P.G. Stanwood, 263–82. Binghamton, NY. Medieval & Renaissance Texts & Studies, 1995.
– 'Milton on Heresy.' In *Milton and Heresy,* edited by Stephen B. Dobranski and John P. Rumrich, 21–38. Cambridge: Cambridge University Press, 1998.
– 'Dominion as Domesticity: Milton's Imperial God and the Experience of History.' In *Milton and the Imperial Vision,* edited by Balachandra Rajan and Elizabeth Sauer, 25–47. Pittsburgh: Duquesne University Press, 1999.

Mukherjee, Ramakrishna. *The Rise and Fall of the East India Company*. Bombay: Popular Prakashan, 1973.

Murry, John Middleton. *Keats and Shakespeare: A Study of Keats' Poetic Life from 1816 to 1820*. London: Oxford University Press, 1958.

Newton, Thomas, editor. Milton, *Paradise Lost*. 1749. In *Milton 1732–1801: The Critical Heritage*, edited by John T. Shawcross, 153–68. London: Routledge and Kegan Paul, 1972.

Norbrook, David. 'The True Republican: Putting the Politics Back into Milton.' *Times Literary Supplement* no. 4844 (2 Feb. 1996): 4–6.

– *Writing the English Republic: Poetry, Rhetoric and Politics 1627–1660*. Cambridge: Cambridge University Press, 1999.

Nyquist, Mary. 'Reading the Fall: Discourse and Drama in *Paradise Lost*.' *English Literary Renaissance* 14 (1984): 199–229.

– 'The Father's Word/Satan's Wrath.' *Publications of the Modern Language Association of America* 100 (1985): 187–202.

– 'The Genesis of Gendered Subjectivity.' In *Re-membering Milton: Essays on the Texts and Traditions*, edited by Mary Nyquist and Margaret Ferguson, 99–127. New York: Methuen, 1987.

– 'Gynesis, Genesis, Exegesis, and the Formation of Milton's Eve.' In *Cannibals, Witches, and Divorce: Estranging the Renaissance*, edited by Marjorie Garber, 147–208. Baltimore: Johns Hopkins University Press, 1987.

Nyquist, Mary, and Margaret W. Ferguson. Preface, *Re-membering Milton: Essays on the Texts and Traditions*, edited by Mary Nyquist and Margaret W. Ferguson, xii–xvii. New York: Methuen, 1987.

Owenson, Sydney (Lady Morgan). *The Missionary*. 2nd ed. London: J.J. Stockwell, 1811.

Parker, William Riley. *Milton: A Biography*. 2 vols. Oxford: Clarendon, 1968.

Patrides, C. A. *Milton and the Christian Tradition*. Oxford: Clarendon Press, 1966.

– 'An Open Letter on the Yale Edition of *De Doctrina Christiana*.' *Milton Quarterly* 7 (1973): 73–4.

– 'The Nature of Inconclusiveness: The Achievement of Balachandra Rajan.' Unpublished.

Patterson, Annabel. *Reading Between the Lines*. Madison: University of Wisconsin Press, 1993.

Pattison, Mark. *Milton*. 1887, Repr. New York: AMS Press, 1968.

Plutarch, *Moralia*. Translated by Frank Cole Babbitt. Cambridge, MA: Harvard University Press, 1949.

Polydorou, Desma. 'Gender and Spiritual Equality in Marriage: A Dialogic Reading of Rachel Speght and John Milton.' *Milton Quarterly* 35 (2001): 22–32.

Pope, Elizabeth. '*Paradise Regained': The Tradition and the Poem.* Baltimore: Johns Hopkins University Press, 1947.

Pound, Ezra. *The Spirit of Romance.* London: J.M. Dent, 1910.

– *Make It New.* London: Faber and Faber, 1934.

Quint, David. *Epic and Empire: Politics and Generic Form from Virgil to Milton.* Princeton: Princeton University Press, 1993.

Radzinowicz, Mary Ann. *Toward 'Samson Agonistes': The Growth of Milton's Mind.* Princeton: Princeton University Press, 1978.

Raleigh, Walter. *Milton.* 1900. New York: Benjamin Bloom, 1967.

Raleigh, Sir Walter. *The History of the World.* 1621. Edited by C.A. Patrides. London: Macmillan, 1971.

Rapaport, Herman. *Milton and the Postmodern.* Lincoln: University of Nebraska Press, 1983.

Ravenstein, Ernest George. *A Journal of the First Voyage of Vasco da Gama,* London: Printed for the Hakluyt Society, 1898.

Reichert, John. '"Against His Better Knowledge": A Case for Adam.' *English Literary History* 48 (1981): 83–109.

Representing Ireland: Literature and the Origins of Conflict, 1534–1660, edited by Brendan Bradshaw, Andrew Hadfield, and Willy Maley. Cambridge: Cambridge University Press, 1993.

Revard, Stella P. 'Eve and the Doctrine of Responsibility in *Paradise Lost.' Publications of the Modern Language Association of America* 88 (1973): 69–78.

Robinson, Henry. *Liberty of Conscience: Or the Sole Means to Obtaine Peace and Truth.* March, 1644.

Roe, Thomas. *The Embassy of Sir Thomas Roe to the Court of the Great Mogul 1615–19.* Edited by William Foster. London: Hakluyt Society, 1899.

Rogers, John. *The Matter of Revolution: Science, Poetry, and Politics in the Age of Milton.* Ithaca: Cornell University Press, 1996.

The Romantics on Milton: Formal Essays and Critical Asides, edited by Joseph Wittreich. Cleveland: Press of Case Western Reserve University, 1970.

Rumrich, John P. 'Uninventing Milton.' *Modern Philology* 87.3 (1990): 249–65.

– 'Milton's God and the Matter of Chaos.' *Publications of the Modern Language Association of America* 110.5 (1995): 1035–46.

– *Milton Unbound: Controversy and Reinterpretation.* Cambridge: Cambridge University Press, 1996.

– 'Milton's Arianism: Why It Matters.' In *Milton and Heresy,* edited by Stephen B. Dobranski and John P. Rumrich, 75–92. Cambridge: Cambridge University Press, 1998.

Safer, Elaine B. '"Sufficient to Have Stood": Eve's Responsibility in Book IX.' *Milton Quarterly* 6 (1972): 10–14.

Said, Edward W. *Orientalism.* New York: Pantheon Books, 1978.

– *The World, the Text and the Critic.* Cambridge, MA: Harvard University Press, 1983.

– *Culture and Imperialism.* New York: Alfred A. Knopf, 1993.

Sauer, Elizabeth. 'The Politics of Performance in the Inner Theater: *Samson Agonistes* as Closet Drama.' In *Milton and Heresy,* edited by Stephen B. Dobranksi and John P. Rumrich, 199–215. Cambridge: Cambridge University Press, 1998.

Saurat, Denis. *Milton: Man and Thinker.* London: Jonathan Cape, 1925.

Scammell, Geoffrey Vaughan. *The World Encompassed: The First European Maritime Empires, c. 800–1650.* Berkeley and Los Angeles: University of California Press, 1981.

Schwartz, Regina M. *Remembering and Repeating: Biblical Creation in 'Paradise Lost.'* Cambridge: Cambridge University Press, 1988.

Sellin, Paul R. 'John Milton's *Paradise Lost* and *De Doctrina Christiana* on Predestination.' *Milton Studies* 34 (1996): 45–60.

– 'The Reference to John Milton's *Tetrachordon* in *De Doctrina Christiana.*' *Studies in English Literature* 37 (1997): 137–49.

– 'Further Responses.' *Milton Quarterly* 33 (1999): 38–51.

Sewell, Arthur. *A Study in Milton's 'Christian Doctrine.'* London: Oxford University Press, 1939; Hamden, CT.: Archon Books, 1967.

Shakespeare, William. *Love's Labour's Lost.* 1906. Edited by Richard David. 5th ed. London: Methuen, 1956.

Shelley, Percy Bysshe. *Prometheus Unbound.* Edited by John Zillman. Seattle: University of Washington Press, 1959.

– *Shelley's Poetry and Prose: Authoritative Texts and Criticism.* Edited by Donald H. Reiman and Sharon B. Powers. New York: Norton, 1977.

Shoulson, Jeffrey. *Milton and the Rabbis: Hebraism, Hellenism, and Christianity.* New York: Columbia University Press, 2001.

Shullenberger, William. 'Wresting with the Angel: *Paradise Lost* and Feminist Criticism.' *Milton Quarterly* 20 (1986): 70–85.

Sims, James H. 'Camoëns' *Lusiads* and Milton's *Paradise Lost*: Satan's Voyage to Eden.' In *Papers on Milton,* edited by Philip M. Griffith and Lester F. Zimmerman, 36–46. Tulsa: University of Tulsa Press, 1969.

– 'Echoes of Camoens' *Lusiads* in Milton's *Paradise Lost* (1–4).' *Revista Camoniana* 3 (1971): 135–44.

– 'Camoëns, Milton, and Myth in the Christian Epic.' 79–87. *Renaissance Papers.* Durham, N.C.: Southeastern Renaissance Conference, 1972.

– 'Christened Classicism in *Paradise Lost* and *The Lusiads.*' *Comparative Literature* 24 (1972): 338–56.

– '"Delicious Paradise" in *Os Lusiadas* and in *Paradise Lost.*' *Ocidente* (Lisbon), special issue (Nov. 1972): 163–72.

– 'The Epic Narrator's Mortal Voice in Camões and Milton.' *Revue de Litterature Comparée* 51 (1977): 377–84.

– '*Os Lusiadas*: A Structural Prototype of *Paradise Lost.*' *Explorations in Renaissance Culture* 4 (1978): 70–5.

– 'A Greater Than Rome: The Inversion of a Virgilian Symbol from Camões to Milton.' In *Rome in the Renaissance: The City and the Myth*, edited by P.A. Ramsey, 333–44. Binghamton, NY: Center for Medieval and Early Renaissance Studies, 1982.

– 'Milton as a Camoist.' In *Performance for a Lifetime: A Festschrift Honoring Dorothy Harrell Brown: Essays on Women, Religion, and the Renaissance*, edited by Barbara C. Ewell, Mary A. McCay, and Georgiann L. Potts, 205–22. New Orleans, LA: Loyola University, 1997.

Sirluck, Ernest. '*Paradise Lost*': *A Deliberate Epic*. Cambridge: W. Heffer and Sons, 1967.

Skinner, Quentin. *Liberty Before Liberalism*. Cambridge: Cambridge University Press, 1998.

Smith, Adam. *The Wealth of Nations*. 1776. Edited by Edwin Cannan. New York: Random House, 1994.

Smith, Logan Pearsall. *Milton and His Modern Critics*. 1941. Hamden, CT: Archon Books, 1967.

Smith, Nigel. '*Areopagitica*: Voicing Contexts, 1643–5.' In *Politics, Poetics and Hermeneutics in Milton's Prose*, edited by David Loewenstein and James Grantham Turner, 103–22. Cambridge: Cambridge University Press, 1990.

Southey, Robert. *The Curse of Kehama*. In *The Poetical Works*. Vol. 8. London: Longman, 1847; rept Georg Olms Verlag, 1977.

Spenser, Edmund. *The Faerie Queene*. Edited by Thomas Roche. New Haven: Yale University Press, 1981.

Steadman, John. *The Hill and the Labyrinth: Discourse and Certitude in Milton and His Near-contemporaries*. Berkeley and Los Angeles: University of California Press, 1984.

Stein, Arnold. *Answerable Style*. Minneapolis: University of Minnesota Press, 1953.

Steiner, George. *After Babel: Aspects of Language and Translation*. New York: Oxford University Press, 1965.

Stevens, Paul. 'Milton and the New World: Custom, Relativism, and the Discipline of Shame.' In *Milton and the Imperial Vision*, edited by Balachandra Rajan and Elizabeth Sauer, 90–111. Pittsburgh: Duquesne University Press, 1999.

Summers, Joseph. *The Muses Method: An Introduction to 'Paradise Lost.'* Cambridge, MA: Harvard University Press, 1962.

Svendsen, Kester. *Milton and Science.* Cambridge, MA: Harvard University Press, 1956.

Swiss, Margo. 'Repairing Androgyny: Eve's Tears in *Paradise Lost.*' In *Speaking Grief in English Literary Culture: Shakespeare to Milton*, edited by Margo Swiss and David A. Kent, 261–83. Pittsburgh: Duquesne University Press, 2002.

Tennyson, Alfred. 'To Virgil.' In *The Poems of Tennyson*, edited by Christopher Ricks, 1311–13. London: Longmans, 1969.

Tillyard, E.M.W. *Milton.* London: Chatto and Windus, 1930.

– *The English Epic and Its Background.* London: Chatto and Windus, 1959.

Tomlins, Jack E. 'Gil Vicente's Vision of India and Its Ironic Echo in Camões "Velho de Rosselo."' In *Empire in Transition: The Portuguese World in the Times of Camões*, edited by Alfred Hower and Richard A. Preso-Rodas, 170–6. Gainesville: University of Florida Press, 1985.

Virgil. *The Aeneid.* Translated by Robert Fitzgerald. New York: Random House, 1983.

Viswanathan, S. 'Milton and Purchas's Linschoten: An Additional Source for Milton's Indian Figtree.' *Milton Newsletter* 2.3 (October 1968): 43–5.

von Maltzahn, Nicholas. *Milton's 'History of Britain': Republican Historiography in the English Revolution.* Oxford: Oxford University Press, 1991.

– 'Acts of Kind Service: Milton and the Patriot Literature of Empire.' In *Milton and the Imperial Vision*, edited by Balachandra Rajan and Elizabeth Sauer, 233–54. Pittsburgh: Duquesne University Press, 1999.

Waldock. A.J.A. *'Paradise Lost' and Its Critics.* 1947. Cambridge: University Press, 1966.

Walwyn, William. *The Compassionate Samaritane.* [June], 1644.

Webb, Phyllis. 'Marvell's Garden.' In *Selected Poems: The Vision Tree*, edited by Sharon Thesen, 33–4. Vancouver: Talonbooks, 1982.

Williams, Roger. *The Bloudy Tenent, of Persecution, for Cause of Conscience Discussed.* July 1644.

Wittreich, Joseph A. *Visionary Poetics: Milton's Tradition and His Legacy.* San Marino, CA: Huntington Library, 1979.

– *Feminist Milton.* Ithaca: Cornell University Press, 1987.

– '"He Ever was a Dissenter": Milton's Transgressive Maneuvers in *Paradise Lost.*' In *Arenas of Conflict: Milton and the Unfettered Mind*, edited by Kristin Pruitt McColgan and Charles W. Durham, 21–40. Selinsgrove: Susquehanna University Press, 1997.

– *Shifting Contexts: Reinterpreting 'Samson Agonistes.'* Pittsburgh: Duquesne University Press, 2002.

– 'Why Milton Matters.' *Milton Studies* 44 (2005): 22–39.

Wollstonecraft, Mary. *A Vindication of the Rights of Woman.* Edited by Miriam Brody. London: Penguin, 1992.

Woodhouse, A.S.P. 'Notes on Milton's Views on the Creation: The Initial Phase.' *Philological Quarterly* 28 (1949): 211–36.

Worden, Blair. 'Milton's Republicanism and the Tyranny of Heaven.' In *Machiavelli and Republicanism,* edited by Gisela Bock, Quentin Skinner, and Maurizio Viroli, 225–45. Cambridge: Cambridge University Press, 1990.

Wright, Julia M. '"Greek and Latin Slaves of the Sword": Rejecting the Imperial Nation in Blake's *Milton.*' In *Milton and the Imperial Vision,* edited by Balachandra Rajan and Elizabeth Sauer. 255–72. Pittsburgh: Duquesne University Press, 1999.

Yeats, William Butler. *The Variorum Edition of the Poems of W.B. Yeats.* Edited by Peter Allt and Russell K. Alspach. New York: Macmillan, 1957.

– *A Critical Introduction.* London: Hutchinson, 1965, 2nd ed., 1969.

Yule, Henry, and A.C. Burnell. *Hobson-Jobson: A Glossary of Colloquial Anglo-Indian Words and Phrases and of Kindred Terms, Etymological, Historical, Geographical, and Discursive.* Edited by William Crooke. New Delhi: Munshiram Manoharlal, 1994.

Index

of, 25; of empire, 131; English, 29, 31; hierarchic relations in, 51; history of, 30; of inheritance, 49; nature of, 8, 62, 108; of poet in exile, 158; possibility of, 20–1; recovery of order in, 23; Romantic, 65; search and vision, 17; shifts within, 58; source of energy of, 28–9; truths of, 14. *See also* epic

politics: chaos and, 87; in context of poem, 42; effects on criticism, 11–12; of India's independence, 88; Milton's modernity and, 152; of reading, 10, 18, 66–9; and relationship with aesthetics, 5; and resistance to temptation, 95; of the right hand, 147; separation of civil and religious power, 143–4

Pope Alexander IV, 79

Pope Innocent IV, 78–9

Pope Urban VIII, 73

Portugal, 74, 85, 95, 124–5, 127–8

postcolonialism, 7, 47, 65; history of study of, 124; informing criticism, 12; politics of reading, 64, 66–9; self-other model, 98

postmoderism, 154

poststructuralism, 47, 65

Pound, Ezra, 49

power, 80, 88; of God, 95; imperial, 97; separation of civil and religious, 143–4; world, 100

Prester John, 126

prevarication of Raphael, 19–20

prophet, Milton's definition of, 18

Protestant Christendom, 48, 77, 91n30, 158

Protestant empire, 104

Ptolemaic universe, 58, 85

Puritan dilemma, 107

Puritanism, 144

pursuit of glory, 100

pygmies, 73

Quint, David, 67, 94

Radzinowicz, Mary Ann, 35, 155

Rajan, Balachandra, 103, 155; on authorship of *Christian Doctrine,* 156–7; avant-garde criticism, 159; contribution to Milton studies, 3–4, 7; ideological shift in *Paradise Lost,* 158–9; mediation of, 154; Milton in exile, 158; politics of criticism, 11; role in Milton scholarship, 155–6

– scholarship: 'Banyan Trees and Fig Leaves,' 12, 72; 'Browne and Milton: The Divided and the Distinguished,' 8; *The Dark Dancer,* 3, 11; *The Form of the Unfinished,* 7–8, 46; *The Lofty Rhyme,* 6–7, 46, 93; 'Milton, Eliot, and the Language of Representation,' 8; 'Milton, Humanism, and the Concept of Piety,' 17; *Milton and the Imperial Vision,* 13, 93; 'Osiris and Urania,' 8; 'The Overwhelming Question,' 10; '*Paradise Lost*: The Uncertain Epic,' 8, 46; *'Paradise Lost' and the Seventeenth Century Reader,* 6–7, 33, 46, 64; 'Surprised by a Strange Language,' 10; 'To Which Is Added *Samson Agonistes,*' 46; *Under Western Eyes,* 7–8, 123

Raleigh, Walter, 82, 90n22, 107, 140, 151

Ramist logic, 50

Rapaport, Herman, 65

reading: and act of writing, 33; assumptions of, 62; climates, 3, 14, 18,